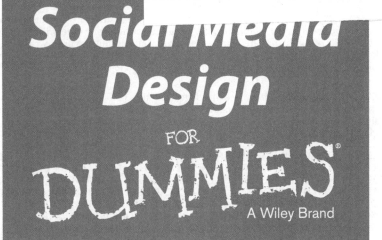

Social Media Design

FOR DUMMIES®

A Wiley Brand

by Janine Warner and David LaFontaine

FOR DUMMIES®
A Wiley Brand

Social Media Design For Dummies®

Published by: **John Wiley & Sons, Inc.,** 111 River Street, Hoboken, NJ 07030-5774, www.wiley.com

Copyright © 2014 by John Wiley & Sons, Inc., Hoboken, New Jersey

Published simultaneously in Canada

No part of this publication may be reproduced, stored in a retrieval system or transmitted in any form or by any means, electronic, mechanical, photocopying, recording, scanning or otherwise, except as permitted under Sections 107 or 108 of the 1976 United States Copyright Act, without the prior written permission of the Publisher. Requests to the Publisher for permission should be addressed to the Permissions Department, John Wiley & Sons, Inc., 111 River Street, Hoboken, NJ 07030, (201) 748-6011, fax (201) 748-6008, or online at http://www.wiley.com/go/permissions.

Trademarks: Wiley, For Dummies, the Dummies Man logo, Dummies.com, Making Everything Easier, and related trade dress are trademarks or registered trademarks of John Wiley & Sons, Inc. and may not be used without written permission. All other trademarks are the property of their respective owners. John Wiley & Sons, Inc. is not associated with any product or vendor mentioned in this book.

For general information on our other products and services, please contact our Customer Care Department within the U.S. at 877-762-2974, outside the U.S. at 317-572-3993, or fax 317-572-4002. For technical support, please visit www.wiley.com/techsupport.

Wiley publishes in a variety of print and electronic formats and by print-on-demand. Some material included with standard print versions of this book may not be included in e-books or in print-on-demand. If this book refers to media such as a CD or DVD that is not included in the version you purchased, you may download this material at http://booksupport.wiley.com. For more information about Wiley products, visit www.wiley.com.

Library of Congress Control Number: 2013952429

ISBN 978-1-118-70781-4 (pbk); ISBN 978-1-118-70779-1 (ebk); ISBN 978-1-118-70784-5 (ebk)

Manufactured in the United States of America

10 9 8 7 6 5 4 3 2 1

Contents at a Glance

Table of Contents

Introduction

You're not supposed to judge a book by its cover, but most people do. The same holds true on social media sites. You might think that you should be judged for the quality of your written posts or the experience you list in your profile, but the reality is that the first impression you make in social media is based on how good your photos and graphics look and how well you've designed your profile.

Today's social media sites aren't just limited to short written messages. You can post photos, graphics, video, and audio to illustrate a point. Social media has evolved from a novelty used by a few early adopters to an essential communication tool used by hundreds of millions of people around the globe. Along the way, social media has become an increasingly important way to build personal and professional networks, search for jobs, find long lost friends, and so much more.

In *Social Media Design For Dummies*, our goal is to help you make a great first impression by showing you how to make the most of the design features on social media sites such as Facebook, Twitter, LinkedIn, Google+, YouTube, Pinterest, and Tumblr.

Throughout this book, you'll find detailed instructions as well as inspiring examples of how to create professional, inventive, and playful designs. Whether you're using social media to build your brand, develop your business, or just keep up with friends and family, creating a great design is not just about making you look good — it's a key part of building credibility online. So read on to find out how to create great social media designs that will help you build connections and enhance your online interactions.

About This Book

We designed *Social Media Design For Dummies* to help you quickly find answers you need when you need them. You don't have to read through this book cover to cover, and you certainly don't have to memorize it. Consider this a quick study guide and a reference you can return to whenever you need it. Each section stands alone, giving you easy answers to specific questions and step-by-step instructions for common tasks.

Want to find out how to change the background image on your Twitter page, add a cover image to your Facebook design, or link all your social media sites on RebelMouse? Jump right to the pages that cover those features. (*Hint:* The Table of Contents and index can help you find the sections that interest you most.) Don't worry about getting sand on this book at the beach or coffee spilled on the pages at breakfast. We promise: It won't complain!

Icons Used in This Book

on the web

This icon steers you to helpful things online: templates, help, great examples, site guidelines, and more.

remember

This icon reminds you of an important concept or procedure that you'll want to store away in your memory banks for future use.

technical stuff

This icon signals technical stuff that you may find informative and interesting although not essential. Feel free to skip over this information.

tip

This icon indicates a tip or technique that can save you time or money — or even a headache — later.

warning

This icon warns you of any potential pitfalls and gives you the all-important information on how to avoid them.

Beyond the Book

With a topic this big, we couldn't fit everything we wanted to include in the book. You'll find additional material in the following places:

 Cheat Sheet: Find tips and tools that can help you create, manage, and build great social media profiles, pages, and groups.

www.dummies.com/cheatsheet/socialmediadesign

▶ **Online articles:** Find tips for crafting great posts, protecting your privacy, and making it easy for web visitors to share your content on social media sites.

`www.dummies.com/extras/socialmediadesign`

▶ **Templates:** You'll find templates designed to help you create great profiles for Facebook, Twitter, YouTube, and other social media sites on author Janine Warner's website at

`www.digitalfamily.com/social`

Where to Go from Here

To familiarize yourself with the latest in social media websites and strategies, don't skip Chapter 1, which provides an overview of all the sites covered in this book and also helps you sort through the many options available. If you're ready to dive in and start creating a killer Facebook page for your business right away, jump ahead to Chapter 5. If you want to find out about a specific trick or technique, consult the Table of Contents or the index; you won't miss a beat as you work to make those impossible web design deadlines. Most of all, we wish you great success in all your social media endeavors, and we welcome the chance to connect with you.

Profile photo displays at 160 px but Facebook requires you upload an image at least 180 px

Your Name Here

Timeline   About   Friends 2,513   Photos 111

☆ Friends   Message   Give Gift

More ▾

Part I

Getting Started with Social Media Design

Chapter 1: Find an overview of the many different types of social media sites and the value of creating a consistent design that makes you (or your business) easily recognizable across different sites.

Chapter 2: Find an introduction to working with design tools, such as Photoshop or Photoshop Elements, how to work with the templates included in this book, and a few tips about developing great social media designs.

Chapter 3: Discover how online design principals can be used to improve your social media profiles and pages.

Visit www.dummies.com/extras/ socialmediadesign for great Dummies content.

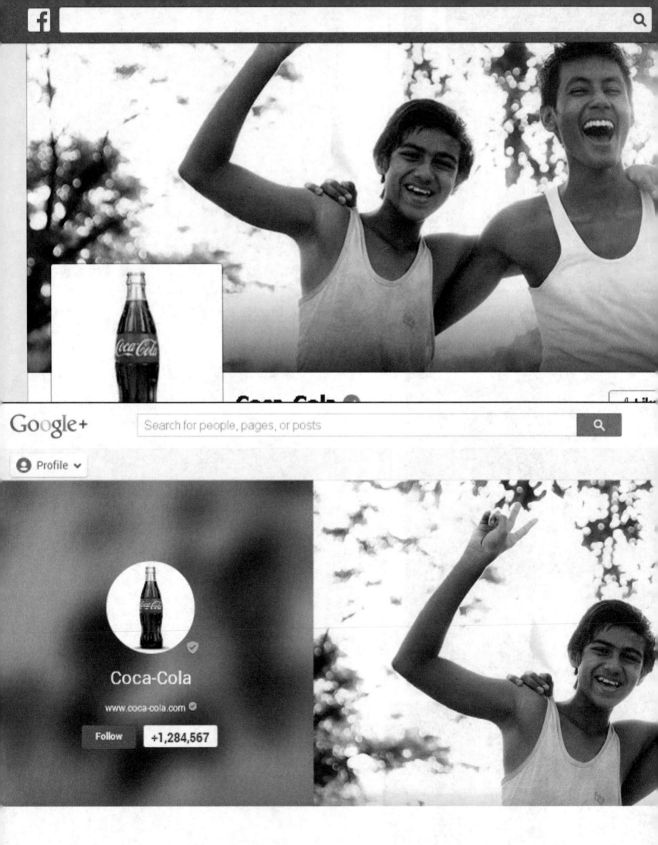

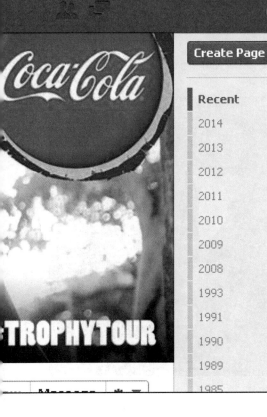

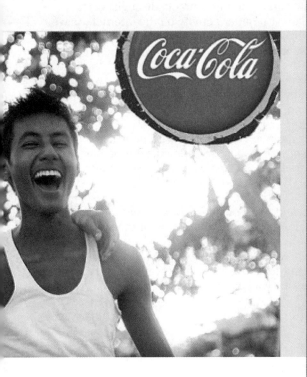

CHAPTER 1

Creating a Consistent Design for All Your Social Sites

In This Chapter

● There are many social media sites to join — you don't have to choose just one!

● Expand your social media presence with Share, Like, and Follow buttons.

● You can consider joining social bookmarking sites, too.

● Be sure to research effective social media designs.

*S*ocial networking — the art of meeting and building contacts through social media websites — has become the most popular activity on the Internet. As we live more of our lives online, social networks have become a powerful way to build connections, attract new clients, find discounts, or get a new job.

On the most popular social media sites, you can create personal profiles as well as professional pages, which are an increasingly important way to drive traffic to your website and promote your business, brand, or organization.

As social media has evolved, it's no longer enough to simply have a presence on each social site. Similar to the evolution of web design, social media design has become increasingly complex, and visitors to social media sites are becoming more discerning.

Today, how you present yourself, your brand, your business, or an organization on your social media is a key part of any marketing strategy, job hunt, or quest for new friends.

This chapter is about helping you stand out from the crowd by creating a great social media design. Figure 1-1 shows an interesting Facebook design.

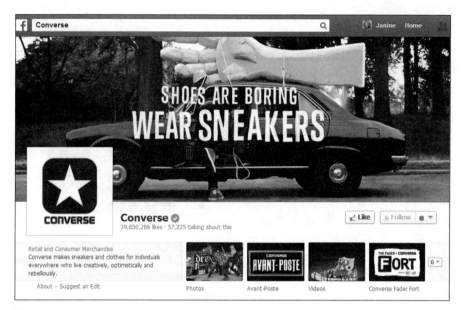

Figure 1-1

tip

If you're looking for advice on how to use the top social media platforms, consult *Facebook All-in-One For Dummies* by Melanie Nelson and Daniel Herndon, *Twitter For Dummies* by Laura Fitton, and *Pinterest For Dummies* by Kelby Carr.

Choosing the Best Social Media Sites

With so many social media sites to choose from, how do you decide which one(s) is (are) right for you? The following is an overview of the relative strengths and specialties of some of the top social media platforms.

The examples in the sections feature the profiles of our friend Erin Manning because she has created a consistent look across her many social media sites. Erin is a photographer, photography instructor, and fellow Wiley author. She takes her brand very seriously and has crafted an image that she is careful to protect and manage consistently across all of her social media sites, as well as her website, which is shown in Figure 1-2. As you can see in Figures 1-3 through 1-8, she uses similar colors, and even the same photos in many cases, to make it easy to recognize her brand on the many different social media sites she uses.

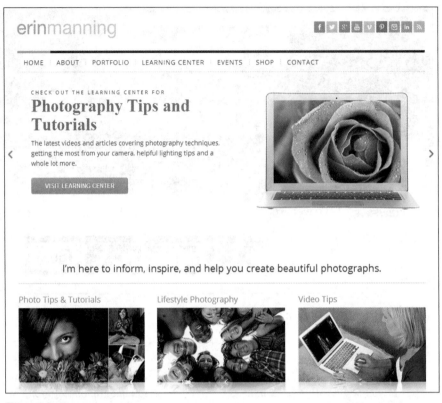

Figure 1-2

Erin Manning (http://erinmanning.com)

Facebook

www.facebook.com

Facebook wins top place as the largest social networking site on the web, and its broad appeal makes it an excellent place to promote your website. Facebook was originally considered a vanity site and a place for college students, but its professional power has grown with its ever-expanding audience. With more than 1 billion members, Facebook is by far the most important, and most active, of the social media sites to date.

You can create a Facebook Profile, Page, or Group, and there are many options for customizing the designs. Erin's Facebook profile is shown in Figure 1-3.

We talk more about how to set up your Facebook Pages in Chapters 4 and 5.

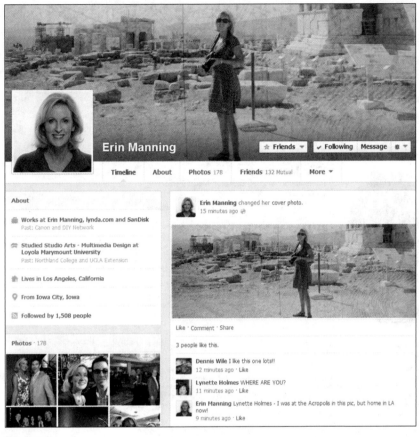

Figure 1-3
Erin Manning (`http://erinmanning.com`*)*

LinkedIn

`www.linkedin.com`

LinkedIn is the site for professional connections and online business networking. If you're online to develop business contacts with other professionals, especially if you're job hunting or trying to attract new business clients, LinkedIn is a powerful place to promote yourself and your website.

remember

Unlike Facebook, LinkedIn is all business.

tip

You get only one small profile image on a LinkedIn profile. Be sure to use the same profile image you use for your other sites for consistent branding.

Erin uses the same profile picture on LinkedIn that she uses on some of her other social sites, as shown in Figure 1-4, and it makes her easily recognizable.

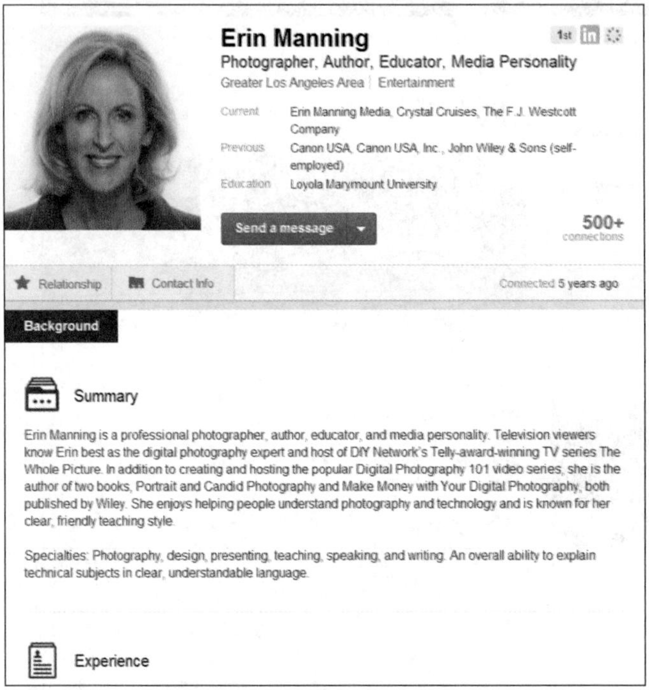

Figure 1-4

Erin Manning (`http://erinmanning.com`)

We show you how to create your LinkedIn presence in Chapter 8.

Twitter

`https://twitter.com`

Twitter has evolved into an international force to be reckoned with. A microblogging platform, Twitter makes it easy to connect with people and share brief bursts of information *(tweets)*. Twitter limits you to no more than 140 characters per post, but that brevity seems to be the secret to Twitter's success. Athletes, celebrities, politicians, and all types of so-called experts use Twitter to connect directly with their audiences, one brief message at a time.

remember

It takes a while to get the hang of the terse, abbreviation-heavy Tweetspeak language, which includes the use of special characters, such as the hashtag (#) to indicate a topic (such as `#socialmedia` in posts about the social media) or the at sign (@) in posts about a person (as in, follow me `@janinewarner`).

People tend to update Twitter more frequently than other services, making it a great place to follow trends, news events, and other information in real time. Like all social networks, Twitter is constantly evolving, so read other people's posts for a while to get the hang of it before you start to participate. Follow a few friends or experts to see how they use the service.

Twitter offers two areas where you can control the design of your site: the background and the main cover image, located at the top center of a profile. In Erin's case, she chose a simple illustration as the background, as shown in Figure 1-5, and uses the same photograph for her Twitter cover image that she uses in her Facebook design, which again makes her easily recognizable across her various profiles.

Turn to Chapter 6 to find out how to set up your Twitter profile.

Google+

`www.plus.google.com`

The newest entry in the social media scene is Google's competitor to Facebook, known as Google+. Launched in the summer of 2011, Google+ quickly turned into a must-have for every self-respecting web geek because membership was initially limited only to people who were invited.

The principal difference between Google+ and other social networking sites (such as Facebook) is that Google+ starts out by encouraging you to put your friends into *circles,* which provides a way to organize the people you know into categories, allowing you to choose what information and updates you share with each group.

Google+, now open to everyone, has become one of the top social media platforms, dwarfing many of its competitors and leveraging the power of the Google brand. In the case of Google, you can include a very large photo at the top of your profile. As you can see in her Google+ profile in Figure 1-6, Erin is making herself easy to recognize by using the same image she uses in her Facebook and Twitter profile designs.

Chapter 9 is where to go to set up Google+.

Figure 1-5

Erin Manning (`http://erinmanning.com`)

Pinterest

`www.pinterest.com`

This highly visual site exploded on the social media scene and became the fastest-growing site in 2012. Especially popular among designers, artists, fashionistas, and other creative people, Pinterest makes it easy to "pin" and share images in collections (*boards*). In her Pinterest profile, as shown in Figure 1-7, Erin showcases her photo tips as well as her fashion sense.

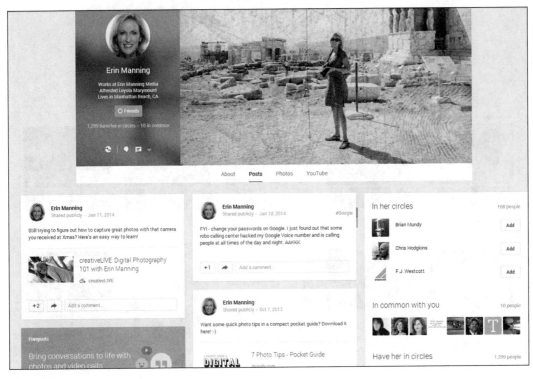

Figure 1-6

Erin Manning (`http://erinmanning.com`*)*

Even though Pinterest is a platform that thrives on the visual, user profiles are not the focus. Pinterest profile pics are incredibly small compared with the other images on the page, and Pinterest allows users to post only a brief, limited bio.

We show you how to use Pinterest in Chapter 10.

YouTube

`www.youtube.com`

YouTube is a global giant, so people use the name "YouTube" generically to refer to all kinds of videos on the web. Owned by Google, YouTube is not only one of the most popular social media sites, but it's also the world's second-most popular search engine. YouTube has become the default place users around the world turn to when looking for Internet video.

From her television appearances to video tapes of speeches to training videos for companies like lynda.com and creativeLIVE, Erin has plenty of video to showcase on YouTube, but she also uses a few still images from her website to decorate her YouTube channel, as shown in Figure 1-8. Chapter 7 shows you how to use YouTube.

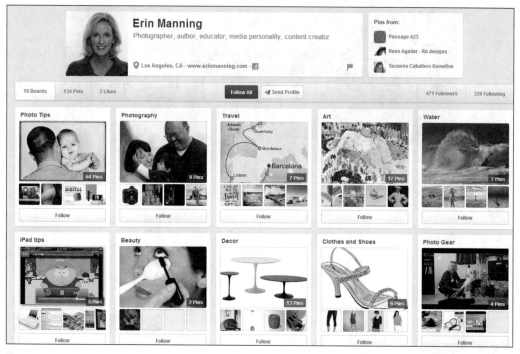

Figure 1-7

Erin Manning (http://erinmanning.com)

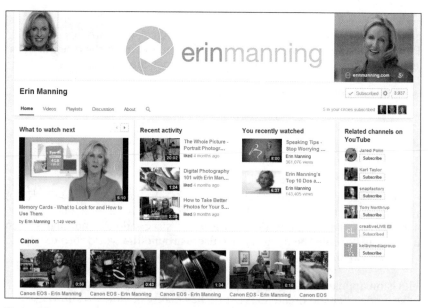

Figure 1-8

Erin Manning (http://erinmanning.com)

POSTING TO SOCIAL SITES

Creating a great social media design is just the first step. You also need to update your pages and profiles by regularly posting and tweeting. Here are a few ideas:

- **Share a favorite link or hot news item in your specialty area.** Odds are that many people in your networks on Facebook, Twitter, and LinkedIn share your interests.

- **Share or retweet something someone else has posted.** Passing along a great post is the highest compliment you can give in social media, and if you liked what they had to say, chances are that your friends will, too.

- **Be personable but not too personal.** You want to be authentic and relatable, but oversharing is the fastest way to lose followers.

- **Ask a question related to your latest book, research project, or business venture.** While writing this book, we asked our friends and followers to send great social media designs to feature in our book.

- **Make updating your status at least a weekly habit.** Just be careful not to flood your social networks with trivial or mundane posts. If you post more than a few times a day, make sure your followers welcome your status updates and find them helpful, interesting, or at least entertaining. Consider creating an editorial calendar for your social media properties to remind you to post often, but not too much!

Spreading the Love with Social Media Share Buttons

In addition to creating great designs for your social media profiles and pages, you can also include social media icons and links on your website or blog.

The two distinct ways to link to social media sites are

- **Like and Follow links:** When you include Like and Follow links on your website (see Figure 1-9), you link to your own profiles on Facebook, Twitter, and other social sites, and invite your visitors to connect with you. When visitors follow this kind of link, they are given options specific to each site, such as clicking the Like button on your Facebook page, clicking the Follow button on your Twitter profile, or subscribing to your YouTube channel.

Figure 1-9

- **Share links:** In contrast to Like and Follow links, Share links invite your visitors to share what's on your website with their friends and followers. In Figure 1-10, you see what happens when a user clicks the Share button for Facebook on the DigitalFamily.com website. In the Share This Link Facebook window open in Figure 1-10, you can see that the headline and the main image from the article are included and will be added to the post box. Above that information is a field (look for `Write something`) where the users can include their own comments as they post a story. When users click the Twitter button, a similar box opens with text for a tweet, which the user can edit before posting.

Click to share.

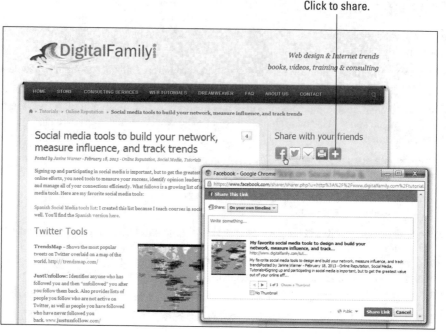

Figure 1-10

Janine Warner (www.digitalfamily.com/social-design)

Which option is best for your website or blog? We recommend using both. Including social media share buttons is one of the best ways to attract new visitors to a website or blog because you empower every visitor to your site to easily share your content with their friends and followers. The type of social media button shown in Figure 1-10 is best included with each individual post or article on your site.

tip

> Including Like and Follow buttons is a great way to build your network. These buttons are generally best included on the front page of your site, on the about page, and with your biography or other personal information.

You'll find many services designed to help facilitate the connection between your site and social media sites, but some of the most popular are

▶ **AddThis:** (www.addthis.com) Sign up for a free account on the AddThis website (shown in Figure 1-11), and you can easily create social media Share buttons as well as Like and Follow links. More than 14 million websites use this popular service. To add social buttons to your website, you simply copy and paste a little code from their page into yours.

tip

If you use WordPress, look for the AddThis plugin in the Plugin Directory to add social media buttons.

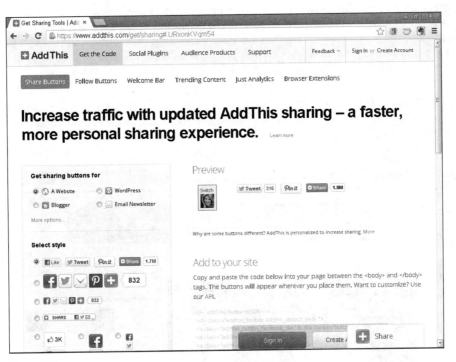

Figure 1-11

▶ **ShareThis:** (www.sharethis.com) Designed to work with a wide variety of website and blogging programs, ShareThis makes it easy to sign up for an account and then add a toolbar with social media sharing buttons to your web pages.

▶ **AddToAny:** (www.addtoany.com) Offering a widget that you can add to almost any website or blog, use AddToAny to create an account and then copy and paste code from AddToAny into the code in your website or blog.

Why would you choose one social media sharing site over another when they all so seem so similar? The biggest consideration is aesthetic. Visit all three sites and decide which one you think has the best-looking social media button designs. Look over their specific features and analytics, too. These services change rapidly, so make sure the one you choose supports all of the social media sites you use.

HOW BIG DO YOU MAKE YOUR SOCIAL MEDIA ICONS?

There is a common notion on the web (and elsewhere) that bigger is better. When it comes to social media icons, though, studies suggest that the best size for social media buttons is somewhere between really big and really small. The best social media icons should be large enough to identify on any page, but not so big that they draw your users' attention away from the content they came to see in the first place.

Another good practice is to make sure that every page with shareable content has a set of social media sharing buttons in the same place. Whether you place social buttons at the top, bottom, or middle of the page depends on your design and how the buttons work with the other content on your site, but most studies suggest they are most effective when they appear higher on the page. Making sure the buttons are always in the same place makes it easier for visitors to find them, which means they are more likely to share your content when they feel inspired to do so.

A typical article on *The New York Times* website, such as the one shown in this figure, includes images, ads, and many other distracting elements. The social media icons are relatively small, but they are consistently placed in a prominent location where they are easy to find.

Using Social Bookmarking Sites

In this book, we focus on social media sites that offer greater design opportunities, such as Facebook, Twitter, and YouTube, but we'd be remiss if we left out social bookmarking sites completely.

Social bookmarking sites rank the popularity of web pages by the number of votes they get. As a result, these sites are excellent resources if you want to keep up with what's popular online. Most enable anyone to vote on a site.

Although these sites have limited options when it comes to designing a profile, sites like Delicious, like Janine's shown in Figure 1-12, do enable you to upload an image and a short biography. You can also typically include your site URL, making these platforms a great way to drive traffic to your content.

Figure 1-12

A few of the most popular social bookmarking sites and services (with more sure to come) are

▶ Delicious (https://delicious.com)

▶ StumbleUpon (www.stumbleupon.com)

▶ reddit (www.reddit.com)

warning

Although you can submit your own web pages on any of these sites, that practice is generally frowned upon, and you can be banned if you do it too frequently. Your one vote won't make much difference, so it's best just not to do it.

tip

A better method to generate votes is to add a button to your website from each of these services so that visitors can easily vote for you. If you're a blogger, you can add a button each time you post. You can get the buttons (chiclets) for free and add them to your pages by simply inserting a little code you generate on the social networking site.

Gathering Ideas for Your Social Media Designs

One of the best ways to get ideas for designing your social media pages and profiles is to visit the websites of people and businesses you admire. Click the social media links on their sites and study what works and what doesn't in their designs. In particular

 Ask yourself what you like about each design and why you like it.

 Consider the choice of photos and illustrations. Do the pictures make you want to get to know them? Does the background or other illustration add credibility or showcase their talents?

 Pay special attention to how individuals and brands describe themselves. Many social media sites restrict your descriptions to just a few words or a sentence or two. Study how others introduce themselves to get clues about how to sum your own profile text in just a few words.

 Determine whether you can easily find the information you're most interested in and whether you think they did a good job of introducing themselves or promoting their business, brand, or organization.

remember

Sometimes the best way to get ideas for your own profile is to look at someone else's site and then return to yours with a fresh perspective. Social media sites are changing all the time. Keeping an eye on what others are doing is a great way to stay informed about new design options and creative ways to introduce yourself online.

CHAPTER 2

Checking Out Design Tools

In This Chapter

- Take the right design approach that fits your social media goals.

- You need to resize graphics for optimum online display.

- Take some time to compare free and premium image editors.

- See how to choose the best image format.

- Sometimes using a drawing instead of a photo is an artistic choice.

PNG-24
153.4K
29 sec @ 56.6 Kbps

Before we can start showing you all the wonderful ways that you can customize your social media profiles, invest a little time upfront in the tools and techniques you'll need. We start this chapter with suggestions for how to choose the right tools and then how to use a program like Adobe Photoshop (shown in Figure 2-1) to create optimal graphics for the web.

Finding the Social Media Design That Fits

First things first. Choose whether you want a beautiful but restrained photo for your social media design, or possibly an image that tells more about you. Throwing caution to the wind and taking the risk of using a quirky image that expresses some deep emotion takes real courage. Should you play it safe in social media or make yourself memorable?

Many creative people struggle with this question, zig-zagging among using a design that features a formal business logo, one that's more personal, or one that takes a risk with its edgy design. As you consider what's right for you, consider your audience.

Figure 2-1

remember

If you're using social media for personal reasons, you may think you can be more casual and playful. That said, many professionals choose to reveal a little more about their personal lives on Facebook than say, LinkedIn. If you're using social media professionally, consider what you want to be known for and how to best build your reputation. If you're a designer or photographer, showcase your talents with a quirky or eye-catching design. If you work at a company where you want to convey to your clients that you will give them the kind of out-of-the-box thinking that doesn't involve using clichés like "out-of-the-box thinking," you may be best served by taking more risks and being more experimental and creative.

Serhan Koçak produced one of the most creative Facebook cover designs we've found so far — a great way to show off his talent as an art director. His memorable design, shown in Figure 2-2, has earned him a spot on a number of Best of Facebook lists around the web.

tip

For a complicated idea like Figure 2-2, don't be afraid to ask for a little help. Serhan asked his friend, Serdar Yilmaz, a copywriter, to help come up with the idea and take the photos. He then used Photoshop to get them positioned just right before uploading them to Facebook.

Figure 2-2

Serhan Koçak (`https://www.facebook.com/serhankocak`); photos by Serdar Yilmaz

Making a composite image like this requires that you have some skill at selecting and extracting a subject in an image-editing program like Photoshop. Sections later in this chapter show you how to use some of the key features in Photoshop, including the Save for Web dialog to optimize images as JPEGs or PNG files for the web, and how to turn a photo into a work of art. In Chapter 3, you find instructions for extracting portions of an image and combining multiple images into a montage image.

Here are some circumstances where you might not want to take risks with your design, and you're probably better off sticking with a more formal social media profile design:

▶ **You're just getting started.** When you first start using social media, it's a good idea to begin slowly and devote some real consideration as to how much of your private information gets revealed to the world.

▶ **You're job hunting.** A growing number of potential employers search social media sites when considering candidates. Don't assume that just because you're connected to friends and family only, your potential employer (or the company that does background checks for them) won't find a way to view your profile. If you are looking for a new job, you want to keep your social media nose clean.

▶ **You're looking for clients.** If you run your own business, work as a consultant, speaker, real estate agent, or any other profession that requires you attract your own clients, make sure you create a profile that represents the quality and integrity of your business. Figure 2-3 shows the Google+ profile of a public-relations firm that shows a simple, straightforward design.

▶ **You have a job that requires trust.** You're an attorney, an accountant, a teacher, a doctor, or someone who works at a place where security is important, such as a bank, power plant, or security firm. More than a few people have been fired from their jobs because they posted something on social media that led their employers to lose confidence in them.

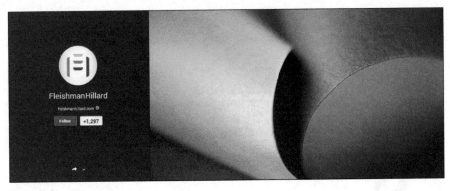

Figure 2-3

If you're a photographer whose hard drives are overflowing with beautiful, innovative images that you can adapt to a social media profile, then you can just start rummaging around through Lightroom, Aperture, or whatever photo-organizing software you use. But for the rest of us, acquiring images to achieve eye-catching designs requires a little planning and preparation.

In the example shown in Figure 2-2, Koçak's design works because he planned the photo session in advance, and carefully staged and shot two pictures he could then combine. First, he had his friend Serdar Yilmaz photograph him loosely clenching his fist and looking down at the imaginary space below it, as shown in Figure 2-4.

Figure 2-4
Serhan Koçak; photos by Serdar Yilmaz

Then he had his friend take a picture of him standing on his right foot, with his hands thrown up in the air, and head cocked to the side.

Before he combined the two images in Photoshop, he cropped out the background and turned the photo of him standing on one foot upside down, as shown in Figure 2-5.

Figure 2-5

Serhan Koçak; photos by Serdar Yilmaz

What makes this Facebook design work so well is that Serhan had a clear vision before he started. He took two relatively easy-to-capture photos and then made a few minor adjustments in Photoshop, like rotating the smaller image 180 degrees. The final effect (shown in Figure 2-6), works so well because the two images look convincing together.

Figure 2-6

Serhan Koçak; photos by Serdar Yilmaz

tip

When shooting photos to achieve a special composite, be sure to capture a variety of poses and expressions. The more choices you have when it comes time to edit, extract, and combine photos, the less risk you run of having to go back and reshoot the entire thing.

Another quirky combination is demonstrated in Figure 2-7, where Sune Adler Miltersen seems to be cowering from a giant cat. This is a slightly simpler photo composite, achieved by taking a close-up of a pouncing cat, and then using a funny mugshot of Sune looking up and to his left to create the illusion.

Figure 2-7
Sune Miltersen Adler (www.facebook.com/sunemiltersen)

technical stuff

Choosing a single-color background when you shoot your photos to use in a special-effect profile, as shown in Figures 2-4 and 2-6, makes it easier to extract your subject.

In her Facebook design, Rachel Brenke showcases her specialized talent for helping creative professionals with everything from basic legal permission forms to more serious matters, as shown in Figure 2-8.

Rachel Brenke is a photographer and an attorney, and her inviting pose in her photos gives her Facebook profile a warm and friendly feeling. Using both color and black-and-white images gives the design a creative touch.

Figure 2-8
Rachel Brenke http://rachelbrenke.com/

Finding the Right Design Tool

Tons of image-editing and design tools are available. Here are the leading tools we recommend and how to use them to design your social media presence. All these programs are available for Mac and Windows.

Photo-editing software

Just about every social media platform requires a profile photo, and photo-editing software comes in handy. At the very least, you will want to resize, crop, and color-correct your profile pictures; if you have advanced skills and are ready to try something a bit trickier, extract a subject from a photo to assemble fun collages.

▶ **Adobe Photoshop:** Photoshop is a widely used standard among graphics professionals. You can create original artwork, edit and enhance photographs, and so much more. Photoshop has a wealth of powerful painting and selection tools, special effects, and filters that enable you to create images far beyond what you can capture on film or create with many other illustration programs. With the Adobe Creative Cloud subscription model, you can sign up for a couple of months at about $19 per month to use Photoshop, and then discontinue the service.

   `www.adobe.com/products/photoshop`

▶ **Adobe Photoshop Elements:** If you don't need all the bells and whistles offered in the full-blown version of Photoshop, Photoshop Elements is a remarkably powerful program that tries to automate a lot of common tasks for beginners. If you're a professional designer, you're best served by Photoshop. For the hobbyist or small business owner who wants to create good-looking images without the high cost and learning curve of a professional graphics program, Elements is a great bargain.

`www.adobe.com/products/photoshop-elements`

 Apple iPhoto: This user-friendly image editor is part of the iLife bundle that Apple loads onto its computers. The tools and functions of iPhoto aren't as robust as many of the other programs listed here. For example, you can't work with multiple layers or do sophisticated image extractions, animations, or pixel-perfect retouching work. However, if you're a beginner and find the profusion of tools that crowd the margins of the more advance image-editing programs to be daunting, the fast, simple options in iPhoto may be perfect for you. As you can see in Figure 2-9, you can crop, straighten, and do basic adjustments to your photos. You can also apply some quick filters that allow you to mimic some of the popular Instagram effects on your photos.

`www.apple.com/mac/iphoto`

Figure 2-9
© istockphoto.com/Alex Nicada

▶ **GIMP:** No, this has nothing to do with an unfortunate character from Quentin Tarantino's *Pulp Fiction* movie. GIMP (short for GNU Image Manipulation Program) is increasingly the choice of photographers and graphic artists outside the United States, who can't afford Photoshop or its professional competitors. While the phrase "You get what you pay for" used to hold true with GIMP, recent upgrades to the underlying source code have made this free program a legitimate alternative. However, if you're used to the tools and techniques that work in Photoshop or other professional programs, GIMP takes some getting used to. Basically, because of patent and intellectual property copyrights, the GIMP programmers were forced to do elaborate workarounds to achieve the kinds of effects that other programs allow you to do with the click of a button. But if you have patience, and more time than money, GIMP allows you to achieve stunning effects without having to shell out such steep licensing fees. See Figure 2-10 for an example of the fairly sophisticated interface and tools that come with GIMP.

```
www.gimp.org
```

Figure 2-10

© istockphoto.com/STV

on the web

Run a Google search for "GIMP image galleries" to see what gifted individuals have created.

Drawing programs

The other broad category of design tools allows you to sketch or draw anything from a simple cartoon-like caricature to a full-fledged work of art. You can create surprisingly complex drawings in the photo-editing programs we mention earlier, but professionals use drawing programs.

▶ **Adobe Illustrator:** Use this powerful drawing program to create anything from a logo design for a local pizzeria to blueprints for the latest experimental Formula One dragster.

The major difference between Illustrator and the photo-editing software packages is that Illustrator works with what are known as scalable vector graphics (SVG) files, which are images that can be resized infinitely with no loss of quality. For your purposes, that would mean that a company logo that was created in Illustrator big enough to be blown up and printed on a billboard, could also be shrunk down small enough to fit in a 2"-square profile photo box on a social media site. If you're a good artist and love to draw (or even doodle), Illustrator can help you take your creations and make them suitable for use on the web.

`www.adobe.com/products/illustrator`

▶ **Inkscape:** This is a free alternative to Illustrator, in much the same way that GIMP provides a free alternative to Photoshop.

Inkscape may not have the sophisticated tools that Illustrator boasts to produce slick graphics that can be used on broadcast TV, in magazines and billboards all from the same file, but it does allow you to work with SVG files without having to invest in expensive software. Just as with GIMP, users around the world are turning to Inkscape to create illustrations.

`http://inkscape.org`

▶ **Adobe Fireworks:** Fireworks was one of the first image-editing programs designed to create and edit web graphics. Unfortunately, Fireworks was one of the casualties of Adobe moving to the Creative Cloud model of distributing and selling software. Created by Macromedia, Fireworks was popular among web designers and graphic artists for providing something of a bridge between Photoshop and Illustrator, mixing elements and functions of both in a way that was especially useful on the web.

At the time of the writing of this book, Fireworks is still available in its last incarnation, as part of the CS6 software suite, and can still perform functions that are not yet included in the Photoshop and Illustrator CC editions.

`www.adobe.com/products/fireworks`

tip

Illustrations, such as the one shown in Figure 2-11, are otherwise known as *line art.*

Figure 2-11

tom mccain (`http://crittur.com`)

MOTION-GRAPHICS AND ANIMATION PROGRAMS

Don't overlook motion-graphics and animation programs that you can use to create images that dance onscreen or that play short video clips in an endless loop. Flash animations are rapidly falling out of favor, but the venerable animated GIF has recently come back into vogue, particularly on social media sites like Tumblr. Some motion-graphics and animation software programs include

- After Effects
- Motion by Apple
- Fusion
- Nuke

warning

Myspace imploded in part because of the headache-inducing overkill in the use of animations. Now most social media sites restrict the amount of animation you can employ on your profile pages. Tumblr is one of the few sites that throws the doors wide open to user-generated animations.

Although there are tactics that you can use to insert an animated GIF into your Twitter or Facebook profile (such as uploading a normal image and then "editing" it by replacing it with an animation), this kind of an end-run around the rules may result in your images being removed, and even having your account suspended.

Creating and Optimizing Web Graphics

The most important thing to keep in mind when creating images for the web is that you want to *optimize* your images: that is, make your file sizes as small as possible so that they download as quickly as possible. This becomes particularly important when you're working with social media sites where users are increasingly accessing and viewing your profile on mobile devices. Devices have slower connection speeds, smaller memory, and weaker graphics cards — meaning large and complex graphics that work fine on the desktop can bring a mobile browser to its knees.

remember

How you optimize an image depends on

- How the image was created
- Whether you save it as a JPEG, PNG, or GIF

You find instructions for optimizing images with Photoshop in the sections that follow, but the bottom line is this: No matter what program, format, or optimization technique you choose, your biggest challenge is finding the best balance between small file size and good image quality.

Essentially, the more you optimize, the faster the image will download, but the compression and color reduction techniques used to optimize images can make them look terrible if you go too far.

As a general rule, take care of any editing — such as resizing, adjusting contrast, retouching, or combining images — before you reduce an image size or optimize it because you want to work with the highest resolution possible when you're editing. You find instructions for resizing an image in the next section and instructions for optimizing in the sections that follow.

Resizing graphics and photos

Resizing is important for two reasons:

▶ The images must be small enough to be displayed well on a computer monitor.

▶ You want the images to download quickly.

tip

The smaller the image file size, the faster it will download.

Although some social media sites allow you to change the display size of an image, you get much better results if you change the dimensions of an image upfront in a photo-editing program such as Photoshop.

Reducing an image's size for use on the web requires two steps:

1. Reduce the resolution of an image, which changes the number of pixels in the image.

   When you're working with images for the web, you want to reduce the resolution to 72 pixels per inch (ppi). If you're wondering why 72, see the sidebar that's appropriately named "Should I use 72 ppi or a higher resolution?"

2. Reduce the image's physical size by reducing its dimensions.

   You want to size your images to fit well in a browser window and to work within the design of your site.

Follow these steps to lower the resolution and reduce the size of an image in Photoshop. In Photoshop Elements, Fireworks, or GIMP, you follow a similar process although the specific steps may vary.

1. **With an image open in Photoshop, choose Image⇨Image Size.**

   The Image Size dialog box opens, as shown in Figure 2-12. Note the high resolution (240 Pixels/Inch) and large height and width (1698 x 1131). This photo is clearly too big to use on most social media sites.

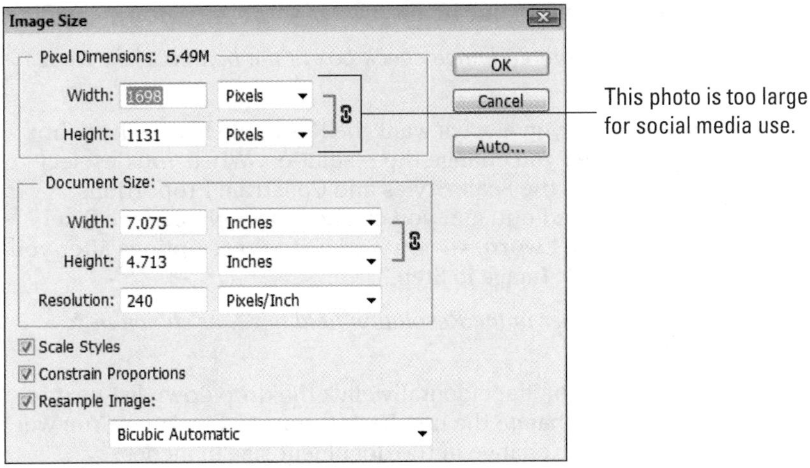

Image Size

Pixel Dimensions: 5.49M

Width: 1698   Pixels ▼
Height: 1131   Pixels ▼

OK
Cancel
Auto...

This photo is too large for social media use.

Document Size:

Width: 7.075   Inches ▼
Height: 4.713   Inches ▼
Resolution: 240   Pixels/Inch ▼

☑ Scale Styles
☑ Constrain Proportions
☑ Resample Image:
   Bicubic Automatic ▼

Figure 2-12

tip

If you don't want your original image to lose quality (or you just want to play it safe), make a copy of your image and resize the copy for your profile image.

SHOULD I USE 72 PPI OR A HIGHER RESOLUTION?

For years, most web designers have saved images for the web at a resolution of 72 pixels per inch (ppi). Most computer monitors displayed no more than 72 ppi, so any resolution higher than that was wasted on the web, and you'd be making your visitors download more pixels than they could see.

One of the emerging questions on the web is whether designers should start increasing the resolution of the images to keep pace with the higher resolution offered by the new breed of mobile devices, such as the Apple iPhone and iPad with ultra–high-density pixel resolution, Retina display, and widescreen monitors.

Of course, other manufacturers followed suit, and the 72 ppi standard is quickly becoming outdated. Most modern computer monitors can display images at 96 ppi to 100 ppi resolution or higher.

So what should you do?

Well, when you upload your images to social media sites, those images are resized to 72 ppi by default. When you think about it, this makes sense, given that every image stored on Facebook, Twitter, Google+, or whatever takes up storage space on a server somewhere, and these companies need to minimize their overhead costs.

Therefore, even if you've saved your images at one of the higher resolutions coming into use, that image will still be downgraded to 72 ppi. As with everything related to social media, this is subject to change with little or no notification. If you're really concerned with ensuring that your profile is future-proofed, you can save a version of your designs in a higher resolution so that it's ready for the day that social media sites start to switch over to 96 ppi or 100 ppi as a standard.

2. Change the resolution of your image.

a. Deselect the Resample Image check box at the bottom of the Image Size dialog box.

For best results, you always want the Resample Image check box deselected when you change the resolution. When you deselect Resample Image, the Scale Styles and Constrain Proportions options are grayed out, and you can no longer change the Pixel dimensions. Don't worry — you work with these options after you turn on Resample Image in Step 3.

b. Change the number in the Resolution field to 72, as shown in Figure 2-13.

Make sure you don't accidentally click the drop-down list next to Resolution and change the numbering units to Pixels/cm. You will notice a dramatic change in the document size in inches.

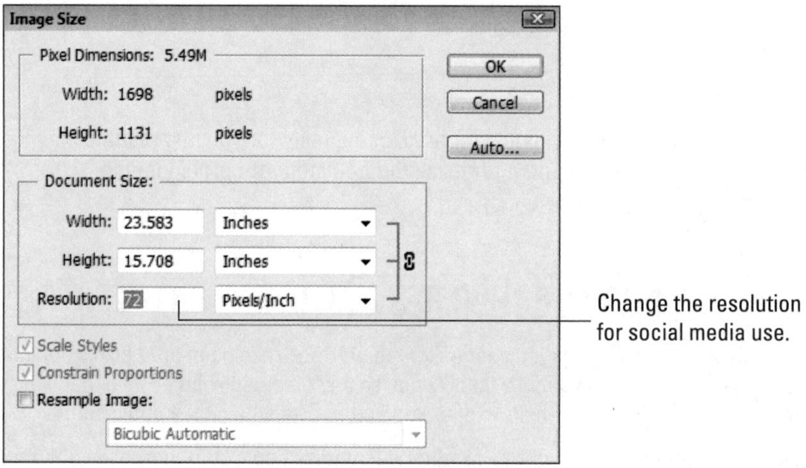

Change the resolution for social media use.

Figure 2-13

3. Change the image size.

a. Select the Resample Image check box.

remember

With the Resample Image check box deselected, you can't change the Pixel Dimensions, so it must be checked when you change the image size.

b. Enter a height and width for the image in the Height and Width fields.

As shown in Figure 2-14, change the size of this image to 851 pixels wide, which is the recommended width for a Facebook cover image. If the Constrain Proportions check box at the bottom of the dialog box is selected (as it is in this example), any changes you make to the height automatically affect the width (and vice versa) to ensure that the image proportions remain constant. We prefer to work this way, but if you do want to change the image and not maintain the proportions, deselect this check box.

warning

Releasing proportionality means that your image can get squished and distorted.

Note also the drastic change in the file size for this photo. Previously, it was 5.49MB, but after the resizing process, the new size is 1.38MB.

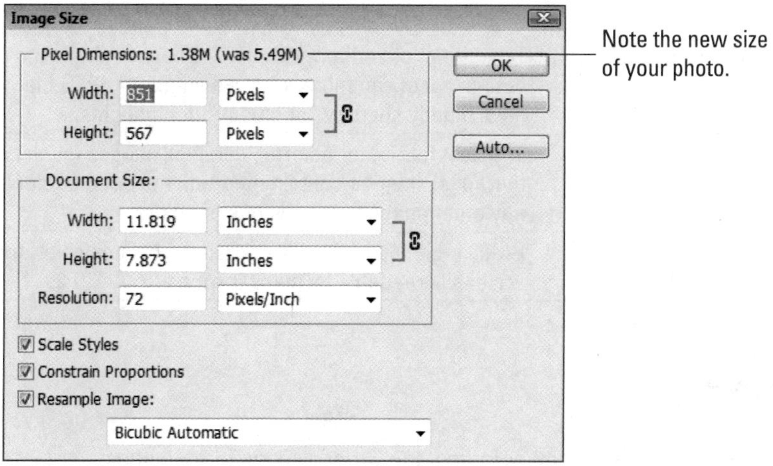

Note the new size of your photo.

Figure 2-14

4. **Click OK.**

warning

Saving the file at this stage is optional and not necessarily recommended because the final Save for Web export that comes next generates a new version.

If you want to return the image to its previous size, choose Edit⟹Undo Image Size. Be aware that when you save the image, though, the changes become permanent.

Choosing the best image format

One of the most common questions about images for the web concerns when to use GIF or PNG and when to use JPEG. Table 2-1 provides the simple answer.

Table 2-1	Image Formats
Format	*Best Use*
GIF (.gif)	For line art (such as one- or two-color logos), simple drawings, animations, and basically any image that has no gradients or blends. GIF is also the best format for displaying an image with a transparent background.
Animated GIF	The simplest way to add animation to a web page.
PNG (.png)	Generally produces better-looking images with smaller file sizes than GIF for the same kinds of limited-color images.
TIFF (.tif)	High-quality image files, commonly used by print shops.
PSD (.psd)	Images saved in PSD format after being edited allow you to go back and make further changes to the image, or reverse changes that they made (either by deleting adjustment layers or finding a previous restore point).
Camera RAW (.raw or .dng)	Talented photo editors can use Camera RAW files to pull details out of situations where a standard JPEG file would have muddy shadows or blown-out highlights.
JPEG (.jpg or .jpeg)	The best format for colorful, complex images (such as photographs); images containing gradients or color blends; and any other images with millions of colors.
BMP	BMP, or bitmap image files, are used by many platforms and are easily readable by many devices.

remember

Here are additional takeaways about the various image format types:

- One advantage that PNG files have over the more common JPEG files is that PNG files can have transparent areas, where the underlying colors or patterns on a web page can show through.

- PSD files are the complex, uncompressed, and multilayered files created by Photoshop. Most social media sites don't accept PSD files, so you have to save your creation into GIF, JPEG, or PNG file format.

- TIFFs are often uncompressed and include multiple layers, resulting in large file sizes.

- RAW or digital negative files are uncompressed files saved by high-end digital cameras. They contain a wider range of color and tones than a JPEG and thus have a larger file size. However, after tweaking the image, you will have to save Camera RAW files to a format that social media sites will accept.

Saving images for the web: The basics

If you're new to saving images for the web, the following basics can help you get the best results from your files, your image-editing program, and ultimately your web pages:

▶ **Convert an image from any format into the GIF, PNG, or JPEG format.** For example, turn all your TIFF, BMP, RAW, and PSD image files into a web-friendly file format.

▶ **Optimize images that are already in GIF, PNG, or JPEG format.** Even if your files are already in a web-friendly format, following the upcoming instructions in this chapter to optimize images with Adobe's Save for Web & Devices dialog box (or similar if you're using non-Adobe software) further reduces file sizes for faster download over the Internet.

▶ **Use different programs to create web graphics.** Photoshop is one of the most popular ones to use. Under the File menu in Photoshop (and Photoshop Elements), you'll find the Save for Web & Devices option. Fireworks provides a similar feature, and although each program's dialog boxes are slightly different, the basic options for compressing and reducing colors (which are covered in this chapter) are the same.

See the upcoming sections "Optimizing JPEG images for the web" and "Optimizing images in GIF and PNG formats" for details about using the Save for Web & Devices feature.

remember

Make image edits before you optimize. When you're editing, using the highest quality image possible is always best. Make sure to do all your editing, sharpening, and resizing before you use the Save for Web option. Similarly, if you want to make further changes to an image after you optimize it, you'll achieve the best results if you go back to a higher resolution version of the image rather than editing the version that's been optimized for the web. When you use the Save for Web & Devices feature, Photoshop creates a new copy of your image and leaves the original unchanged.

Optimizing JPEG images for the web

The JPEG format is the best choice for optimizing continuous-tone images, such as photographs and images with many colors or gradients. When you optimize a JPEG, you can make the file size smaller by applying compression. The more compression, the smaller the image — but, if you compress the image too much, the image can look terrible. The trick is finding the right balance, as you discover in this section.

If you have a digital photograph or another image that you want to prepare for the web, follow these steps to optimize and save it in Photoshop. In Photoshop Elements, Fireworks, or GIMP, the process is similar although the specific steps may vary.

1. **With the image open in Photoshop, choose File⇨Save for Web & Devices.**

2. **In the top-left corner of the dialog box, choose either the 2-Up or 4-Up tab to display multiple versions of the same image for easy comparison.**

   In the example shown in Figure 2-15, we opt for 2-Up, which makes it possible to view an image from iStockphoto.com of a colorful tile lizard created by Antoni Gaudí on the top, with the bottom showing a preview of the same image as it will appear with the specified settings. The 4-Up option, as the name implies, displays four different versions for comparison.

3. **On the right side of the window, just under Preset, click the small arrow to open the Optimized File Format drop-down list and choose JPEG.**

4. **Set the compression quality.**

   Use the preset options Low, Medium, High, Very High, or Maximum from the Compression Quality drop-down list. Or use the slider just under the Quality field (top right of the screen) to make more precise adjustments. (The slider appears when you click the arrow.) Lowering the quality reduces the file size and makes the image download more quickly.

Choose 2-Up or 4-Up.   Choose a compression value.   Choose a format.

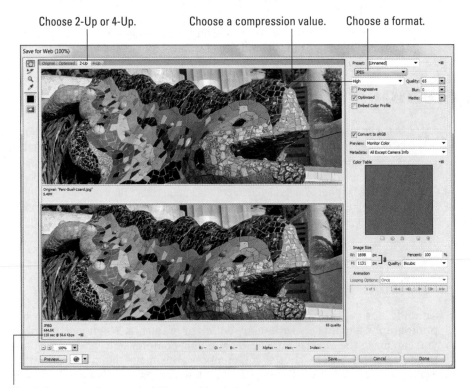

Watch the connection speed while you make choices.

Figure 2-15

Photoshop uses a compression scale of 0 to 100 for JPEGs in this dialog box, with 0 the lowest possible quality (the highest amount of compression and the smallest file size) and 100 the highest possible quality (the least amount of compression and

warning

If you lower the Quality number too much, the image will look blurry and blotchy.

the biggest file size). Low, Medium, and High represent quality values based on the amount of compression. The more the compression applied, the lower the image quality.

5. **Specify other settings as desired.**

   The compression quality and file format are the most important settings.

6. **Click Save.**

   The Save Optimized As dialog box opens.

7. **Enter a name for the image and save it to a folder on your hard drive where you will be able to quickly find it when you need it.**

   Photoshop saves the optimized image as a copy of the original and leaves the original open in the main Photoshop work area.

Repeat these steps for each image you want to optimize as a JPEG.

technical stuff

At the bottom of the image preview in the Save for Web & Devices dialog box, Photoshop includes an estimate of the time required for the image to download at the specified connection speed. In the example shown in Figure 2-15, the estimate is 118 seconds at 56.6 Kbps. As you adjust the compression settings, the size of the image changes and the download estimate will automatically adjust. You can change the connection speed used to make this calculation by clicking the small arrow just to the right of the connection speed and using the drop-down list to select another option, such as 1.5 Mbps for cable/T1 modem speed. Use this estimate as a guide to help you decide how much you should optimize each image.

Optimizing images in GIF and PNG formats

If you're working with a graphic that can be displayed in 256 colors or less — such as a logo, cartoon character, or drawing — your best bet is to use the PNG format and reduce the total number of colors used in the image as much as possible to reduce the file size.

To help make up for the degradation in image quality that can happen when colors are removed, GIF and PNG use a dithering trick. *Dithering* involves alternating pixels in a checkerboard-like pattern to create subtle color variations, even with a limited color palette. The effect can smooth the image's edges and make it appear to have more colors than it actually does.

To convert an image to a GIF or a PNG in Photoshop, follow these steps. In Photoshop Elements, Fireworks, or GIMP the process is similar although the specific steps may vary.

1. **With the image open in Photoshop, choose File⇨Save for Web & Devices.**

   The Save for Web & Devices dialog box appears.

2. **In the top-left corner of the dialog box, choose the 2-Up or 4-Up tab to display multiple versions of the same image for easy comparison.**

   In the example shown in Figure 2-16, we chose 4-Up, which makes it possible to view the original image (in the upper-left corner) as well as three different previews of the same image. (Refer to Figure 2-15 for an example showing 2-Up.)

Check the settings for your chosen image.

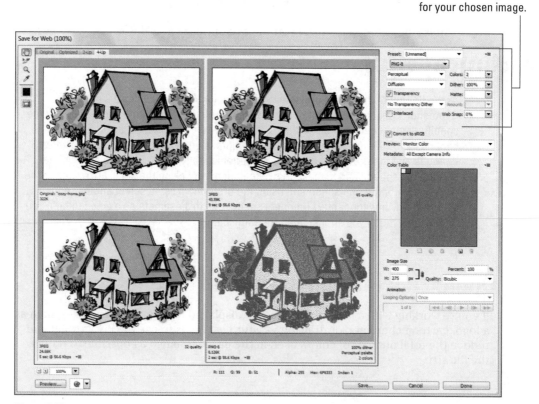

Figure 2-16

tom mccain (http://crittur.com)

3. **Click to select any of the four preview images to see the size and adjust its settings.**

The size, format, and other settings of the selected image are shown in the top right of the dialog box. Reducing the number of colors and other options can dramatically affect the image.

For example, the fourth version (bottom right of Figure 2-16), shows the image with only two colors showing. In the other three squares, the image includes more colors — and although they look better, the file size will be larger.

tip

Changing the preview images in the 4-Up view enables you to compare the original image with up to three different versions using different Colors, Transparency, and other settings, covered in the steps that follow.

4. **On the right side of the dialog box, just under Preset, click the small arrow to open the Optimized File Format drop-down list and choose PNG-24.**

The PNG-24 option produces a better quality image. The quality of the image declines quickly as you reduce the number of colors in the file or change the format to GIF. However, you also reduce the file size.

5. **In the Colors box, select the number of colors, as shown in Figure 2-17.**

The fewer colors you use, the smaller the file size and the faster the image will download.

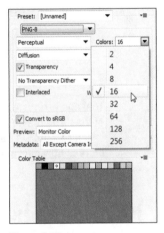

Figure 2-17

warning

If you reduce the colors too much (as in the bottom-right preview shown in Figure 2-16), you lose details. The ideal number of colors depends on your image. You want as small an image as possible, but if you reduce the number of colors too far, your image will look terrible.

6. **If you want to maintain a transparent area in your image, select the Transparency check box.**

Any area of the image that was transparent when you created the image in the editor appears transparent in the preview window. If you don't have a transparent area in your image, this setting has no effect.

Using transparency is a good trick for making text or an image appear to float because a transparent background doesn't appear on the web page. You can select transparency as a background option in the New dialog box when you create a new image in Photoshop or Photoshop Elements.

7. **Specify other settings as desired.**

   The remainder of the settings in this dialog box can be left at their defaults in Photoshop.

8. **Click Save.**

   The Save Optimized As dialog box opens.

9. **Enter a name for the image and save it into a folder that you can quickly and easily locate when it comes time to upload to your chosen social media site.**

Repeat these steps for each image you want to optimize as a GIF or PNG for your site.

Trial and error is a great technique in the Save for Web & Devices dialog box. In each of the three preview windows displaying optimized versions the drawing of the house in Figure 2-16, we use fewer and fewer colors, which reduces the file size with an increasingly degrading effect.

How small is small enough?

After you know how to optimize GIFs and JPEGs and appreciate the goal of making them as small as possible, you may ask, "How small is small enough?" The answer is mostly subjective, but the following points are good to remember:

▶ **The larger your graphics files, the longer people have to wait for them to download.**

▶ **Most social media sites place strict limits on the size of images that they allow you to upload.** You may have an amazing panorama that you shot from the North Rim of the Grand Canyon, but if Facebook rejects that 100MB file, you'll have to reduce the file size. The best ways to do that are to crop the image, increase compression, or scale down the image by reducing the pixel height and width.

▶ **Make sure to test your image on a variety of different devices and platforms.** With more and more people using mobile devices to access social media, your profile images need to be legible even on the small screens (viewports) of smartphones and tablets. An image that looks great on the 23" desktop monitor — where you likely designed it — may be a muddled mess on a tiny handheld device screen.

Working with Easy Drawing Tools

If you have a steady hand and some artistic talent, you may want to try your hand at sketching something that represents how you want to present yourself to the world. Keep reading for tips on how to achieve some cools looks by using a feature of Adobe Illustrator called Live Trace.

With some time and practice, you'll be able to produce artwork from an ordinary photo that looks a little like the famous "Hope" poster used by President Obama's campaign in 2008. Or you can strip your portrait photo to its most basic curves and lines, and then use the Fill and Paintbrush tools to do the equivalent of paint-by-numbers on your own portrait.

Follow these steps for a good start on using Illustrator to achieve a cool look quickly:

1. **Open a standard portrait (it can be in JPEG, PNG, or just about any other image format) in Illustrator.**

   As you can see in Figure 2-18, we start with a simple portrait photo, suitable for Twitter, Pinterest, YouTube, or many other social media sites.

Figure 2-18

Figure 2-19

2. **Click the image to make it active.**

   A thin blue box appears around the image, and you can now edit the image. See Figure 2-19.

3. **Using either the Preset drop-down menu on the top status bar, or the drop-down menu that appears next to the Preset option in the Image Trace panel, click the Default option to convert your photo to line art.**

   The image is converted to a simple black-and-white sketch, as shown in Figure 2-20. If you don't like this effect, simply press Ctrl+Z (on a Mac, ⌘+Z) or choose Edit⇨Undo Image Tracing to undo the action.

Figure 2-20

4. **From the drop-down menu next to the Image Trace button on the toolbar, choose how you want to convert your photo to line art. If you want to exert more control on the Image Trace process, choose Window⮞Image Trace to open the Image Trace panel.**

tip

The panel can be docked with the other panels on the right-hand side, or you can float it around your screen wherever you like.

If you just want to do a simple conversion, ignore the more complicated options in the panel and just use the drop-down menu that appears in the top status bar.

5. **To take total control of how the image looks, choose the Image Trace option you like best and then choose Object⮞Image Trace⮞Expand.**

You see all the paths that Illustrator has broken your image into, as shown in Figure 2-21. You can now select each area in your photo, and paint, use a Fill tool, or replace the color to customize your image. This "paint by numbers" approach can get quite complex.

Figure 2-21

For an oil painting look: Choose 16 Colors from the Image Trace drop-down menu. This reduces the number of colors displayed in the image to only 16, while converting the image to look as though it had been painted by hand.

For a monochromatic look for your image: Choose 6 Colors from the Image Trace drop-down menu. You get the same smooth lines and slightly "creamy" look for your image as when choosing 16 Colors, but the color palette will be reduced to only six colors.

The biggest benefit of converting an image using Image Trace is that the image can now be blown up or reduced in size without affecting the quality. This means that if you're using a photo for your company logo, you can now produce a version of it that could be enlarged to put on a billboard or poster in your place of business, as well as reduced to a diminutive size that could be put on your business card (or Twitter profile) without damaging the quality.

CHAPTER 3

Advanced Design Concepts

In This Chapter

● Use free, web-based photo-editing software to create a customized image.

● Use an image editor to extract a subject from the background.

● Use a template to create a social media design in Photoshop or another image editor.

This chapter shows you simple image editing techniques that you can do to make your social media design shine. Then we show how to take your social media profiles to the next level by shooting eye-catching photos, extracting the subject from a photo, and then blending it into a new photo collage that will impress your friends and contacts.

For much of what we demonstrate in this chapter, access to professional tools (such as a good dSLR camera and professional photo-editing software, such as Photoshop) is pretty much standard operating procedure to achieve good results. Yes, you can probably achieve graphic designs that look a lot like what we're showing off in this chapter with the types of cameras built into smartphones, processed through free software — but that route requires a lot more ingenuity, time, and effort.

This chapter is for when you just want to stretch your boundaries and do something out of the ordinary, like create a collage of images to dress up your social media pages. In her Facebook design, coauthor Janine Warner combines three images to share her personal and professional story (see Figure 3-1). Not only is this a great way to use pictures that you like (but that aren't in the wide, horizontal format favored by most social media sites), but the process for cropping, moving, and combining multiple images into a larger whole is one that after you master it, can be used in many other ways.

Janine Warner

Figure 3-1

Using Free Photo-Editing Software

Not everyone has the time, interest, or budget to invest in photo-editing software such as Photoshop, but that doesn't mean that you can't still create custom images to use across your brand's social media properties.

PicMonkey (www.picmonkey.com) allows you to create a free account before editing images. You can also upgrade ($33 per year) to access additional tools, from a greater range of fonts to photo filters. From the PicMonkey site, select Edit from the horizontal navigation bar at the top of the screen.

Hover your cursor over the Edit button that appears, and you can access the following uploading options:

 Computer

Dropbox

Facebook

Flickr

Opening your image takes you to the editor page (shown in Figure 3-2) where you can begin to play around with the PicMonkey tools. Use the Basic Edits tools (on the left) to

 Crop

Change canvas color

Rotate or straighten photos

Change the exposure

Adjust image color saturation and temperature

Sharpen the image

Resize your image

Figure 3-2

Although the PicMonkey Basic Edits tools are a great starting point to take your images to the next level, that's just the tip of the editing iceberg. More sophisticated tools allow you to do everything from add text to place image stickers and shapes on your photos. You can even create a collage as we discuss later in this chapter. Don't have Photoshop? No problem! PicMonkey also provides collage-creation options.

To get started, select Collage from the horizontal navigation bar. After you select your photos, you can use the following collage tools shown in Figure 3-3:

 Layouts

Swatches

Background

Use the collage tools to create the perfect size and style collage for your social media pages. The Layout menu even offers a FB Cover option, automatically providing you with the correct size for your Facebook Cover Photo and offering four style options from which to choose.

After you create your collage, select Edit at the top of the editing screen (see Figure 3-3) to send your collage to the PicMonkey Edit menu. You can now add text, overlays, and other goodies to your collage.

Figure 3-3

Extracting a Subject from a Photo

For the heavy-hitting, time intensive photo-editing techniques, you really need a photo-editing program. (See Chapter 2 for an overview of several good ones.) In this chapter, we use Photoshop.

One of the most useful skills is the ability to make an accurate, high-quality selection of a subject in a photo. A good selection allows you to

▶ Apply styles to specific parts of a photo.

▶ Take portions from a variety of images and arrange them into an entirely new composition or collage.

Selecting something out of a photo sounds like it would be easy. Most people who have played with Photoshop or another image-editing program have blundered their way through the process, usually by hit-and-miss use of obvious tools such as the Magnetic Lasso or Eraser tools. But in practice, it can be very tricky, and we've all seen enough "crude Photoshops" where some nitwit has cut and pasted an inappropriate head on a celebrity's body.

Here are some basics about the "major player" Photoshop tools. Other photo-editing software programs have similar tools.

▶ **Eraser:** Use the Eraser to remove pixels on the active layer. You can also tell the Eraser not to bother pixels of a certain color, or set it to function only on the pixels that are active in a certain layer. So, say you're building a photo collage and want to touch up some stray hairs that have gotten into your picture without also getting rid of the background; in that case, set the Eraser to delete pixels that are the same color as the strands of hair.

▶ **Magic Wand:** Use the Magic Wand to select pixels of a certain color range and select pixels that are noncontiguous. The contiguous option allows you to select either all the specified color that appears in the image, or only that color that appears in one area (such as getting rid of a green sign in the background without also getting rid of the lawn under your subject's feet). The color range allows you to specify what shade of color you want.

▶ **Quick Selection:** Use the Quick Selection tool to click and drag around an area to indicate a selection. Photoshop engineers have developed sophisticated behind-the-scenes analysis tools that allow the program to find and recognize the edge that separates your subject from the background.

▶ **Lasso:** The Lasso tool is one that most beginners use because it's the easiest to understand. Just click and start dragging around an object. Depending on how steady your hand is and how accurate your mouse movements are, you can do a pretty good job of cutting out only the parts that you want. This technique is slow and painstaking, and if you make an error, you will spend a lot of time trying to clean it up.

▶ **Magnetic Lasso:** This variation of the Lasso tool drops little points on the screen as you drag it around, connecting those points by thin lines. The computer tries to figure out what you're selecting and puts those points on areas that it thinks are dividing lines between what you want and what you don't. So if you start out trying to cut out a person's face from a picture, the Magnetic Lasso tries to help by dropping little points on the edge of the person's hair, cheek, or neck. Where it runs into trouble is when you get to areas where there is no clear differentiation between colors, such as where the shadow under a chin is almost the same color as the background.

▶ **Marquee:** Use the Marquee tool to draw a simple square or circle on the screen, and to select whatever is inside that shape. You can restrict the ellipse into an circle or drag the square into a rectangle, but really, you're not going to be getting very sophisticated with this tool. At least, not at the outset.

▶ **Refine Edge:** This is a tool to use after you make a selection with just about any of the primary tools here. It opens a window where you see a close-up of the subject that you just tried to select, and offers you a number of tools that you can use to try to make the selection cleaner and more accurate.

The following sections show you how to use a few of these tools — Magic Wand, Eraser, Quick Selection, and Refine Edge — to construct the building blocks for your own image collages.

Using the Magic Wand tool to extract a subject

The Magic Wand tool has become the subject of much scorn from photo-editing professionals, who consider it to be the type of thing that is misused by neophytes who produce jagged-edged selections that make the whole profession look bad. The Magic Wand tool has undergone some refinements that have made it much more useful, though. Don't let the mutterings of some old-school curmudgeons on online forums turn you away from using what can be a useful tool.

Follow these steps to extract a subject from a photo, using the Magic Wand tool in Photoshop. For this example, we chose an image with a fairly solid-colored background to work with (see Figure 3-4).

Figure 3-4
© istockphoto.com/Chimneys on Casa Mila by Architect Antoni Gaudí

tip

Photos with complex or busy backgrounds are not good candidates for using the Magic Wand. See the section "Working with the Quick Selection and Refine Edge tools."

1. **With an image open in Photoshop, choose Layer⇨Duplicate Layer, or press Ctrl+J (on a Mac, ⌘+J).**

   A duplicate layer, the same in every detail as your original image, is created in the Layers panel on the right-hand corner.

remember

Create a duplicate layer to work on before you start a complicated edit. That way, if you make a mistake, you can always start over from the original layer. It's also handy to turn off the visibility of the original background layer by clicking the eye icon next to the layer, as shown in Figure 3-5. Some photo editors are able to work without doing this, but we have found that when we make a layer transparent and still see the pixels from the underlying layer, we can get confused.

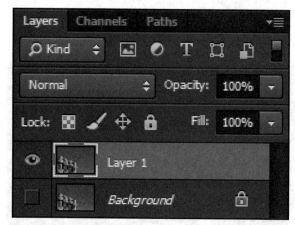

Figure 3-5

2. **Click the Magic Wand tool (or press W if the last tool you used was Quick Selection).**

   The Quick Selection tool is also nested under the Magic Wand tool in Photoshop CS3 and later. For this example, make sure the Magic Wand tool is active. You can tell which one is active by the square dot next to it. We cover how to use Quick Selection later in this chapter.

3. **Click the background area that you want to select. For this example, we click in the blue sky area.**

   As you can see in Figure 3-6, the Magic Wand has done an okay job of selecting blue pixels in the image. However, if we were to use just this selection to try to isolate the Easter Island–looking tan heads, it would be a long and laborious process. Fortunately, by tweaking a couple of settings, we can streamline the process.

4. **Double-click the Tolerance field (beneath the menu bar) to select the number in the box and then type a larger number. Or, hover your mouse pointer over the Tolerance field, click, and then hold down the left mouse button to make the number higher or lower.**

Figure 3-6
© istockphoto.com/Toni Flap

We made our initial selection with the Magic Wand with the Tolerance set to 11. (Your initial Tolerance level will vary, depending on your computer's initial settings, and whether you have changed it in the recent past.) A Tolerance level of 11 means the pixels to be selected are those within 11 shades of whatever color you click (in this case, the color blue). As we point out in Figure 3-6, that resulted in a narrow band of blue being selected.

remember

The higher the Tolerance, the more shades and colors are selected. The lower the Tolerance, the more stringent the selection. The maximum value you can enter is 255 — but at that loose Tolerance, the Magic Wand selects every pixel in the image. And that's not what you want.

5. **With a higher Tolerance set, click again with the Magic Wand to select the background.**

   As shown in Figure 3-7, the higher Tolerance setting (now 70) results in a much wider section of the sky being selected.

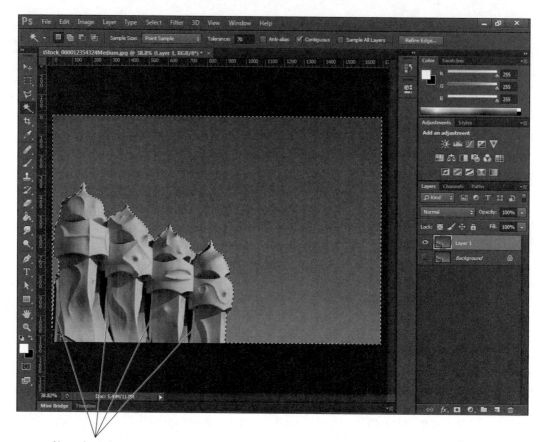

Nonselected parts

Figure 3-7

© istockphoto.com/Toni Flap

However, note the thin segments of blue between the heads — which are patches of blue that are not selected. Sure, you can carefully click and select each individual segment to select it, but here's a simpler way to select those thin blue slices.

6. **Underneath the menu bar, click twice to deselect the Contiguous check box. Then click twice to select the background.**

All the shades of blue that are within the Tolerance settings in the background are selected, as shown in Figure 3-8.

Now selected

Figure 3-8
© istockphoto.com/Toni Flap

If there are colors that are within the Tolerance range that you have set, and you turn off the Contiguous setting, the Magic Wand tool will select them, no matter where they appear in the image.

That means that if you're trying to select the blue sky in the background — and your subject has blue eyes or is wearing a blue shirt — those other blue pixels can wind up being selected.

7. Press the Delete or Backspace key to remove the pixels in the image that you selected.

Photoshop indicates a transparent background to reflect the deletion. It displays a checkerboard of gray and white squares, as shown in Figure 3-9.

Figure 3-9

© istockphoto.com/Toni Flap

Now you can either save the image as a PNG file with the transparency option turned on (see how in Chapter 2), or you can select this extracted subject and paste it into another image to make a collage or composite.

Using the Eraser tool to extract a subject

The Eraser tool is usually limited to those times you've made a mistake and need to scrub away some stray pixels or an effect that you've overdone. The Eraser tool can also be used to make a more complicated selection than can be done with the Magic Wand.

tip

This technique can come in handy if you want to isolate your face from a group shot to use as a profile photo.

The following steps build on the preceding section, showing you how to not only get rid of the pesky blue background, but also how to remove three of the heads, leaving only one.

1. **With an image open in Photoshop, choose Layer⇨Duplicate Layer or press Ctrl+J (on a Mac, ⌘+J).**

2. **Click and hold the Eraser tool to bring up the menu options. Then choose Background Eraser.**

   The Eraser and Magic Eraser tools are also nested under this tool in Photoshop. You can tell which one is active by the square dot next to it.

3. **Below the menus, click to select the Protect Foreground Color option.**

   This option allows you to tell the Eraser tool to get rid of only the pixels in the color ranges you want, while not accidentally erasing the pixels you want to preserve. In this example, we have the blue of the sky that we want to get rid of, while preserving the tan of the heads.

4. **With the Background Eraser tool active, Alt-click (on a Mac, Option-click) on the color you want to preserve.**

   The cursor changes from a circle with a crosshair in it to an eyedropper, as shown in Figure 3-10. Use this to select a color in the area that you want to preserve.

Figure 3-10
© istockphoto.com/Toni Flap

tip

One thing that makes the Eraser useful is that you can quickly preserve different colors while isolating your subject from a background. Simply alternate using the Background Eraser with Alt-clicking/Option-clicking colors you want to keep, and you can work with even complex backgrounds where the colors are shifting and changing around the outlines on your subject.

5. **Click and hold, and drag the Background Eraser over the image to remove the background color.**

As shown in Figure 3-11, the Background Eraser removes the blue color, while not erasing the pixels in the tan heads. If all the colors you want to remove are not being erased, adjust the Tolerance, as we describe in Step 4 of the previous section.

Figure 3-11
© istockphoto.com/Toni Flap

tip

You can quickly increase or decrease the size of your Background Eraser by using the bracket ([or]) keyboard shortcuts.

With your subject extracted, further isolate a single element if needed (such as a face) by switching to the regular Eraser tool. Click and hold the Eraser tool, and then start erasing the other faces (or torsos, or whatever) in the image.

warning

The Eraser tool removes all pixels, regardless of color. Watch that you don't get carried away, as in Figure 3-12.

Figure 3-12
© istockphoto.com/Toni Flap

To create a clean line on the extracted image, hold down the Shift key while holding the left mouse key down. Then "scrub" over the image, to force the cursor to erase in a perfectly straight line. This technique is useful if you want to have profile photo with a straight edge. as shown in Figure 3-13.

Like with a Magic Wand image, an extracted subject can be saved as a PNG file with the Transparency option turned on (read about that in Chapter 2), or you can select this extracted subject and paste it into another image to make a collage or composite.

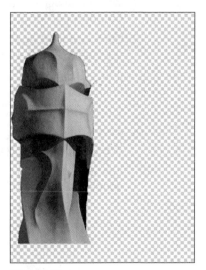

Figure 3-13
© istockphoto.com/Toni Flap

Working with the Quick Selection and Refine Edge tools

Think of the Quick Selection tool as having the computer act a little like a more coordinated older sibling, helping their kid brother cut only the sports hero they idolize out of the newspaper. Photoshop tries to guess what you're trying to isolate from the rest of the image, and draws a border between the subject and the background.

Photoshop Elements also sports this tool, although some users claim that the full version of Photoshop is much more precise in its selection. GIMP has a Foreground Select and Fuzzy Select tool that together come close to emulating the functionality of Quick Selection.

technical stuff

The Quick Selection tool works by applying sophisticated analytics to the image, looking for similar textures in an image, and interpolating the difference between these areas and other areas. For example, it looks for things like the difference between stiff, bristly hair on a horse's back, and the patchy, mottled appearance of a cloudy sky to figure out where the border between the horse and the sky should be drawn.

In this example, we use another lovely Gaudí image. It's not suitable for making a selection with the Magic Wand or Eraser tools because of the wild variety of colors on the giant tile lizard (see Figure 3-14) as well as on the stairs, railings, grass, and stone columns surrounding the subject.

1. **With an image open in Photoshop, choose Layer⇨Duplicate Layer or press Ctrl+J (on a Mac, ⌘+J).**

2. **Click and hold on the Magic Wand tool to bring up its submenu. Choose the Quick Selection tool.**

   It looks like a paintbrush with a dotted circle around the end, and its keyboard shortcut is W.

   The mouse pointer should change to a circle with a crosshairs in the middle.

3. **Click and hold the left mouse button on the subject in your image and start carefully dragging it around the perimeter of the subject in your image.**

   Photoshop will start drawing dotted lines over what it thinks the borders of your subject should be (see Figure 3-15).

Figure 3-14
© istockphoto.com/KarSol

A selection line

Figure 3-15
© istockphoto.com/KarSol

When you're making your selection, pretend that you're painting with your mouse cursor over the subject in your image. Use short strokes and release the mouse button frequently. That way, if Photoshop gets a little over enthusiastic when selecting pixels in your image, you can undo the last small selection by pressing Ctrl+Z (on a Mac, ⌘+Z) while still retaining the careful selection work that you've done so far.

4. **Hold down the Alt (Option) key, and click and drag to deselect areas that aren't part of your subject and that you don't want to include.**

   You can also click the Add to Selection or Subtract from Selection buttons beneath the main menu. These buttons look like the Quick Selection tool but with a plus or minus button added, respectively.

   Look back at Figure 3-15 for a sec. You can see that Photoshop included the white area under the arm of the lizard, on the left side. When you hold down the Alt (Option) key, the plus symbol inside the Quick Selection pointer toggles to a minus sign. That means that everything you now click will be subtracted from the selection.

   Alternate between using the Add to Selection and Subtract from Selection settings to get as close as you can to the edge of the subject you are trying to extract.

5. **When you have the subject in your image selected as well as you feel comfortable with, click the Refine Edge button below the main menu bar.**

   The Refine Edge dialog box opens along with a new window showing your selection against a solid background. You can choose black, white (see Figure 3-16), or a silhouette. Choose the option that best helps you see the contrast between the selection and the background.

   On our example, stray pixels remain near the snout of the lizard, as well as under the chin, and stray lines are coming off the arms. If the selection is too rough and there are too many stray pixels (or big missing pieces from your subject) — like our example — click Cancel and return to using the Quick Selection tool to further refine your extraction.

6. **Refine the edge.**

   a. *Click the Refine Radius Tool in the Refine Edge dialog box (the paintbrush squishing down on a dotted line, on the left edge).*

   The mouse pointer changes to the circle with a plus sign inside it.

   b. *Paint over the edges of your subject where Photoshop hasn't quite gotten the dividing line between your subject and the background correct.*

   As you click and drag over the outlines of your subject, you will see the background of the photo show through, as seen around the paw of the lizard in Figure 3-16. When you release the mouse button, Photoshop will attempt to refine the edge even further.

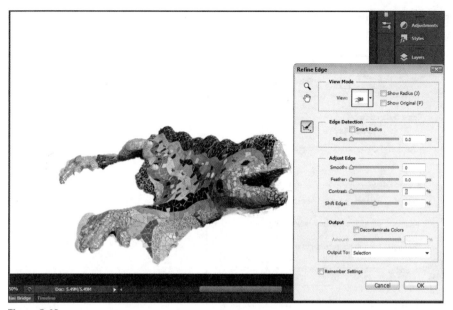

Figure 3-16

© istockphoto.com/KarSol

If you overdo this, and your image starts to look faded-out and vague, just click the Cancel button and start again.

7. **To further refine the edge, still in the Refine Edge dialog box, adjust the sliders for Smooth, Feather, and Contrast.**

   - *Smooth* creates a more clean, sinuous line in areas where the Quick Selection tool might have left jagged edges.

   - *Feather* softens the border between your subject and background.

   - *Contrast* makes the edge between your subject and the background more clearly defined.

   Play around a bit with the sliders to get an edge you're satisfied with, finding a balance between a smooth (but somewhat ill-defined) and a sharp (but rough and artificial-looking) edge.

8. **When you're satisfied with your selection, choose the appropriate Output To option and then click OK.**

   The choice you should make depends on your expertise with Photoshop and Layer Masks. If you're a beginner and don't know much about layer masks, just choose New Layer, as shown in Figure 3-17. To create an entirely new image file, choose New Document.

   Layer masks are handy if you want to continue to work with the underlying image, as we show in the next lesson, but they can be hard for a beginner to grasp.

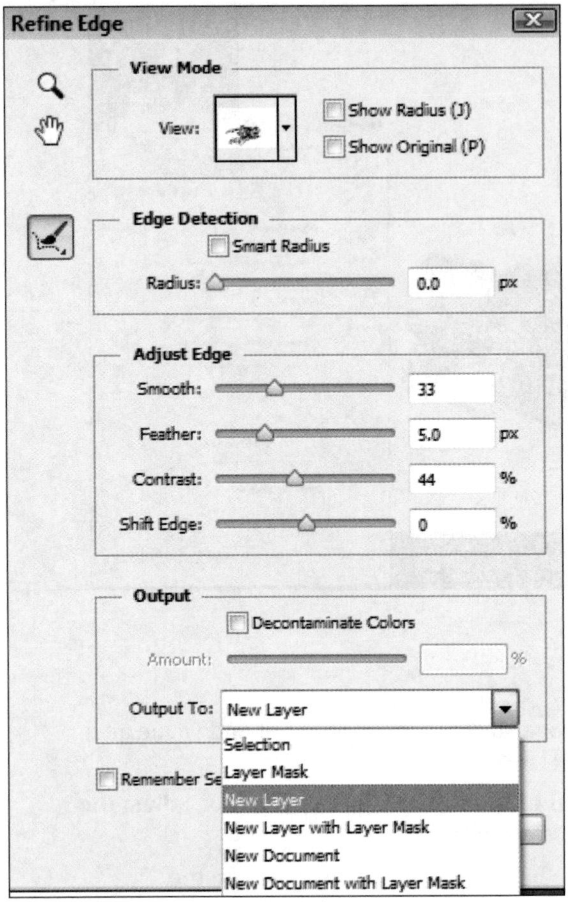

Figure 3-17

Combining Images to Create Collages

After you extract your subjects, crop your photos, or create a cool drawing, the next step is to combine and arrange them to form a new collage to upload to your social media profile.

If you are creating a design for a specific social media site, it's helpful to start with a template to guide the arrangement, sizing, and placement of images. In the exercise that follows, we show you how to create a Facebook cover design that combines multiple images.

on the web

We created a template you can use for your Facebook cover image. You can download it at www. digitalfamily.com/social.

You need photo-editing software that gives you precise control over multiple layers, allowing you to move, resize, and crop multiple images, such as Photoshop (shown in the following steps), Photoshop Elements, or GIMP. (Sorry, iPhoto users.)

You could get a little more fancy, but here is a simple way to combine multiple images into a template in Photoshop:

1. **Open a social media profile template, such as the Facebook template you can download from our site, in your favorite image editing program.**

   For this example, we use Adobe Photoshop CC, as shown in Figure 3-18.

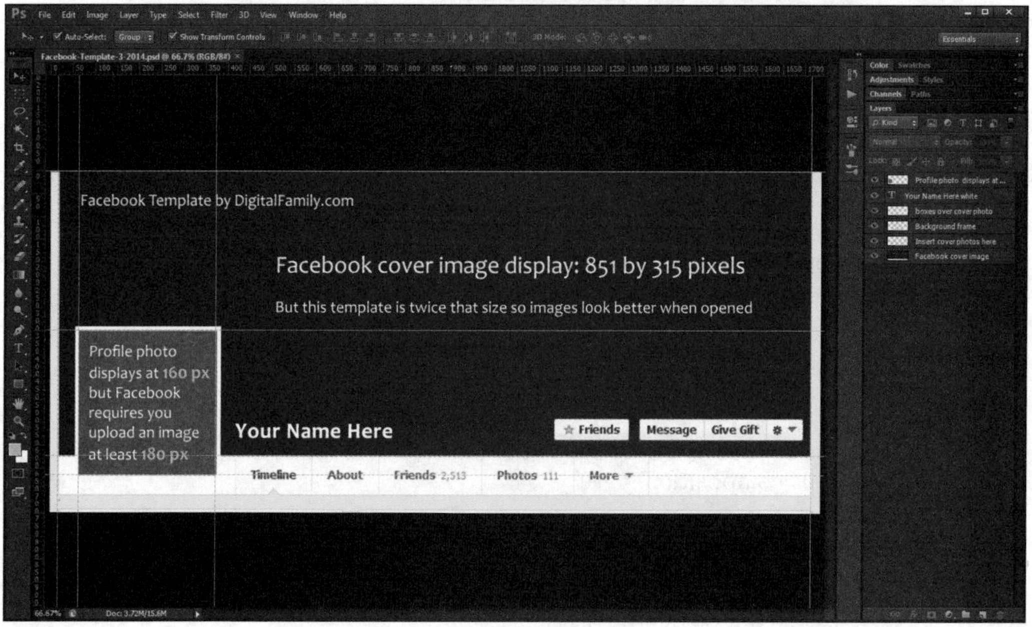

Figure 3-18

2. **Open each of the images that you want to assemble into a collage. Copy and paste each image into the template.**

   Alternatively, you can choose File⇨Place, navigate to your stored images, click to choose each one in turn, and then click the Place button in the Place dialog box. We prefer to use Place when importing multiple images into a new composition, as shown in Figure 3-19, because it's more efficient and requires fewer steps than opening each image before you can copy and paste.

Figure 3-19

3. **The selected image(s) are added to the template, with resizing handles active on the corners, as shown in Figure 3-20. To resize or move the photo**

   • *Resize:* Click and drag the little square boxes on the corners of the image to resize the photo to fit the template.

   • *Rotate:* Click and drag outside the photo box to rotate the photo.

   • *Move:* Click and drag inside the photo box to move the photo in your composition.

4. **Repeat Steps 2 and 3 to add as many images as you want to fill in the space in the template.**

   Click and drag to position the images; click and drag the corners to resize them within the template area.

   Don't worry if they bleed over the edges a little, as you can see in Figure 3-21. We show you how to fix that in the next step.

remember

You can click and drag to reorder the photos in the Layers panel. This will affect which photos appear to be "on top" of each other.

Images that are listed above other images in the Layers Panel are displayed so they will overlap in the workspace. By changing the overlap of images, you can preserve details in one layer while obscuring things in another.

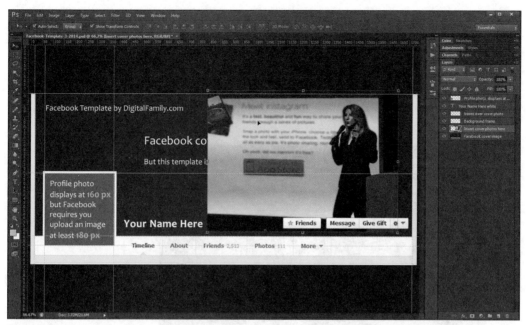

Figure 3-20

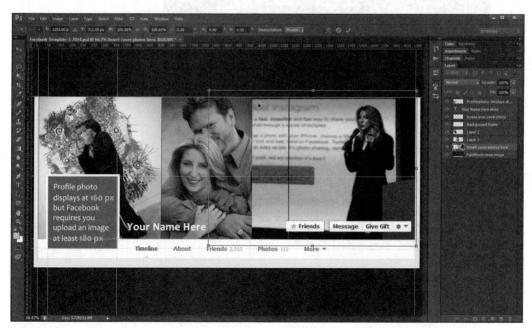

Figure 3-21

5. **Arrange the layers in the Layers panel to preview how your design will look on Facebook.**

   In the Layers panel, make sure the layers are arranged so that the layer named Background frame is at the top of the layer stack, but just below the layer named Profile image. With these layers in position, you should get a good idea of how your cover image and profile image will fit together when uploaded to Facebook (see Figure 3-22).

Figure 3-22

remember

To prevent the template from appearing in the version you upload to Facebook, you'll want to turn all of the layers off, except the ones in your cover design, when you save the image after you're done.

6. **Click the Zoom tool (it looks like a magnifying glass and the keyboard shortcut is Z) and adjust the size of the image as necessary.**

   Double-click on the zoom tool to set the image to 100%. Click the image with the Zoom tool selected to enlarge it. Alt (or Option) click to reduce the size.

7. **Save your work.**

The next step is to crop just the part you'll upload, but you may want to preserve your design at this point so that you can come back and edit it again later.

8. **Crop just the part of the image that will serve as your Facebook Cover design.**

   a. Select the cropping tool from the toolbar.

   b. Click and drag to position the crop marks around the image, or images you've assembled in the template, as shown in Figure 3-23.

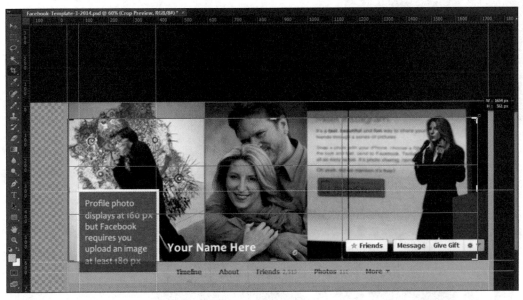

Figure 3-23

   c. Click and drag the corners to resize them within the template area.

   d. Turn off the profile image layer and any other layers from the template that are visible by clicking the small eye icon next to each layer in the Layers panel, as shown in Figure 3-24.

   e. When you have the cropping tools set, double click in the middle of the selected area to complete the crop.

9. **Choose File⇨Save for Web.**

   The Save for Web dialog opens, as shown in Figure 3-25.

10. **Adjust the settings and then click Save.**

    Photoshop saves a copy of the image and prompts you to give it a name.

11. **Enter a name and click Done to save the image and close the dialog.**

You find more detailed instructions for the Save for Web dialog box in Chapter 2.

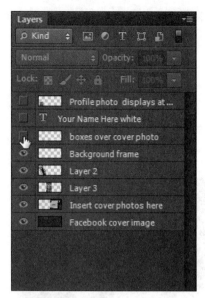

Figure 3-24

Figure 3-25

Part II
Creating Designs on the Top Social Sites

Chapter 4: Explore how to create a great Facebook profile design.

Chapter 5: For businesses, celebrities, and anyone else with more than 5,000 friends, see how to design a Facebook Page.

Chapter 6: Check out the design options for the micro-blogging site, Twitter.

Chapter 7: Find out how to dress up your online video pages on YouTube.

Visit www.dummies.com/extras/socialmediadesign for tips on how to create attractive social media content.

Sven De Bruyne

Janine Warner

Timeline   About   Friends 2,617   Photos 118

About

🗎 Author & creator of DigitalFamily.com at DigitalFamily.com and Author at John Wiley & Sons
Past: University of Southern California and CNET

🎓 Studied Journalism at University of Massachusetts Amherst
Past: City High School

🏠 Lives in Los Angeles, California

📍 From Ann Arbor, Michigan

💗 Married to David LaFontaine

Photos · 118

🗎 **Status**   📷 Photo   📍 Place   📖 Li

What's on your mind?

Janine Warner
3 hours ago

Happy Mother's Day Malinda McCain!

(This is one of my all time favorite pho

Up

CHAPTER 4

Fashioning a Fantastic Facebook Profile

In This Chapter

● Before starting your Facebook design, check out what other Facebook users do.

● Understand Facebook design rules so you can creatively exploit them.

● You, too, can design your own Facebook Profile.

● The last step is uploading your Profile and cover photos for everyone to see.

Janine

Timeline

Facebook is the unquestioned 800-pound gorilla of the social media world. A key part of making a good first impression on Facebook is creating a great Profile design.

Our goal with this chapter is to inspire you with a collection of Facebook Profile designs that are beautiful, provocative, playful, or just well-played — and then guide you through the process of creating a design that fits your personality or whatever message you want to convey on Facebook.

For example, in the playful design shown in Figure 4-1, Mohammad L. Azzam (http://facebook.com/mr.5416) makes it appear that he's holding a lollipop just out of his own reach. Designs like this one are created by combining two photographs, each uploaded separately, but carefully positioned to work together on Facebook. You find instructions for how to create your own Profile design at the end of this chapter.

Figure 4-1
Mohammad L. Azzam (www.facebook.com/mr.5416)

on the web

You can download our Facebook template from our website at www.digitalfamily. com/social and use it as you follow along with the step-by-step exercise at the end of this chapter.

Choose the version of the template you want by clicking the link that corresponds to the format you prefer and then use the instructions that follow to create your own design.

Looking Good on Facebook

Take a fresh look at your friends' Facebook Profiles and then revisit your own. Even the most clever, well-crafted text update pales in comparison to a striking image. Friends will Like, share, and comment on a cute picture of a pet, dramatic landscape, or new Profile photo far more readily than they will on posts that are just text.

tip

When you change your Profile photo, the photo is added to your Timeline automatically and displayed to all your friends on Facebook as a post. In Figure 4-2, the latest post in the Timeline is also the Profile photo.

remember

The *Timeline* is the entire collection of pictures, text, and videos that you post on Facebook — essentially, everything that appears below the Profile and cover images.

Figure 4-2 shows how your Profile picture, cover image, and Timeline work together.

Profile image   Cover image

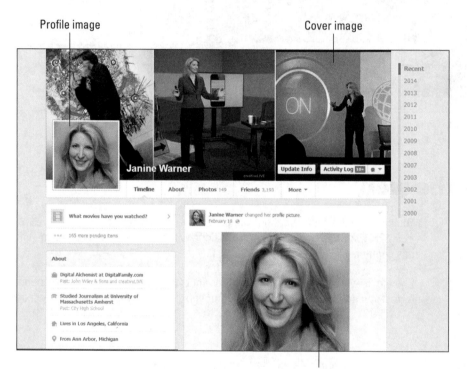

Timeline

Figure 4-2

Janine Warner (www.facebook.com/janine.warner)

Comparing Timeline, cover, and Profile images

Two kinds of images get displayed at the top of your Facebook Profile:

 Your Facebook *Profile picture* (the small image included at the top of your Profile, as well as with all your posts)

 Your *cover image* (the big photo you can add to the top of your Facebook Profile)

These two images are quite literally the face that you display to the world. Which images you choose and how you position them will have a significant impact on the first impression you give when your Profile is visited.

Sizing images for your Facebook design

As you see in Figures 4-3 through 4-5, the top of a Facebook Profile is made up of two images. One of the key design challenges you face when you create a cover design is the fact that these are two separate graphic elements, each of different sizes and dimensions. The Profile photo is a perfect square, but the cover image is wide and horizontal.

Edit Profile Picture

Choose m Photos...

Take Photo...

Upload Photo...

Edit Thumbnail...

Remove...

Figure 4-3
Janine Warner

Further complicating matters, Facebook displays the Profile picture in your cover design at 160 x 160 px. However, Facebook requires that you upload a Profile picture at least 180 x 180 px because in some parts of Facebook, the images are displayed in a larger size.

Similarly, Facebook displays the large cover image at 851 x 315 px, but if you click the cover image after it's placed in the cover design on Facebook, it opens in a much larger window. That means if you want your cover image to look its best, you need to upload an image that is larger than the display size.

The different sizes used by Facebook for your Profile and cover images can make positioning a bit complicated. To help you with this challenge, we designed a template twice the display size as the images at the top of your Profile on Facebook. (You find instructions for how to use the template later in this chapter.)

Profile image goes here.   Cover image

Figure 4-4

Janine Warner

Figure 4-5

Janine Warner

After considerable testing, we found that uploading larger images works well as long as you keep the aspect ratio (the proportional relationship between the width and height) the same.

If you upload a cover image that is smaller than 851 x 315 px, Facebook stretches it to fit the display area. But if you upload a larger cover photo, Facebook reduces the image to fit the 851-px-wide display area in your Profile, and you have the benefit of the larger size when someone clicks it.

warning

If the aspect ratio is not the same, Facebook crops the image to fit the space, but you can adjust the cropping area when you upload the image.

CHOOSING PAGES, PROFILES, OR GROUPS

Here's a brief description of how you should use each of these accounts:

- **Profiles**: In a nutshell, Profiles are for individuals. You're supposed to use your real name in your Profile and manage it yourself. Everyone who uses Facebook must have a Profile, and you need to have a Profile to create a Facebook Group or Page.

- **Groups**: Anyone can create a Group on Facebook on any topic, and Groups can be managed by one or more people. Groups are designed to foster discussion and are ideal for professional associations, Little League teams, and just about any topic of interest you want to build a community around.

- **Pages**: Designed to broadcast information to a large audience, Facebook Pages are the best option for big brands, actors, authors, businesses, and anyone else with a large following. Pages may be created and managed only by official representatives of a brand, but they can be managed by more than one person. This figure shows the Facebook Page created by the video training company, creativeLIVE.

Remember: None of these are mutually exclusive. You can create a Facebook Profile for your consulting business, or you can create a Facebook Page for an individual (especially if that individual is a celebrity with a lot of fans).

creativeLIVE (www.creativelive.com)

Be sure to consider that even though your Profile picture and cover photo will primarily be viewed together, both images can also be seen individually in other areas of Facebook. You may not want to create or select a Profile or cover image that makes sense only when viewed on your Profile page. See the "Creating Your Own Profile Design" section for steps on how to do it.

technical stuff

To view the designs on Facebook, you'll need to use a computer monitor capable of displaying at least a 1024 x 768 px screen resolution. Most modern computers come with widescreen monitors capable of displaying images and video at far higher resolutions, but if you're still hanging on to a very old computer with a display limited to 800 x 600 px, you may have to scroll around to see the entire image at the top of each Facebook Profile.

Admiring Inspiring Facebook Designs

The best way to get started creating your own Facebook design is to study some of the best designs other people have created.

We've organized our favorites into four categories:

▶ **Playful and creative designs:** Combine a Profile picture with a cover image in a way that creates a playful or startling design. Despite the inherent limits of Facebook Profile designs, many creative designers have found ways to create the illusion that they're using only one image by using a portion of the larger image in the Profile position. Others use programs like Photoshop or Photoshop Elements to combine multiple images into one big image to upload to Facebook.

The key to creating a composite image like these examples lies in being able to take a carefully posed series of photographs, and then to process them in an image-editing program to extract elements from each image, and then to place each image in careful position with each other. (You learn more about how to set up an image like this and edit them in an image-editing program in Chapter 3.)

▶ **Photographic designs:** Photographers have an advantage because they have so many images. Many change the image on a regular basis to showcase their work because the large cover photo serves as an ideal place to display a portfolio. If you don't have your own pictures, though, you can use stock photography sites available online.

▶ **Business and professional designs:** Many small business owners, consultants, speakers, attorneys, and other professionals use their Facebook Timeline designs to build their brands, showcase their talents, or boost their credibility.

Chapter 5 shows off Facebook Pages, which is what Facebook recommends for big brands, celebrities, and others with large followings.

▶ **Designs that tell a good story:** Some of the best Facebook Profiles are especially good at telling the story of the Profile owner, demonstrating their talents, passions, hobbies, or personal style. Consider using photos that illustrate your favorite hobbies, or other elements that help your connections quickly and easily learn something important about you.

remember

Don't be confused by the three types of Facebook accounts. In this chapter, we focus on Facebook Profiles. To learn more about the differences among the three types of Facebook accounts, see the sidebar "Choosing Pages, Profiles, or Groups."

Kay Int Veen

In this design, shown in Figure 4-6, Kay Int Veen (`www.facebook.com/kayintveen`) seems to be peeking out from behind the page. This illusion was created by integrating a white bar that seems to be part of the Facebook page design with an image, cleverly posed to fit the space. He then added a collage of images on the left-hand side. In this case, there is no interaction between the Profile photo and the other photos; but the generous amount of white space between the two elements helps them work well in the shared space.

Figure 4-6

Kay Int Veen (`www.facebook.com/kayintveen`)

Sven De Bruyne

In this design, Sven De Bruyne (www.facebook.com/svendebruyne) took a photo of himself looking off to the side, flipped it upside down, and repeated it in the Profile and cover photos, as shown in Figure 4-7. Because he appears to be looking from one image to the other, the combination creates a dramatic effect. It's a challenge not to let your own eyes dart between the images in this design.

Figure 4-7

Sven De Bruyne (www.facebook.com/svendebruyne)

tip

Facebook designs that integrate the cover image and Profile photos are especially effective. Notice that adding a white bar to the bottom of his image makes it look like Kay is coming out of the page, instead of just floating above it in Figure 4-6. Sven achieves a similar effect in Figure 4-7.

Gilad Koriski

As you see in the two Profile designs shown in Figure 4-8, Gilad Koriski created dramatically different Facebook Profile designs and showcased the diversity of his photography by simply changing his Profile and cover images.

Jasper Johal

This single, simple, stop-motion photo of a dancer swirling her skirts with a strong light shining through from the background creates an eye-catching cover design, as shown in Figure 4-9.

Jasper Johal (www.jasperphoto.com) specializes in photographing yoga and dance, so this dark angel is not only a great way to demonstrate that he has a great eye for capturing physical action, but the subject matter is also thematic for his business.

Figure 4-8
Photography by Gilad Korisiki (http://koriski.com)

Figure 4-9
Jasper Johal Photography (www.jasperphoto.com)

Colin Smith

Photographer and Photoshop instructor Colin Smith (author, trainer, digital artist, and founder of PhotoshopCAFE.com) inflicts this freaky vision of what would happen if giant wasps outfitted with gas masks broke out of a mutant research lab. This cover design showcases his talent and warped imagination, as shown in Figure 4-10.

Figure 4-10
Colin Smith

This cover image also serves as a great advertisement for Colin's video training programs, which teach how to create complex composite images like this one. Apparently, he's been hanging around some strange underground science installations for inspiration.

Jérôme Vadon

Using a mix of photos and hand-drawn illustration, digital designer Jérôme Vadon (`http://jerome.vadon.fr`) cleverly constructed a tag cloud of words that he considers relevant to his design ethos. Figure 4-11 shows off his design.

Figure 4-11
Jérôme Vadon (`http://jerome.vadon.fr`)

technical stuff

A *tag cloud* is a visual representation of keywords, commonly used on websites and blogs that display the most important words in larger sizes or with a distinguishing color.

The tag cloud is connected to the Profile picture by an arrow leading to his smiling face in a carefully cropped Profile photo. He's also done a great job of aligning the edge of his face in the portrait almost perfectly with the top of his head in the larger banner.

Ken Riddick

A glance at Ken Riddick's Facebook design, shown in Figure 4-12, tells you volumes about his life and priorities. The dive photo illustrates his passion for scuba diving and underwater photography, and the Profile picture of him and his wife makes it clear that he's married and enjoys tropical excursions.

Figure 4-12

Ken Riddick (www.kenriddick.com)

tip

If your primary use of Facebook is personal, use your Profile design to share something about your hobbies, passions, sports, and relationships.

Kare Anderson

Professional speaker and author Kare Anderson emphasizes "communicating to connect" in her consulting and speaking business. She also believes in empowering others to help tell your story and her design reflects that philosophy — by using photos and testimonials from her clients to describe the quality of her work, shown in Figure 4-13.

Figure 4-13

Kare Anderson (www.sayitbetter.com)

You can mimic the look of your website in your Profile and cover images if your goal is to create a consistent design across your sites. Here, the look of her Profile also mimics the colors and style of Kare's website, which uses similar design elements.

FINDING THE FACEBOOK IMAGE THAT FITS YOU

It can be difficult to choose between a beautiful but restrained photo for your cover image, or an image that tells more about you. Throwing caution to the wind and taking the risk of using a quirky image that expresses some deep emotion takes real courage for most of us. Should you play it safe in social media, or make yourself memorable?

If you're using social media professionally, consider what you want to be known for and how to best build your reputation. If you are a designer or creative, you may want to showcase your talents with a quirky or eye-catching design. If you're a financial planner and your clients are looking for someone who is reliable and trustworthy, you may be best served by a simple photograph of the view from your office or an image of a local landmark.

Amanda Cey

In her Facebook design, shown in Figure 4-14, Amanda Cey (founder and owner of ABCey Events) uses a photo of a crowd lined up on a red carpet waiting to get into an event. Amanda is an event planner, and the image instantly suggests she's good at gathering a crowd. The sinuous line of people in the photo also does a great job of leading your eye right to Amanda's Profile picture.

Figure 4-14
Amanda Cey `(http://abcey.com)`

Following Facebook Design Rules

Although Facebook says it wants to encourage all users to express their creative imaginations when designing Profiles, the company has instituted a number of rules about what you can and cannot include in a cover image or Profile design.

Most of the rules are designed to keep spammers, trolls, and overly enthusiastic marketers in line, but some of the rules may surprise you. Unfortunately, a few bad eggs on the Internet are making things a lot stricter for all of us.

warning

Even if you aren't trying to do something nefarious, like sell a fake prescription drug, you want to avoid doing anything that makes it look like you're breaking the rules. *Facebook can freeze your Profile or close your account.*

AVOIDING BAD FACEBOOK DESIGNS

If you wouldn't go out in public looking disheveled, don't let your Facebook Profile introduce you that way. (If you do prefer the disheveled look, by all means play it up on your Timeline. Just make sure that's the impression you want to give your visitors.)

Many Facebook users post a Profile photo that's only slightly better than their passport photo or a school picture. Too many people opt for the simplest, quickest cover image: a photo that may say little about who they are or what they do or care about. Worse, some people post photos that are blurry, badly cropped, or just not very good looking.

Also beware of Facebook cover images that are given away by big companies as part of an advertising campaign. A professionally designed banner created by your favorite car or cola company might be an easy choice, but your little Profile photo will almost certainly get lost when it's up against a big commercial message. When you opt for the visual impact of someone else's design, your Facebook banner is no longer an expression of who you are or what you are all about.

Here are the Facebook rules about what you can't have on your Timeline. (***Disclaimer:*** These rules are subject to change, and we recommend you consult the Facebook help files for the latest updates.)

▶ **Do not use anything that infringes another person's copyright.** That means cartoon characters, movie posters, and just about anything from commercial media is a big no-no.

▶ **Do not encourage other people to upload your cover photo to their personal Timeline.**

▶ **Your cover image can't be deceptive or misleading.** No promising a cure for cancer, earning a million dollars an hour for working from home, or promising instant worldwide fame for liking your Profile.

▶ **Facebook frowns on your having an arrow pointing at the Like button.** Having said that, Facebook has moved that button so that it appears only on Pages now.

▶ **Facebook will remove posts and Profiles if they are deemed to be racist, abusive, or sexist.**

Creating Your Own Profile Design

In this final section, we show you how to put all this information into practice with step-by-step instructions for designing your own Profile by creating a cover image and Profile picture in the correct size and dimensions.

To help guide your work, we created a template you can use to position and size your images. We created the template and made it available in three common image formats (.psd, .tiff, and .jpg) so you can choose the one that works best with the software program you use to design your Profile.

Using an image editor to design a Profile

The following instructions show you how to use our Facebook template to resize and position your cover and Profile pictures for your Facebook design.

tip

You'll find more information about why we recommend Adobe Photoshop and Photoshop Elements, as well as free programs you can use, in Chapter 2.

The following instructions show you how to create your design using the layered version in Adobe Photoshop or Photoshop Elements. Because both versions of Photoshop support the features covered in this lesson, the instructions work with both (although you may have to make minor adjustments if you are using an older version).

Because there are many steps involved in creating a cover image and Profile picture and then uploading them to Facebook, we broke the instructions into sections. You can complete these exercises one after the other or jump directly to any set of instructions.

remember

This template is twice the display size of the images on Facebook. Facebook reduces the size so that the images fit in your Profile and uses the larger versions when the images are viewed in other areas of the site.

BE PERSONABLE BUT NOT TOO PERSONAL

Whether you run a small business or a Fortune 500 company, many analysts agree that your Facebook Profile is at least as important as a business card when it comes to making a good impression on professional contacts.

Although Facebook has become an increasingly important place to promote your professional skills, it's still best known as a social site where people share photos and stories with friends and family. That means most people are more informal on Facebook than they are on a site like LinkedIn, which is designed only for professional networking. (You can learn more about LinkedIn in Chapter 8.)

The best strategy if you want to build a professional Profile on Facebook is to be *personable* without being too *personal.* The key is to be authentic and approachable while avoiding anything that might be deemed objectionable or offensive. If your goal is to represent yourself as a responsible, trustworthy businessperson, don't include images or text that are sexually suggestive, pictures from drunken parties, politically controversial slogans, or any content that's likely to set off an argument in the comments section on your Facebook Profile.

That doesn't mean you can't be a little provocative once in a while, especially if you do it in a way that is consistent with the personality, culture, and expertise of your business.

Creating a cover image in Photoshop

Follow these instructions to create your own Facebook design using Adobe Photoshop:

1. **In Photoshop, choose File⟹Open and select the `Facebook-Timeline-Template.psd` file.**

   The template opens in the Photoshop workspace, as shown in Figure 4-15.

2. **Choose Window⟹Layers to open the Layers panel.**

   The Layers panel opens on the right side of the Photoshop workspace and displays all seven layers included in the `Facebook-Template.psd` file.

3. **Choose File⟹Open and then open the image you want to use as your main cover image.**

   The image opens in the Photoshop workspace.

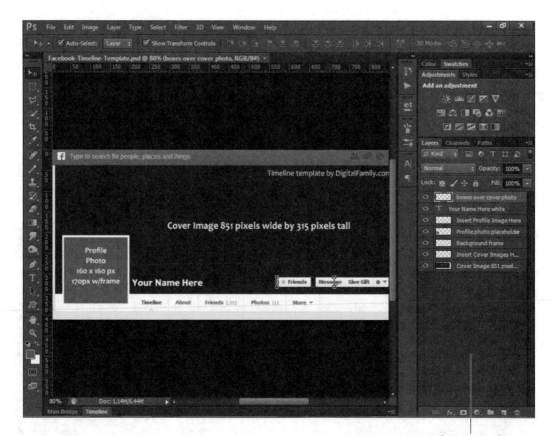

Layers panel

Figure 4-15

4. **Choose Image⇨Image Size.**

5. **In the Image Size dialog box that opens, change the height and width of the image; see Figure 4-16.**

technical stuff

Ultimately, the cover image displays at exactly 851 x 315 px to fit the space at the top of your Facebook Profile. However, this template is twice that size, so you should set the width of your cover image to 1702. You can resize the image before or after you paste it into the template file, which you do in the next steps. However, if the cover image is significantly larger than the template, resizing it after you paste it into the template file is difficult. For best results, get the cover image close to the final size while still leaving a little room to move the image around in the template and get things lined up the way you want them.

Image Size	
Pixel Dimensions: 1.55M (was 4.88M)	
Width: 200 Pixels	OK
Height: 600 Pixels	Cancel
	Auto...
Document Size:	
Width: 12.5 Inches	
Height: 8.336 Inches	
Resolution: 72 Pixels/Inch	
☑ Scale Styles	
☑ Constrain Proportions	
☑ Resample Image:	
Bicubic Automatic	

Figure 4-16

6. **Copy the image you want to use as your cover image.**

   You can copy the image whatever way you prefer. One way is to press Ctrl+A (on a Mac, ⌘+A) to select the image, and then press Ctrl+C (on a Mac, ⌘+C) to copy the image.

7. **Click the tab in your image-editing program that has your Facebook Timeline Template open in it to make it active in the workspace.**

   The template becomes visible in the Photoshop workspace.

8. **Click to select the Insert Cover Images Here layer, and then paste the image you copied into the template, as shown in Figure 4-17.**

   The template includes a layer named Insert Cover Images Here (Figure 4-17) to help you position the cover image so that it sits behind the Profile photo and border of the Facebook design area. This makes it easier to position the image and see how the two images will work in relationship to one another in the following step.

tip

If your cover image isn't on the correct layer, it may cover up the template, or it may not be fully visible. If that's the case, you need to move it to the correct layer. Choose the Move tool from the Tools palette and then click the cover image layer to select it; drag it until it's below the Frame Should Surround Cover Image layer. Similarly, you can click to select the image itself in the main workspace and drag it until it's in the desired position in the template.

Figure 4-17

Adding a Profile picture

If you're creating a design that combines your Profile and cover image, you'll need to add a Profile picture to your template file to position the two images in relation to one another.

With the template file open, follow these steps to add and position a Profile picture. Remember to begin with a cropped photo as discussed previously:

1. **Choose File⇨Open and open the image you wish to use as your Profile picture.**

   The image opens in the Photoshop workspace.

2. **Choose Image⇨Image Size and enter 160 pixels in the Height and Width fields.**

tip

You can also change the size of an image by using the Canvas size options by choosing Image⇨Canvas size. When you change the size via the Canvas Size dialog box, the image is automatically cropped to fit the size, which can make it easier to make it a perfect square.

3. **Copy the Profile picture.**

Press Ctrl+A (on a Mac, ⌘ +A) to select the image; then press Ctrl+C (on a Mac, ⌘+C) to copy the image.

4. **Click the tab in your image-editing program that has your Facebook Timeline Template open in it to make it active in the workspace.**

The template becomes visible in the Photoshop workspace.

5. **Click to select the Insert Profile Image Here layer and then paste the image you copied into the template.**

The template includes a layer named Insert Profile Image Here to help you position the Profile picture so that it sits over the cover image and the Profile frame.

6. **Choose the Move tool from the Tools palette, and then click the Profile picture layer and drag it into position.**

Continue to move the Profile and cover images around until they are positioned the way you want them in relation to each other, as shown in Figure 4-18.

Figure 4-18

Illustration by tom mccain (www.crittur.com)

7. **After you size and position the cover image and the Profile picture just right, choose File⇨Save for Web & Devices and save a copy of the file with a new name.**

Saving a copy of the template with your photos is optional, but it will ensure that you can go back to the template after you crop and export the background image if you want to create a different design or make a mistake and want to try again.

Optimizing the cover image with the Save for Web dialog box

After you get your cover and Profile pictures positioned where you want them, optimize the cover image before you upload it to Facebook in the steps that follow.

Remember that your cover image needs to first be cropped to 1702 x 630 px. Use the guidelines in the template, or crop right along the edge of the Facebook frame around the cover image to crop just the cover image.

tip

> If you have trouble getting the cover image cropped exactly to 1702 x 630 px, enlarge the image in the workspace so that you can more precisely control the Crop tool. You can also use the Canvas Size dialog box to adjust the exact size of the cover image.

1. **Click the small eye icon next to each layer in the Layers panel to turn off all the layers** *except the layer with the cover image,* **as shown in Figure 4-19.**

Figure 4-19

When you finish turning off all the other layers, only the cover image will be visible in the workspace.

2. **Choose File⇨Save for Web.**

The Save for Web dialog opens.

In previous versions of Photoshop, this dialog was called Save for Web & Devices. The name may be different in different versions, but the dialog box itself and its features have not changed.

3. **Choose JPEG or PNG from the Image Format drop-down list, as shown in Figure 4-20.**

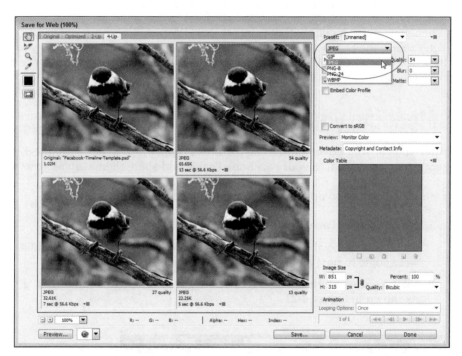

Figure 4-20

If the image is a photograph or other image with millions of colors, choose JPEG. If the image is a logo or cartoon that uses fewer colors, choose PNG.

4. **If you choose the JPEG format, adjust the quality settings to apply compression and reduce the image size. If you choose the PNG format, reduce the number of colors.**

See Chapter 2 for more details about reducing the file size when you save images for the web.

5. **After you get the settings the way you want, click Save As, and then give the image a new name.**

A copy of the image is saved, the Save for Web dialog box closes, and the cover image is ready to be uploaded to Facebook.

Getting your Profile photo the right size

Although your Profile picture in your Facebook design is displayed at 161 x 161 px, Facebook requires that you upload the image in a larger size. Facebook recommends that you upload a version of your Profile that's 180 x 180 px because within many places in Facebook, your Profile picture is sometimes displayed at that larger size. We found Profile pictures look even better when they are uploaded at 320 x 320 px.

This can be confusing, especially if you're trying to create a complex design that requires that your cover image and Profile photo fit together just right. That's why we designed our Facebook Timeline Template with the Profile picture set to 320 x 320 px while keeping its position in relation to the cover image.

When you upload an image that is larger than 180 pixels, Facebook resizes it for you. You can use the Facebook cropping tools to make final adjustments after you upload it, which is a fine option — as long your Profile photo doesn't need to be positioned perfectly against your cover image.

Uploading your images to Facebook

After you get your cover and Profile pictures cropped, sized, and optimized, you're ready to upload them to your Facebook Profile and share them with all your friends.

Follow these steps to upload your Profile pictures to Facebook:

1. **Log in to your Facebook Profile account.**

   There is no special login for this. Just log into Facebook as you would if you were going to post an update or do anything else with your account.

2. **Click your name in the top right of the Facebook page to open your Profile, as shown in Figure 4-21.**

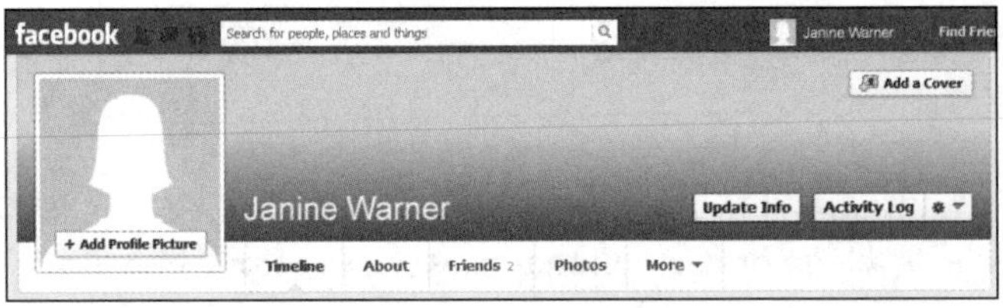

Figure 4-21

You need to ensure that you're on your own Profile page, not viewing someone else's page or viewing the stream of new posts.

3. **Let Facebook know whether you're adding a cover image for the first time or replacing an existing image:**

   • *If you're adding a cover image for the first time:* Click the Add a Cover button, as shown in Figure 4-21, and skip to Step 4.

   A drop-down menu opens giving you a few options, as shown in Figure 4-22.

Figure 4-22

   • *If you're replacing an existing cover image:* First roll your cursor over the existing cover image to make the Change Cover button appear. Then click the Change Cover button.

   A drop-down menu opens giving you a few options, as shown in Figure 4-22.

4. **Choose Upload Photo.**

   The Upload Photo dialog box opens.

5. **Navigate to find your cover photo, click to select it, and then click Open.**

   The cover photo you selected is automatically uploaded to your Facebook Profile. After a few seconds, the image appears in the cover photo space, and over the image, text appears with the message Drag to Reposition Cover, as shown in Figure 4-23.

Figure 4-23
Janine Warner

remember

If you upload an image that is larger than 851 x 315 px, Facebook will resize it to display properly in your Profile page.

warning

When you change your Facebook cover image, it is also posted to your Facebook feed and made visible to all your friends.

6. **Click and drag anywhere on the cover image to adjust its positioning.**

   If your cover is exactly the size we recommend — 1702 x 630 px — it should fit the space perfectly. If it's larger, you may want to click and drag it around until you are happy with how it's cropped to fit in the space.

7. **Click the Save Changes button to save your cover image and publish it on your Facebook Profile.**

8. **If you're adding a Profile picture for the first time, click the Add Profile Picture button (refer to Figure 4-21) and skip to Step 11.**

9. **If you're replacing an existing Profile picture image, roll your cursor over the existing Profile picture to make the Add Profile Picture button appear. Then click the Edit Profile Picture button.**

   A drop-down menu opens, as shown in Figure 4-24.

Figure 4-24

10. **Choose the Upload Photo option from the Add Profile Picture drop-down menu if you are uploading an image for the first time. Choose Edit Profile Picture if you are replacing your Profile picture.**

    The Upload Photo dialog box opens.

11. **Navigate to find your Profile photo. Click to select it and then click Open.**

    The Profile photo you selected is automatically uploaded to your Facebook Profile. After a few seconds, the image appears in the Profile photo space, and Facebook may display a warning or other message noting that your Profile photo is public, as shown in Figure 4-25.

Figure 4-25

Illustration by tom mccain (www.crittur.com)

remember

From time to time, Facebook changes its privacy options and policies for how it manages how and where images are displayed.

We always recommend that you review the privacy options for your Facebook Profile on a regular basis. You'll find these options by clicking the small gear-shaped icon at the top right of your Profile, as shown in Figure 4-26.

Figure 4-26

FINDING FRIENDS ON FACEBOOK

If you want to find a Friend on Facebook or visit any of the Facebook Profiles featured in this chapter, enter the name of the person in the Search field at the top of Facebook, as shown in this figure.

Lesa Snider (http://photolesa.com)

CHAPTER 5

Polishing Your Look on a Facebook Page

In This Chapter

- Maximize Facebook to promote your business or organization.

- Use Facebook Page tools to create your Page design.

- Plan your design to communicate consistent branding across social media platforms.

Facebook is increasingly used by successful professionals for marketing, recruitment, organization, and sales. In this chapter, we explore how consultants, small business owners, authors, and many others are creating Pages on Facebook. We explain the differences between a Page and a Profile and show you how you can use graphic design to communicate directly with your users.

In this chapter, you find how you can design a Page, which is what Facebook recommends for big brands, celebrities, and others with large followings. We also take a look at what makes a Facebook Page different from a Profile as well as how to use your Facebook Page to present a consistent look to your audience and customers.

Managing your Facebook Page can be a time-consuming task, but starting off with a beautiful and appropriate design can set the tone so your friends and fans know what they're getting when they visit your page. See Figure 5-1.

remember

Profiles and Pages are not mutually exclusive. You can create a Facebook Profile for your consulting business, or you can create a Facebook Page for an individual (especially if that individual is a celebrity with a lot of fans).

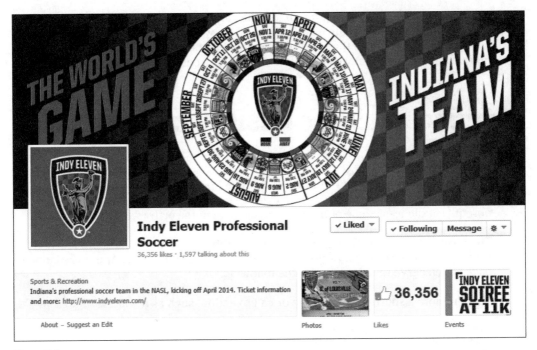

Figure 5-1

Facebook Pages come with their own set of terms and guidelines. For the complete rules, visit `www.facebook.com/page_guidelines.php`.

Getting Professional with Pages

A Facebook Page is a wonderfully flexible thing because it can serve as a meeting place for millions of eager followers of a rock band to discuss the minutia of a concert appearance, or allow a brand to run a worldwide contest to see who can come up with the best 30-second video ad to launch a new product.

Facebook has rolled out some changes to how Pages function, and some of these changes have sparked user outrage and controversy. Chief among these rumblings was a change that affected how popular brands are allowed to use Facebook's messaging functions to communicate with their fans.

Basically, Facebook started charging Page operators who were sending millions of messages to their fans. On the one hand, Facebook is a business, after all, and Page operators were getting a service for free by using Facebook like a dedicated e-mail messaging platform, even though brands otherwise have to pay thousands of dollars for such a service. But on the other hand, the sudden imposition of control over whether, how, and how frequently Page operators were allowed to contact their fans was a rude awakening. In the words of one rock band manager, "We woke up one morning to discover that we no longer owned the attention of our fans. Facebook did."

Inspiring Business Designs on Facebook

Before diving into the basics of creating a solid Facebook Page, take a look at some brands that make the most of Facebook with pages of their own. Individuals and organizations from bloggers to work-from-home Etsy shop owners to international brands use Facebook to connect with existing customers and fans as well as their potential audiences. Some of them are doing so in noteworthy ways.

The basics of a Facebook Page aren't radically different from the look and feel of a Profile, but a Page does allow you to create a unique landing page. And these landing pages often serve to help you with the following:

- Promote a short-term initiative or call to action, such as a contest or special offer.
- Introduce the brand to new fans.
- Display branding consistent with the brand's other social media properties.
- Drive the visitor to Like the page rather than just visit.
- Explain tabs on the page.

Scholastic

www.facebook.com/scholastic

Scholastic is a recognizable brand that most of us in the United States grew up with. With the FACE Literacy Initiative landing page (https://www.facebook.com/Scholastic/app_286153118166140) on its Facebook Page (see Figure 5-2), Scholastic uses Facebook not just to connect with legions of fans but also to make a very specific call to action. Note the prominently placed FAQ link for more on the initiative and also the call to action placed above the fold for fans to join its initiative.

Nike

www.facebook.com/nike

The managers of the Nike Facebook Page, as shown in Figure 5-3, have opted to keep it simple and follow their highly recognizable branding. As you scroll down the page, images are big and bold, playing on the familiar Just Do It theme. Rather than create flashy graphics or complicated calls to action, Nike instead sticks to motivational themes, inspiring athletes around the world.

Figure 5-2

Figure 5-3

warning

Keep this in mind when building your Facebook Page: *You are working on a platform that you do not own.* Facebook can (and does) unilaterally impose changes to the terms of service that affect how you can operate.

We suggest that you use Facebook Pages as an additional way that you interact with your customers, fans, and friends — and that you maintain your own website or other means of interacting with them, just in case you have to "go it alone" for a while.

Volkswagen

www.facebook.com/volkswagen

Just as you'd expect from the famous German engineering auto-industry giant, the Volkswagen international Facebook Page (see Figure 5-4) features a slick design and streamlined graphics. Several tabs share the same cover image, which is the highly recognizable VW logo. The cover photo on display at the time this book was written shows a forward-thinking image focused on (what else?) their cars. The prominent colors in the image reflect the silver and blue of the logo, which is used as the Page's profile picture.

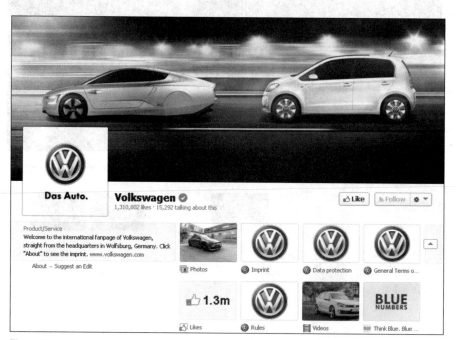

Figure 5-4

tip

Page Profile pictures are displayed at 160 x 160 pixels (px) on your Page just as they are on your Profile page, as we explain in Chapter 4. You must, however, upload a picture that's at least 180 x 180 px. Facebook recommends using a square picture, but Facebook also provides you with the opportunity to crop your picture after upload.

Nesting Place

www.facebook.com/pages/Nesting-Place/116713278381310

The blogger behind Nesting Place (known to most as "The Nester") brings her design background to the creation of her simple yet popular Facebook Page shown in Figure 5-5. With more than 20,000 Likes at the time this book was written, this Page certainly doesn't have the same following as a big brand. Still, loyal followers of this blog will recognize the colors and style of the blog immediately when visiting this Facebook Page, which features uncluttered, décor-focused images along with the fun-loving personality of the author.

Figure 5-5

On Wings of Hope

www.facebook.com/OnWingsOfHopeFilm

Pages are also great for promoting creative projects, such as the documentary film, *On Wings of Hope* (see Figure 5-6). Although documentary projects like this one don't always attract a huge audience, the film's creator, Pascal Depuhl, used Facebook to help build a loyal and supportive following and get the film featured in the Palm Beach International Film Festival.

Figure 5-6

Pascal Depuhl, www.depuhl.com/

Colorado Moms

www.facebook.com/ColoradoMoms

Creators of this website geared toward parents in Colorado chose to create a Facebook Page design that highlights their home state rather than their homepage. Although the site's logo is featured in the profile picture, the cover photo on the Page is a collage featuring photos from around Colorado (see Figure 5-7).

Figure 5-7

Mom Prepares

www.facebook.com/momprepares

MomPrepares.com is a website focused on the trend of "prepping." This blog Page is another great example of how powerful it can be to create a collage cover photo and save the Profile photo as a place to highlight your logo design (see Figure 5-8).

Figure 5-8

Adding a Facebook Tab

Facebook tabs are an integral part of most Facebook Pages, but they are certainly not required. A Facebook tab, very simply, allows you to add multiple and separate pages to your Facebook Page. By default, a Page contains

 A timeline, which is technically a tab

 The Photos tab

You can very easily add additional tabs, such as Likes, Notes, Blog, Videos, and Events, or tabs that showcase other online properties, such as Pinterest and Twitter accounts. This is also where you'll add unique landing pages, as Scholastic has done. Adding a tab on your Facebook Page is easy as clicking the plus sign on a blank tab and selecting the existing app that fits your needs. Many Facebook Pages also include custom apps within the tabs area of their Page, allowing your Page to do everything from administer giveaways to offer special coupons to grow your newsletter database.

tip

The app page width is 810 px. To keep the important information within your app "above the fold," be sure to stay at 500 px in height to accommodate most computer screens. When designing the cover photo for your app's tab, stick with 111 x 74 px to accommodate the tab size.

Creating Facebook tabs with apps

Although you can choose to add Page tabs from the tabs made available by Facebook, not everyone can develop and install custom tabs. To receive permission from Facebook to become an approved app developer, navigate to `https://developers.facebook.com`. There, under the Apps navigation heading, click Register as a Developer.

But maybe you don't want to become an app developer. Luckily, apps are available that can help you take your Facebook Page to the next level without having to build a whole new set of skills. Here is a sampling of what's available.

ShortStack

`www.shortstack.com`

ShortStack provides users with prebuilt templates and themes, allowing you to create a great-looking final product without having to start from scratch. If you have fewer than 2,000 fans, this program is free. Other pricing options range from $25 per month to $250 per month if paid annually.

Tabfoundry

`www.tabfoundry.com`

Tabfoundry is especially user-friendly for Facebook Page administrators who prefer drag-and-drop styling. Want to dig in a bit deeper? Tabfoundry also allows you to add background graphics and change HTML coding. A free version of Tabfoundry is available, but you also have the option of upgrading for $9 per month. This reasonably priced upgrade provides you with an unlimited number of tabs.

DIVING INTO TABS

Don't feel pressured to dive into custom tabs immediately after creating your Facebook Page. It's more important to nail some of the basics, such as your About section, Profile image, and cover photo. After all, these are the ways that you're introducing your brand or business to the Facebook world! Then, after you sort out these basics, spend some time playing with the options available to you in Facebook tabs.

Pagemodo

www.pagemodo.com

This tool costs $6.25 per month for three tabs but also offers a Pro version for $13.25 per month that provides you with unlimited tabs on up to three Pages. Like some of the other options, Pagemodo allows you to get started with templates, but custom options are also available.

Heyo

https://heyo.com

Like Tabfoundry, Heyo is another drag-and-drop app that allows you to upload a background photo or logo. You can also drop in videos and links, allowing you to create an app that meets all of your needs while also providing consistent branding across your social media properties. Heyo offers users a free trial, but after the trial, it costs $25 per month.

Woobox

http://woobox.com

Woobox is especially enjoyed by Page administrators who want to offer coupons, contests, and sweepstakes. This app allows a free trial, and then pricing begins at $1 per month for Pages with 100 fans or fewer. After you hit the big time and you have 100,000 or more fans, you'll pay $249 per month.

Adding a custom Facebook tab

For the purpose of understanding how Facebook tab apps work, take a look at the free tools available from Tabfoundry. To get started, point your favorite browser to www.tabfoundry.com and select Get Started to begin the free level of service. You will be asked to authorize Tabfoundry's management of your Facebook Page, and you must accept in order to use this tool to place a new tab on your Facebook Page.

Tabfoundry displays your account dashboard, which you'll see looks much like your Facebook Page (shown in Figure 5-9).

The Tabfoundry tab creation screen offers a tutorial option on the left side of the screen. For more help, turn to the tutorial.

1. **On your Tabfoundry Facebook Page dashboard, click the Create New Tab icon to begin the creation process. Select from the following options:**

   - Custom tab
   - Quiz contest
   - Photo contest

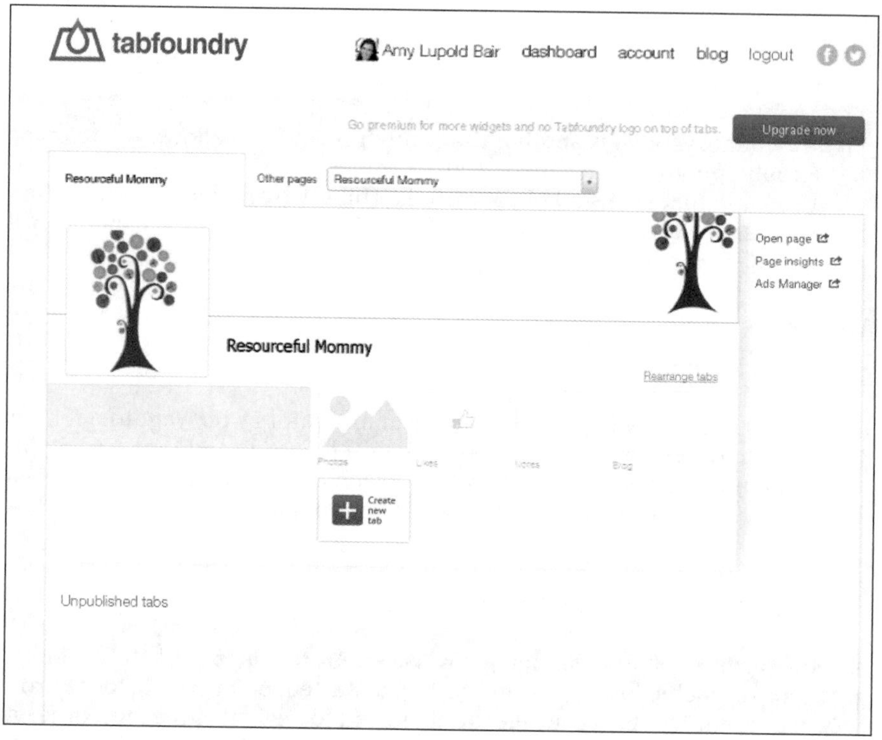

Figure 5-9

2. **Select the Custom Tab option. Then click the Edit Tab button (see Figure 5-10).**

   The tab creation screen opens, as shown in Figure 5-11.

3. **Drag and drop widgets onto the screen — or *canvas*, as Tabfoundry calls it.**

   Widgets include the following:

   - *Basic:* Text, picture, photo gallery
   - *Multimedia:* YouTube, YouTube channel, Vimeo, SoundCloud, LiveStream, UStream
   - *Social:* Instagram, Like button, Share button, Facebook Like box, Facebook comments, Tweet button, Follow button, Twitter stream, Twitter search, Google +1 button, Google+ badge, LinkedIn share button
   - *Tools:* iFrame, HTML box, Google Maps, Button, Countdown, Time reveal, Custom form, MailChimp, AWeber

Figure 5-10

Figure 5-11

For the purpose of these steps, we're assuming you're interested in adding a social media tab to your Facebook Page. We selected Instagram as our social media site of choice.

4. **Sign in to your account (shown in Figure 5-12) and customize the look of your tab.**

You can make a number of changes, including the number of images shown and the outline of the widget.

5. **When finished, click Publish in the upper right of the screen (shown in Figure 5-12).**

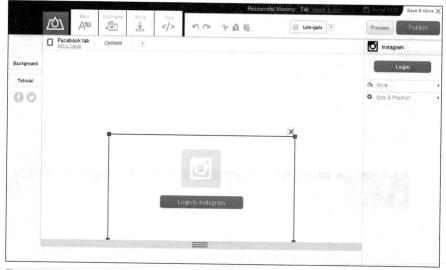

Figure 5-12

Figure 5-13 shows an Instagram custom tab on a Facebook Page.

A custom Facebook tab

Figure 5-13

Keeping Branding Consistent with Pages

A Facebook Page provides you with the opportunity to customize your brand's Facebook presence, but keep in mind the importance of presenting a consistent image across your online properties. When designing your Facebook cover photo and profile image, consider simply using a variation of the images you've already uploaded on other properties.

Coca-Cola is a great example of consistent branding. Navigate to the Coke Facebook page (www.facebook.com/cocacola) and then pop over to its Google+ page at https://plus.google.com/+Coca-Cola/posts. As of this writing, you'll find that both pages have the same profile image and cover photo. You'll also see that both social media properties feature the hashtag #trophytour, using the page design to communicate not just branding but also advertising campaign messaging that's consistent across platforms. Check it out in Figure 5-14.

tip

We discuss Google+ in detail in Chapter 9.

Figure 5-14

remember

While you're creating or changing the design of your Facebook Page, don't forget that you've also probably already created images and profiles on a variety of platforms:

- Twitter (Chapter 6)
- Google+ (Chapter 9)
- YouTube (Chapter 7)

Although you certainly want to be creative and dive into all that Facebook Pages have to offer, glance at your other social media properties before making final Page design decisions.

Tweaking Your Twitter Profile

In This Chapter

- You have a lot of options on how to present yourself on Twitter.

- Profiles, headers, and backgrounds give you a lot of artistic leeway.

- Take a photo on the fly with your smartphone.

T witter, which was born of a failing podcasting service in 2006, has grown steadily to become a worldwide phenomenon relied upon by millions of people for breaking news, sharing photos, and reading the innermost thoughts of presidents, queens, sports heroes, and wanted criminals — all 140 characters or fewer at a time.

However, Twitter is one of the trickier social media sites to design for because of how Twitter profiles are centered within a browser window. The biggest challenge with Twitter is creating designs that look good on both small and large screen sizes. Keep in mind, also, that many Twitter users access the platform via popular apps and websites rather than visiting Twitter.com directly. This further complicates what you need to consider when creating your Twitter profile.

tip

For advice on how use Twitter to build followers and connect with people around the world, for the meaning of common Twitter acronyms (say, RT for *retweet*), or when to use a hashtag (#) to highlight keywords, consult *Twitter For Dummies*, by Laura Fitton, Michael E. Gruen, and Leslie Poston.

Figure 6-1
Scott Clark (www.buzzmaven.com)

Some designers simply create a Twitter page that's optimized for the most popular screen size, which as of this writing is 1366 x 768 pixels (px). That's fine for everyone who uses a monitor of that size, but that approach often leads to very undesirable results for those folks who use a small smartphone screen or a giant computer monitor.

In this chapter, we demonstrate that with ingenuity, creativity, and a little insight into what works best on Twitter, you can produce stunning Twitter page designs that work well across a variety of screen sizes and platforms. Figure 6-1 shows an example of an effective Twitter design, from Scott Clark, online marketing expert.

ANIMATING TWITTER PROFILE PHOTOS

Once upon a time, Twitter allowed you to upload animated GIFs to use as your profile photo. *Animated GIFs* are images created by combining a series of images in the GIF format into one image that play automatically to create a short animation.

In the fall of 2012, Twitter banned uploading any new animated GIFs but allowed some users to preserve their existing animations. Opinions differ as to why this was done. Some people allege that users were abusing the animation function to upload obscene clips, and others claim that the animations were burdening Twitter's servers and contributing to frequent outages. Either way, under Twitter's current guidelines, you cannot use animated GIFs.

We suggest software that allows you to create animated GIFs in Chapter 12; animated GIFs are accepted on Tumblr.

TWITTER'S MOBILE ROOTS COMPLICATE DESIGNS

Twitter was originally designed as a podcast-hosting site, but it has evolved and grown to become a "micro-blogging" site. It's now a worldwide phenomenon where people post breaking news, upload photos, and share everything from news updates to their innermost thoughts, limited to no more than 140 characters at a time.

The leaders (the presidents or prime ministers) of more than 125 countries have Twitter accounts (although it's debatable how many of those tweets sent are really done by these world leaders and how many are posted by a harried subordinate, furiously punching away at the keys of a smartphone), which are followed by about 52 million of their citizens.

Unlike just about every other social media service that we cover in this book, Twitter has its roots firmly planted in the mobile web. The 140-character limit came about because 160 characters was the sendable limit via SMS message from a mobile handset. (The remaining 20 characters are reserved for reasons that are too technical to go into here.)

And because Twitter is so tied to the mobile web, Twitter's designers have consistently worked to make the site visible on the smaller-resolution smartphones and tablets as well as on the larger monitors of regular computers.

The result of this evolution means that while a Twitter profile will load and run on virtually any browser environment, the fluid resizing and position of static elements on the profile make it particularly tricky to come up with a design that is both eye-catching and that works on every conceivable platform.

Comparing Twitter Image Options

The biggest challenge with Twitter designs is figuring out how to juggle the space constraints and how best to position the three separate images you're allowed to use on your Twitter profile, as shown in Figure 6-2.

Here are the three primary Twitter images you can design:

- ▶ **Profile photo:** Most Twitter users (also known as "Tweeple") opt for a simple *mugshot* (a photo of their face), as shown in Figure 6-2. Instead of a photo, you may prefer to use an illustration or a logo. This image appears with your tweets in your followers' message stream and is also used by Twitter in a wide variety of ways. If you use your Twitter identity to log in to other services (such as to comment on a blog, or sign up to attend a meeting), this photo is the one that appears.

- ▶ **Profile header:** This is the image that appears around your photo in the central box on your Twitter profile page, as shown in Figure 6-2, with a few words of information about yourself, a general location that you can set, and a link to a website. Because the header is a larger image (currently, 1252 x 626 px, although Twitter has been known to change this unpredictably), you can take advantage of this section to express your creativity.

Profile header

Profile photo

Twitter background extends
behind entire page.

Timeline

Figure 6-2

Twitter page of author Janine Warner (https://twitter.com/janinewarner)

> **Twitter background:** The background image fills the background of the page
> and surrounds your profile photo and header (as shown in Figure 6-2). The
> background photo appears only when a user clicks through to view your
> Twitter page. Positioning your background image is the most challenging
> because the visible amount of the background depends on the size of the
> screen.

All your text and image posts combine to create your *Twitter timeline,* also shown
in Figure 6-2. You can't change the design of the timeline area of your page, though.
The timeline comprises your posted tweets, arranged in descending order, with the
most recent tweet on top. If you scroll down the page, the elements to the left of the
header and timeline move off the page. However, the main timeline column remains
centered in the page, so any background design that you create should take this into
consideration.

THE MANY WAYS TWITTER USES YOUR PROFILE PHOTO

Twitter profile photos appear in many places and are displayed in different sizes in different sections of Twitter, including

- On your home page, at 128 x 128 px

- Next to each of your tweets in your followers' timelines, at 48 x 48 px

- In the Who to Follow box next to the timelines (if you're lucky or good enough to be suggested by Twitter), at 33 x 33 px

- In the Following column, at 25 x 25 px, which appears when you log in to your home page on a browser and shows little pictures of all the people you follow

Who to follow · Refresh · View all

Kevin Pepin @kpepin   ✕
Followed by Rob Sylvan and others
🐦 Follow

Ps   Adobe Photoshop ✅ @Photos…   ✕
🐦 Follow

CS6   Creative Suite ✅ @Creativesuite   ✕
🐦 Follow

Popular accounts · Find friends

Adobe @Adobe   2h
UK manufacturer @UNICOLmfg switched to @CreativeCloud for teams. Find out why: adobe.ly/18ZCl3l #CreativeCloud
Expand

Adobe @Adobe   4h
Behind the Project' #Behance feature with Steve Simpson: adobe.ly/15ADu2Y pic.twitter.com/jS8WOlb7OP
📷 View photo

When you click the profile photo on someone's profile page, it displays at the maximum size of 520 x 520 px.

Uploading Profile Photos

Despite its small size, your profile photo is the most important element of your Twitter profile design. In this section, you find instructions for uploading and positioning a profile image.

Twitter allows you to upload images of any height and width, as long as the file size is 2MB or smaller. After you upload a profile image, you can resize and move the image around to better fit the space.

However, for best results, we recommend that you first crop your photo into a perfect square and then resize it to 520 x 520 px using an image editing program such as Adobe Photoshop, as shown in Figure 6-3. This size is the largest size that your profile image will be displayed on Twitter.

Figure 6-3

Follow these instructions to upload your image to Twitter:

1. **Click the Edit Profile button, as shown in Figure 6-4.**

   Small icons that look like little pencils appear in the top-right corner of the profile image and the header photo, as shown in Figure 6-5.

Figure 6-4

2. **Click the small pencil icon at the top-right corner of the profile image field, as shown in Figure 6-5.**

   A drop-down menu appears under the profile image, as shown in Figure 6-6.

Figure 6-5

3. **From the drop-down menu, choose the Upload Photo option, as shown in Figure 6-6.**

   The Select File dialog box opens.

Figure 6-6

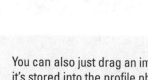

tip

You can also just drag an image from wherever it's stored into the profile photo area of the browser window, shown in Figure 6-6.

4. **Select an image and choose Save.**

   The selected image opens in the Position and Size Your Photo dialog box, as shown in Figure 6-7.

5. **Click the image and drag it to position the image as necessary in the Position and Size Your Photo dialog box.**

tip

If you already sized the image at 520 x 520 px, it fits the space perfectly, as shown in Figure 6-7.

Figure 6-7

6. Click the Apply button.

The Position and Size Your Photo dialog box closes, and the image is automatically inserted into the profile photo space in your Twitter profile page, as shown in Figure 6-8.

Figure 6-8

7. Click the Save Changes button to save your profile.

Your profile image is now visible to all your Twitter followers.

tip

Find instructions for changing your profile image using a smartphone in the "Taking profile photos with a mobile phone" section later in this chapter.

Adding a Header Image to the Top of Your Twitter Profile

In addition to a profile image, you can include a larger image at the top of your profile. Twitter calls the larger image the "header image." Twitter recommends that you use an image in the header that's 1252 x 626 px.

remember

Adding a header image is even more important than including a background image because the header image is displayed more frequently than the background image.

The background image of your Twitter page is visible only when your profile is viewed on a desktop or laptop computer. In Figure 6-9, you see how Adobe Evangelist Paul Trani's (@paultrani) profile appears when displayed on an iPad. Note that his background image isn't visible, but the profile photo and header image are both displayed. The header and profile image are also displayed on smartphones, such as an iPhone.

Figure 6-9

Paul Trani (http://paultrani.com)

Choosing a great header image

You can use virtually any image in your header as long as it's not obscene and doesn't violate Twitter guidelines.

```
https://support.twitter.com/groups/56-policies-violations
```

However, not all images work well in the header area of a Twitter profile. The best header images have these characteristics:

- ▶ The bottom of the image area is dark enough that the white text used to display your title and description is easily readable (as shown in the example in Figure 6-10).

- ▶ The center area of the photo isn't too busy, leaving space for the profile photo to display without covering a key part of the header image or looking crowded. Figure 6-10 shows a great example.

remember

The header photo helps tell your story by conveying information about your personal or professional interests or talents.

Use a background dark enough that white text is readable.

Figure 6-10

Kare Anderson (www.sayitbetter.com)

Uploading a header image to Twitter

Follow these instructions to upload a header image to your Twitter profile page:

1. **Go to your Twitter profile page (`http://twitter.com/yourusername`).**

2. **Click the Edit Profile button at the bottom of the header image area.**

   Small icons that look like little pencils appear in the top-right corner of the profile image and the header photo, as shown in Figure 6-11.

Figure 6-11

3. **Click the small pencil icon at the top-right corner of the header image field.**

   A drop-down menu appears at the bottom of the header image area, as shown in Figure 6-12.

4. **From the drop-down menu, choose Upload Photo, as shown in Figure 6-12.**

   The Select File dialog box opens.

tip

For best results, Twitter recommends you use an image that's 1252 x 626 px.

Figure 6-12

5. **Select any image from where it's stored and choose Open.**

   Alternatively, just drag an image into the header photo area of the browser window, as shown in Figure 6-12, to upload it to Twitter.

   The selected image opens in the header area of your Twitter profile, replacing the previous image, as shown in Figure 6-13.

6. **Click and drag the slider at the bottom of the header image (see Figure 6-13) to size and position the photo as necessary.**

7. **Click the Apply button and then click Save Changes.**

   The slider closes, and the image is automatically inserted into the header space in your Twitter profile page and made visible to your followers.

remember

If you sized the image to 1252 x 626 px, it will fit the space perfectly, as shown in Figure 6-13.

Drag the slider to size and position the image.

Figure 6-13

Adding Background Images

The largest image you can add to a Twitter profile is the background image. It's also the most challenging image in a profile design. Figures 6-14 through 6-16 show examples of different screen resolutions that dramatically change how a background image appears to your followers. In this example, the Twitter background features a photo of Richard Branson, the well-known entrepreneur and owner of Virgin Airlines, looking out the window of an airplane. In Figure 6-14, you see how the designer intended the background to appear and how well it fits the space on the most popular screen resolution today, which is 1366 x 768 px.

Figure 6-14

In Figure 6-15, you see how the background image disappears when the profile is viewed on a monitor with 1024 x 768 px resolution. Having a background disappear on lower-resolution monitors isn't so bad.

Figure 6-15

Figure 6-16 shows what happens when the page is viewed on a large monitor, with a resolution of 1920 x 1080 px. Branson's face is blocked by the Twitter profile. This example demonstrates the kind of unflattering results that can happen when a background image is displayed at different resolutions. If you're encountering this problem, see the upcoming section, "Centering the background image," for a solution.

Figure 6-16

remember

By carefully designing and aligning your background image, you can ensure that visitors to your Twitter profile page will see a pleasing design at any resolution. We recommend that you test your designs at both the highest practical resolution currently in use (1920 x 1200 px) as well as the lowest (currently 1024 x 768 px).

If you have a monitor large enough to support 1920 x 1200 px resolution, you can test your design at smaller sizes by simply dragging the edge of your browser window to make it smaller. If you don't have a large monitor, consider testing your Twitter designs on a friend's computer.

In the sections that follow, you find tips for designing Twitter backgrounds that work on small and large screen sizes.

Positioning background images

There are many ways you can design and position Twitter backgrounds to avoid the problems caused by different displays on different screen sizes. Here are four options that can help you avoid display problems.

Repeating one image or using a series of images

As you can see in Figure 6-17, Dapo Olaopa (@dpencilpusher), shows off his artistic talents by making his background look like a series of doodles from his notebook. This effect is heightened by his use of a blank page and a pencil in his Twitter header.

Figure 6-17
Dapo Olaopa (http://dribbble.com/dpencilpusher)

Author and photographer Syl Arena (@syl_arena) created a grid of tiny images, as shown in Figure 6-18. By using a combination of portraits, company logos, and goofy cartoon images, he constructed a background with a range of colors and styles. Although the design is a little busy, it works well on any screen size and provides followers with a quick insight into his many interests.

Figure 6-18

Syl Arena (http://pixsylated.com/blog/)

Assembling images into a collage

A slightly more sophisticated way to communicate to the world who you are, and what you are all about, is to create a Twitter background design that features photos, knickknacks, and other things that interest you.

These designs are often created to look like a desktop or corkboard with pinned photos or things scattered across the desk. In Figure 6-19, you see an example created by digital marketing pro Scott Clark (@scottclark). Among the items on his virtual desktop, Clark created cryptic messages that look like they were typed on an old-school manual typewriter, as well as maps, images of exotic animals, a worn Indiana Jones–style leather satchel, and (of course) a deadly skeletal robot hand.

remember

Done well, collages like the one shown in Figure 6-19 have a charming, organic quality that makes it feel as if you're peering over the author's shoulder as he works at his desk or in his workshop.

tip

In the design shown in Figure 6-19, Scott Clark cleverly uses a gradient along the right side of the design that fades into a solid color. The effect is that even on a very large monitor, the design doesn't abruptly cut off at the edge of the image but instead fades into the solid background color, making it seem to be part of a larger backdrop.

Figure 6-19

Scott Clark (www.buzzmaven.com)

warning

Be careful to not overdo it and make the background too cluttered and busy.

For the background of his Twitter profile, as shown in Figure 6-20, social media director Sean R. Nicholson (@SocMedSean) uses a collage that includes an iPhone, an iPad, pens, and other things that he holds in his hands to do his work. Making the design even more interesting, he includes reminders scrawled on his left hand that seem to represent a typical to-do list. He gave the entire design a modern look by using a background image that looks like it's made of gritty concrete.

Figure 6-20

Sean R. Nicholson (www.socmedsean.com)

There is no real shortcut to creating a collage like this. To crop each image and position them the way Sean did, you need a good image editor, such as Photoshop. You find instructions for extracting and combining images like this in Chapter 3.

tip

Pay attention to the brightness, contrast, and color balance in all the images that you combine in your design. If you put pictures that are really dark next to photos that were shot under bright lights without balancing them, the effect can be jarring.

Using one dominant image

One of the simplest and most elegant approaches to creating a Twitter background is to use one big image. Photographs of landscapes, skylines, or abstract images work well, and repeating the image in the background and the header is a common and effective trick.

In Figures 6-21 and 6-22, you see how Kare Anderson (@KareAnderson), an author, speaker, and consultant who lives in Sausalito, used a photo of the Golden Gate Bridge for her background and the header in her Twitter page.

Repeating an image the way Kare does in her Twitter profile reinforces the visual effect and helps visitors recognize the background image, even if it doesn't fit on smaller monitors, as shown in Figure 6-22.

Figure 6-21

Kare Anderson (www.sayitbetter.com)

Figure 6-22

Kare Anderson (www.sayitbetter.com)

tip

Using vertically aligned text, such as the design in Figures 6-21 and 6-22, is another way to help ensure your message gets through on small and large screens. Notice that the vertical text with the URL of Kare's website is still visible, even when displayed on a small screen, as shown in Figure 6-22.

Centering the background image

Many of the problems we've shown you with Twitter background images getting cut off or oddly cropped at high or low screen resolutions (such as the one shown in Figure 6-16), can be solved by centering the background instead of aligning it to the left. Figure 6-23 shows a Twitter design with a centered background.

Twitter originally offered only left alignment for background images. You can now center the image by clicking and dragging your image into the position you choose.

Figure 6-23

Erika Barker (www.erikabarker.com)

remember

Centering the background makes a big difference because the middle of the design area — where the timeline, profile photo, and header graphic appear — is always centered, no matter how large or small the screen.

Centering the background means the background stays in the same location relative to the middle area of a Twitter profile, no matter how large or small the screen. That solves many problems that are caused when the background stays aligned to the left, but the centered middle area covers different parts of the background, depending on the size of the screen.

Centering a background image is especially useful when you want to create a design like the own shown in Figures 6-23 and 6-24. Photographer Erika Barker (@erikabarker) creates a clever illusion by using a section of the background image in the header area. The effect appears that the header and background are all one image, even though they were cropped and uploaded separately.

Figure 6-24

Erika Barker (www.erikabarker.com)

However, this kind of integrated design works only if the background and the header image stay the same distance from each other, no matter what the screen size — and that would not work if the background were not centered.

In Figure 6-23, you see what Erika's page looks like on a monitor with the resolution set to 1920 x 1080. In Figure 6-24, you see the same design as it appears on a monitor with the resolution set to 1024 x 768. Despite the significant difference in real estate, the design works in both sizes because the centered background and the centered header line up perfectly on the small and the large screens.

remember

If you create a design that integrates the header and background images, like the one shown in Figures 6-23 and 6-24, keep in mind that the background image doesn't display on mobile devices, so the header image also has to work alone.

In Figure 6-25, you see another example of a centered background design. In this case, the Adobe software company (@Adobe) created an abstract design that echoes the color scheme used in its Creative Suite products. Because the design is centered, the colorful elements continue to surround the Timeline section of the Adobe Twitter page no matter what size screen it displays on.

Figure 6-25

Inserting background images

After you decide on the image you want to use in your background, uploading it to Twitter is relatively easy. Follow these steps to upload and position a Twitter background:

1. **Open Twitter in your favorite web browser and log in to your user account.**

2. **Click the Edit Profile button at the top right of the browser window, as shown in Figure 6-26.**

Figure 6-26

tip

The Edit Profile button looks like a gear.

3. **Click the Design link on the left site of the Account page that opens.**

   The Design Settings open, as shown in Figure 6-27.

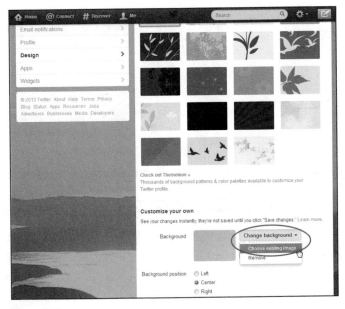

Figure 6-27

4. **In the Customize Your Own section, as shown in Figure 6-27, click the Change Background button.**

   The Change Background drop-down menu opens, as shown in Figure 6-27.

5. **From the drop-down menu, select Choose Existing Image, as shown in Figure 6-27.**

   The Choose File to Upload dialog box opens.

remember

If you want your background image to fill the screen on high-resolution monitors, make sure that it's at least 1400 px wide.

6. **Select any image from where it's stored and choose Open.**

   The selected image is uploaded to Twitter, but it may not be visible until the page is saved.

7. **Choose an alignment option from the Background Position section, as shown in Figure 6-28.**

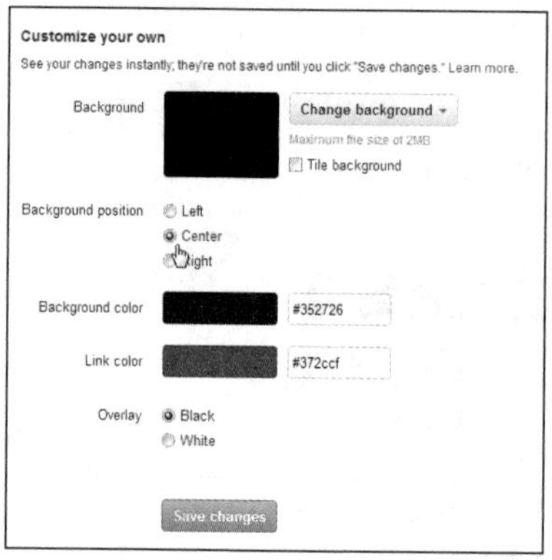

Figure 6-28

8. **Click the Save Changes button.**

   The background is saved and becomes visible in the background of the Twitter page.

9. **To view your Twitter profile, click the Me link at the top of the browser window.**

   Your Twitter profile page is displayed with the new background image in place, as shown in Figure 6-29.

Figure 6-29

Changing Twitter Profile Photos

Most users choose a good portrait as their profile photo and keep it for months or even years. Others change their profile photos as often as they change their socks.

Being consistent has advantages on Twitter because using the same photo makes you more recognizable. That said, using a photo that's more than a few years old can make you look outdated. For most Twitter users, updating your profile photo every six months to a year is a good practice.

Making more frequent profile changes

Changing things more frequently can help keep your profile looking fresh, especially if you're an exceptionally active Twitter user.

Here are a few reasons why Twitter users change profile photos:

▶ **Holidays:** Using a profile photo with a red hat (like the one shown in Figure 6-30), bunny ears, or clown makeup can make your page look more festive during holidays, such as Christmas, Halloween, or Purim.

Figure 6-30

▶ **Special events:** When you're attending a special event, celebrating a birthday, or graduating from college, using a profile photo that includes a graduation cap, birthday hat, or other prop can help you share the excitement with your followers.

▶ **Changing your look:** If you get a new haircut or otherwise change the way you look, updating your profile to reflect your appearance helps keep you recognizable when you meet people in real life.

▶ **Sports:** Adding your team colors or wearing a team jersey or baseball cap is a great way to show you're a fan. Adding a black stripe across your photo can signify that you're in mourning if your favorite sports team loses.

▶ **Seasons:** Using a photo of yourself in a winter hat or your amazing new sunglasses can help illustrate the changing seasons.

tip

Although changing your profile image once in a while is good practice, don't risk losing the attention of your followers just to look up-to-date. We recommend that when you change your profile picture you make sure that your face is still recognizable. Remember that a lot of people scan Twitter, looking for messages from their friends. If you look radically different because you use a profile image that makes it hard to recognize you — such as a moody close-up of just your eyes, a picture of a flower, or a cartoon character — your followers may not be able recognize you, and they may scroll right past your valuable words of wisdom.

If a special event seems to warrant changing your photo to something your followers won't easily recognize, make sure that you alert your friends to the fact that you have a new look. We suggest that you post a tweet explaining why you chose the image.

Taking profile photos with a mobile phone

Twitter has its roots on the mobile web, and many users manage their accounts via mobile phones. Virtually every mobile phone has a fairly decent camera these days, so it's no big surprise that Twitter includes a feature that makes it easy to update your profile with a photo taken with a camera phone.

When you change a profile photo on Twitter, you can upload an existing photo or take a new photo. Although you can use the Take Photo option (which we cover in the following step list) on a computer that has a camera, this feature is primarily used to change profile photos using a camera phone.

Here are instructions for changing your profile photo with a camera taken using the Twitter app on a smartphone:

1. **If you haven't already, download and install the Twitter application on your smartphone**.

2. **Launch the Twitter application on your smartphone and click the Edit button, as shown in Figure 6-31.**

    Hint: The Edit button, which looks like a gear, is on the left side of the screen, just below the number of tweets you've posted.

    The Edit options open, as shown in Figure 6-32.

Figure 6-31

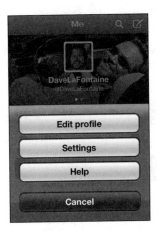

Figure 6-32

tip

Although you can edit your Twitter profile using the web browser on your smartphone, this task works much better using the Twitter app, as illustrated in these steps.

3. **Click Edit Profile, also shown in Figure 6-32.**

    The Edit Profile page opens, as shown in Figure 6-33.

4. **Click your profile photo image, as shown in Figure 6-33.**

    If you don't have a profile image, click the blue box that represents the profile picture.

    Your profile photo options open, as shown in Figure 6-34.

Figure 6-33

5. **Click the Take Photo button, as shown in Figure 6-34.**

   The camera on your phone opens, ready for you to take a photo.

6. **Take a photo just as you would take any photo using your smartphone camera.**

   After the photo is captured, the Retake and Use buttons appear at the bottom of the screen, as shown in Figure 6-35.

7. **Click the Use button (shown in Figure 6-35) to replace your profile photo with the picture you just took.**

   Choose Retake to return to the camera where you can take another photo or cancel.

Figure 6-34

As shown in Figure 6-36 the profile photo is replaced in the header area at the top of your profile, as well as in all the posts you have made on Twitter.

Figure 6-35

Figure 6-36

ecent uploads

How to
Video w

1,516 vie

0:53

Designing websites for the
iPad

151 views   2 years ago

1:52

Intro to Video: Designing
for Multiple Screens with ...

284 views   1 year ago

4:15

esigning for Desktop,
obile & Tablet Devices ...

92 views   1 year ago

Channeling Your Look on YouTube

In This Chapter

- You need to put some thought into your YouTube channel design.

- Check out unique YouTube channel designs.

- Create a custom YouTube channel that reflects you.

- Lure viewers into watching your videos with a custom thumbnail.

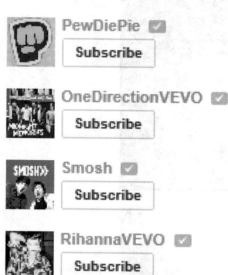

YouTube has grown into a global giant, and the name itself has become shorthand when referring to video on the web. From its launch in 2005, to its acquisition by Google, to its lofty ranking today as the world's #2 search engine, YouTube has become the default place users around the world turn to when looking for Internet video. Figure 7-1 shows how one company uses YouTube.

on the web

We provide a template for you to create your YouTube channel art. You can find it at www.digitalfamily.com/social.

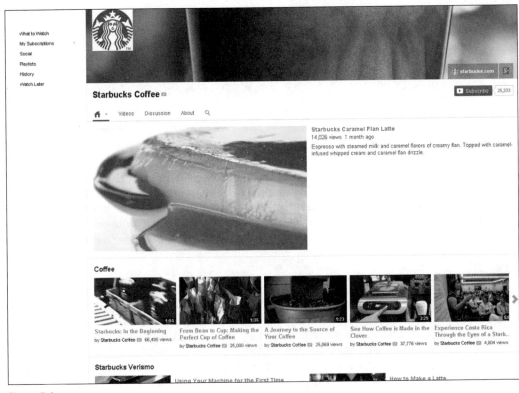

Figure 7-1

In this chapter, we help you understand all the other ingredients that go into crafting your own hit Internet TV channel, such as how to write the kind of description of your videos that entices viewers to subscribe, what kind of trailer you should have to greet visitors to your channel's home page, and how to choose the right thumbnail image to lure viewers into clicking to watch your videos.

Launching Your Own YouTube Channel

Anyone who has a Google account can watch, Like, or subscribe to videos. If you want to upload your creations, comment on other people's videos, or make a playlist, though, you need to create your own channel — a home page for your account that hosts all your videos that you customize to your liking. A channel costs nothing but a few minutes of your time. Creating your own YouTube channel provides you with the opportunity to add to your branding across social media platforms. Similar to Facebook, the design of your YouTube channel features a small profile image and a cover photo that YouTube refers to as channel art. Users can select from existing photo galleries or upload image files.

tip

Ever since the launch of the Google+ social media platform, activities on it and YouTube have been increasingly integrated. If you Like or comment on a video, or upload a video, that's posted to your Google+ feed. For more on Google+, see Chapter 9.

If you already have a Gmail account, you're most of the way there. However, there are some options that you can explore. For example, you can create a channel using your own name (or the "handle" you use in Gmail or Google+), or you can create a channel for your business, or using another name. This, along with the design options, provides you with another opportunity to intentionally brand your YouTube channel to match your website and/or other social media platforms. One thing to note — every newly created YouTube channel automatically comes with a connected Google+ page.

tip

You may need to later tinker with the name for your channel. You can have any name you like, including the names of global brands or celebrities, but Google does have the right to take down abusive or spammy channels. Try to come up with a name for your channel that both describes what your content is going to be, and that sounds interesting enough so that your users will be encouraged to subscribe. This is also an opportunity to keep your branding consistent across sites.

Planning Your Channel

Part of the beauty of YouTube is that it has democratized starting up your very own television network in a way that could never have been anticipated a decade ago. And more than that, plain old broadcast TV networks pale in comparison to the reach and power of YouTube. Billions of people around the world can watch a video, creating instant global pop culture phenomena like Psy, Justin Bieber, and the incomprehensibly popular guys on Smosh.

Creating your own channel on YouTube is about more than just showing off for your friends. In the last few years, YouTube (and its corporate owners at Google) have gotten serious about empowering their power users to monetize their creations.

But before you start getting visions of Hollywood stardom, waving to your screaming fans from red carpet premieres and reserving parking space for your own private Gulfstream V Jet, you're going to need to design a spiffy-looking YouTube channel to entice all your fans-to-be to click to follow you.

warning

For your video creations for YouTube, be sure that you're not infringing on any copyrights. Beginner YouTube copyright mistakes often include casually using a favorite song or a sequence from a favorite movie.

Over the past few years, YouTube has devoted significant resources to building sophisticated tools that allow musicians and filmmakers to automatically find and flag users who pirate their creations. One of the worst impressions you can give a prospective subscriber is to have a trailer or video feed full of blank spaces with the notice, "This video has been removed because its content violated YouTube's Terms of Service."

Making your YouTube videos pay

Producing a decent video can be hard work. You need a video camera or webcam, editing tools, and access to a fast Internet connection to upload your video. And after you go to all that trouble (not to mention all the time you spend bragging about your creation across all the other social media platforms), it's natural to want to get a little something back from YouTube.

The ways to make money on YouTube are limited only to the terms of service and your own imagination. Here are three ways to make money from your video:

 Use video to promote your own product or promote a product for which you are a sales affiliate.

 Create sponsored content for clients.

Become a YouTube Partner and receive ad revenue based on your video's views.

warning

Of these three, only the first one is now frowned upon by YouTube. If your video is nothing more than a blatant commercial for something you're trying to sell, YouTube is likely to remove it for violating its terms of service. Without this policy, YouTube would quickly be clogged up with millions of spammy infomercials. Want to promote a product on your YouTube channel? Find a way to create compelling content that happens to also feature that product. Find out more about the YouTube terms of service and brand guidelines at `www.youtube.com/yt/about`.

Until quite recently, you couldn't charge people to watch your videos on YouTube, whose entire business model was grounded in Google's philosophy that "content wants to be free." In May 2013, Google announced that it was rolling out more than 50 channels that were subscription-only ("paid" channels). The channels, which range from $0.99 to $9.99 per month, feature premium content, such as videos that show you how to fix your Harley-Davidson motorcycle, or full-HD video of classic rock concerts. Keep in mind that it may be a challenge to draw an audience to a fee-based YouTube channel when there's a wealth of free content available to viewers.

YouTube restricts paid premium channels to its trusted Partners. To achieve Partner status, you must apply through the Partner Creator Hub. As of this writing, most subscription channels seem aimed at the family market (such as the *Sesame Street* or the *National Geographic for Kids* channels), but YouTube has invested more than $200 million with dozens of celebrity and high-profile Hollywood figures to start producing original content. Find out more at

```
www.youtube.com/yt/creators/creator-benefits.html
```

But the most common way of monetizing your videos is the same as what is done with traditional TV: advertising. To take advantage of all the various kinds of advertising available for online video (overlays, frames, pre-rolls, and so on), you need to enable ads on your videos. You will also need a Google AdSense account for the money to be deposited into.

For more on how to enable ads on your videos, see the YouTube instructions at

```
https://support.google.com/youtube/answer/94522?hl=en
```

Creating a channel trailer

Just like blockbuster movies generate excitement by pushing out a *trailer* (also known as "Preview of Coming Attractions"), your YouTube channel can start building an audience by greeting visitors with a short video that explains who you are, what you're all about, and why they should subscribe and watch your video creations.

Orabrush Story

We recommend that you take some time to carefully plan what you want to appear in your channel trailer. One good approach that we've seen work is pulling 1-second to 5-second segments from the videos that you have already created, and using those short sequences to form a new Greatest Hits video.

Starbucks: In the Beginning
by Starbucks Coffee ☑ 66,495 views

You can then record a voice-over, narrating those moments and explaining how you shot them, what makes them so special, and how you plan to deliver more content like that. You should also think about creating *bumpers*.

technical stuff

Bumpers are so-named because like on a car, these short sequences come immediately before and after your main video content.

Again, it pays to plan before you shoot such an important video for your channel. Carefully consider what visual impression you want to create in the minds of your viewers. If you are going to have a personal vlog-type channel, consider shooting in a small space to convey a sense of intimacy. On the other hand, if you're going to be recording your extreme sports adventures, shooting footage outdoors, on top of a rock formation that you've just climbed, will show your prospective viewers that you're not just a couch-potato wannabe.

Enjoying Eye-Catching YouTube Channel Designs

Video is, after all, such a visual-heavy medium that it should hardly be surprising that YouTube channel owners spend a lot of time coming up with just the right design. Here is a collection of what we consider to be the best examples to help you get your creative juices flowing.

tip

Recent changes to the YouTube channel page design have stymied a lot of channel owners, causing them to rethink everything from profile images to video descriptions. There are still way too many channels where the header image is a featureless blank, but many of the smaller, independent online video stars are taking advantage of the responsive design possibilities.

iJustine

www.youtube.com/user/ijustine

Quirky comedian, video game geek, and YouTube sensation Justine Ezarik is a genuine online video break-out star. She's turned her "pretty girl who likes to do geeky boy stuff" persona into a cross-platform industry that has major advertisers begging to sponsor her shows, and it earned her guest-starring roles on network TV shows. Justine now has a total of five YouTube channels (iJustine, iJustineGaming, iJustinesiPhone, iJustineReviews, and OtheriJustine) that have garnered more than 450 million views. Figure 7-2 shows her main YouTube channel.

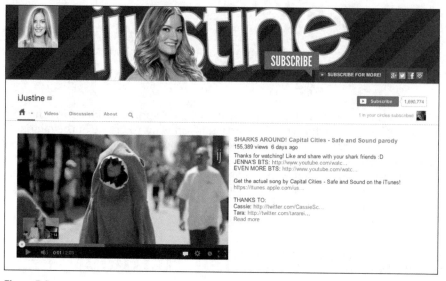

Figure 7-2

`http://www.youtube.com/user/ijustine`

She makes good use of props (such as a video-game controller in Figure 7-3) to give her viewers visual cues as to which of her many channels they have tuned into. She also includes buttons on her YouTube header that not only take users to her other social media profiles, but also to the main channel or to a webstore, where you can buy all kinds of iJustine merchandise.

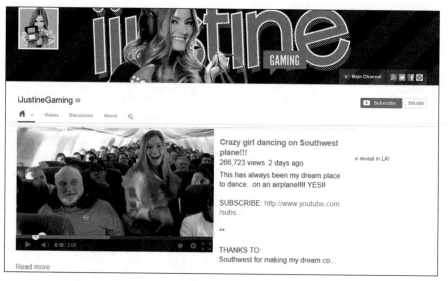

Figure 7-3

iJustineGaming, a popular channel on YouTube

tip

Look for areas where you can cross-brand your sites. The design that Justine uses on her OtheriJustine profile on YouTube is taken from the design that she uses on her Google+ page (see Figure 7-4).

Figure 7-4

iJustineGaming Google+ Page

remember

You don't need to invest in expensive video gear to be a star. Justine shot most of her early videos with a point-and-shoot camera (that included video capability), using a green rug as her backdrop to do green screen work.

ZeFrank

www.youtube.com/user/zefrank1

Another Internet humorist who has rocketed to fame via his hilarious videos, ZeFrank (real name: Hosea Jan Frank) also uses his YouTube profile to give viewers advance warning of his offbeat personality. The simple but powerful close-up of his eyes in Figure 7-5 and the anxious, bemused expression on his face in his profile photo are clues that ZeFrank's videos are what online denizens call "nerdcore humor."

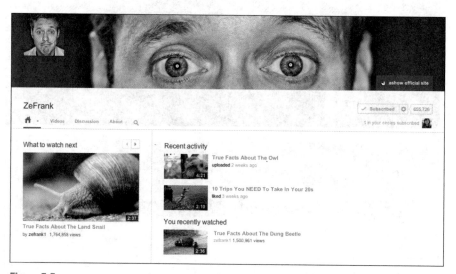

Figure 7-5

Ze Frank (www.zefrank.com)

Orabrush

www.youtube.com/user/curebadbreath

Continuing with the theme of offbeat designs, the YouTube page for Orabrush (shown in Figure 7-6) tackles the underlying issues head-on. The profile photo includes the mad scientist character who is the host of the videos, along with a grimacing actor in a tongue costume. One innovation that earned them inclusion in this list is that they customized their channel page to include a tab called Bad Breath Test, which leads you to the satirical (but informative) video called "How to Tell When Your Breath Stinks." For more on the importance of having a custom trailer to greet your viewers when they land on your YouTube page, see the earlier section, "Creating a channel trailer."

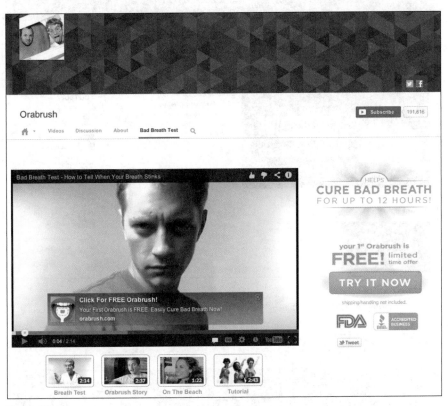

Figure 7-6

Orabrush YouTube Page (www2.orabrush.com)

Eres Lo Que Publicas

www.youtube.com/user/EresLoQuePublicas

www.eresloquepublicas.com

Founded by Roberto Ruz, *Eres Lo Que Publicas* — which means "You are what you publish" — is an educational initiative designed to help young people in Mexico use the Internet and social media more responsibly. See Figure 7-7.

Ruz, director of Responsabilidad Digital, uses his YouTube Channel to promote his speaking and educational business and to attract visitors to his website shown in Figure 7-8. Ruz offers his training program to schools and other education groups and is a popular speaker at events around the world.

Figure 7-7

Eres Lo Que Publicas YouTube Channel by Roberto Ruz (www.youtube.com/user/EresLoQuePublicas)

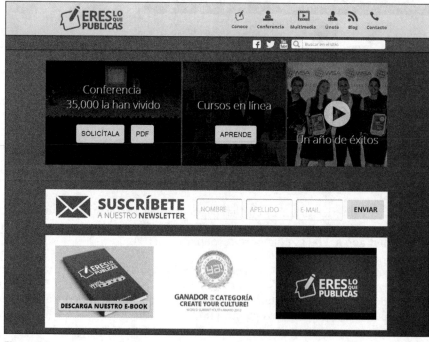

Figure 7-8

Roberto Ruz (www.eresloquepublicas.com)

Customizing Your YouTube Channel

YouTube has rolled out a lot of little extras over the years to allow you to customize the look, feel, and functionality of your YouTube profile. You can create a banner, which YouTube refers to as channel art, that shows up wherever your channel is being accessed from (regular desktop Internet, on mobile devices, or via Google TV). You can also link to your other social media profiles and choose a trailer.

remember

Many customization settings don't have to be chosen right away, but you should at least change your channel artwork from the bland default pattern to something a bit more interesting.

Creating your channel art

The specifications for the channel art on your YouTube channel have changed drastically since YouTube first allowed it to create custom designs.

YouTube is prone to regular design changes, but as of this writing, the channel art template shown in Figure 7-9 will help you design a YouTube page that works on small, medium, and large screens so you can take advantage of the dizzying growth in platforms that viewers now use to watch videos.

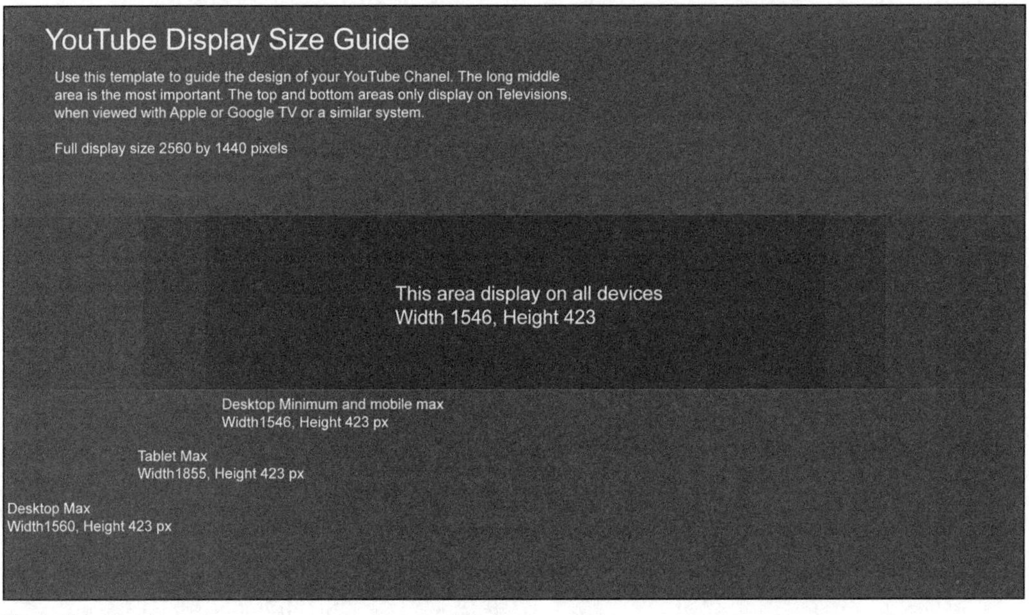

YouTube Display Size Guide

Use this template to guide the design of your YouTube Chanel. The long middle area is the most important. The top and bottom areas only display on Televisions, when viewed with Apple or Google TV or a similar system.

Full display size 2560 by 1440 pixels

This area display on all devices
Width 1546, Height 423

Desktop Minimum and mobile max
Width1546, Height 423 px

Tablet Max
Width1855, Height 423 px

Desktop Max
Width1560, Height 423 px

Figure 7-9

The sudden radical changes to the banner size have left many major broadcasters and brands scrambling to create images that work for the following sizes and platforms. These are the latest recommendations:

▶ **TV, 2560 x 1440 pixels:** We have to assume that YouTube means Google TV, but this is often also the image that is cross-posted to Google+.

▶ **Desktop Max(imum), 2560 x 423:** The horizontal resolution of this specification exceeds the display resolution of even full-HD computer monitors (which are 1920 x 1080).

tip

The latest and most expensive Macs and MacBook Pros have Retina displays that display up to 2880 px, so it would appear that YouTube is future-proofing itself so that its designs still look good when all the other laptop manufacturers adopt this as their standard.

▶ **Tablet, 1855 x 423:** Again, most tablets in use won't display this many horizontal pixels, although the current version of Apple iPad has a maximum resolution of 2048 px.

▶ **Desktop Minimum and Mobile, 1546 x 423:** Despite YouTube saying that this is the "minimum," smaller images in resolution are simply stretched a bit to fit this space, rather than rejected altogether.

▶ **Text and Logo Safe Area:** The center rectangle is where you should concentrate your attention. YouTube has carefully designed its channel pages to be *responsive* — meaning that the images and text scale and rearrange themselves to fit the display area of the device that they are being accessed from. The banner image here is what photo professionals call a *radical horizontal,* which makes things tricky for channel owners who have vertical images, such as portraits or snapshots.

If you have one really big image that perfectly fits this design template, feel free to use it. But if you're like us, you'll probably need to piece a few images together to create the best design for this long, narrow space that needs to adjust to wide and narrow screen sizes. See Chapter 3 for more on how to extract and combine subjects from multiple images to form photo collages.

1. **Open a YouTube template in an image-editing program.**

   In Figure 7-10, you see Janine's Twitter Template open in Adobe Photoshop. You can download templates from the YouTube website in both layered PSD (Photoshop) and PNG formats.

remember

The PSD and TIFF formats are best for editing, but before you upload your images, you'll need to save them as web-friendly JPEGs.

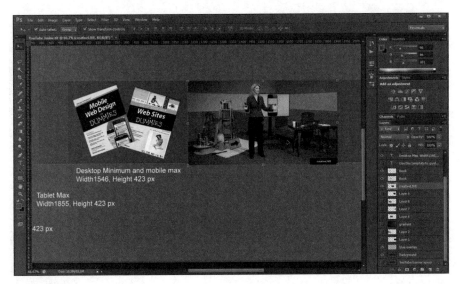

Figure 7-10

2. **Choose File⇨Place.**

   Navigate to the photo you want to add to the composite image you're creating for the top of your YouTube page.

When you upload an image to YouTube, you must use a web-friendly format, such as JPG, GIF, or PNG. YouTube will not accept layered PNG or Photoshop PSD files.

3. **Click a corner handle and resize the image to fit your design.**

4. **Click and drag the image on the template to place it where you want it.**

5. **Add as many photos as you want to fit, resizing each as necessary.**

   As you can see in Figure 7-11, the images are being placed into the central stripe section of the template because that's the only area that will be visible on most devices. Also note that Janine created a simple blue gradient background to fill in the space above and below the narrow center. The full image is displayed only on television sets equipped with Google TV, Apple TV, or a similar system. After you import, place, and size all your photos, they should fit nicely into a layered composite image, such as in Figure 7-11.

tip

Turn on and off the layers containing your new images (or reduce their opacity below 100%) to see how well your design is fitting into your template. You must commit all layers before you can use the Save for Web dialog in the next step.

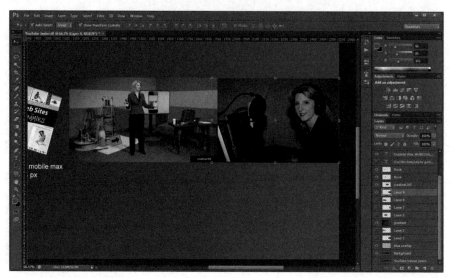

Figure 7-11

6. **Choose File⇨Save for Web and save your creation, as shown in Photoshop in Figure 7-12.**

Figure 7-12

remember

YouTube accepts channel art files with a 2MB maximum only. You may have to tweak the compression settings a bit to get an image that is compatible with these requirements. You find instructions for how to optimize images using the Save for Web dialog in Photoshop and similar programs in Chapter 2.

Uploading your channel art

With your new YouTube channel art created, it's time to upload it to YouTube. You may need to resize it and move it around the interface a bit for it to achieve the effect you're looking for.

If you can't fit the "safe" area into the horizontal stripe in the profile banner template, don't panic. Just backtrack to the image-editing program and make changes to your image based on the problems you see after you upload it to YouTube.

1. **Log in to your Google account.**

2. **Click the down arrow next to your profile in the upper-right corner.**

   The drop-down menu with options to control your YouTube profile appears.

3. **Click My Channel.**

   Your channel administration page opens. If you haven't already uploaded a banner image, the central graphic on the page will prompt you to do so (see Figure 7-13).

   Note: If you've uploaded a banner image, roll your cursor over the cover image, and a drop-down menu appears from which you can select Edit Channel Art to replace the image.

4. **Upload an image to select a photo by dragging an image into the upload area or by clicking the blue Select a Photo button in the middle of the Channel Art screen.**

   The Channel Art window appears, with graphics showing you how your image will look when displayed on different devices. As you can see, YouTube's responsive design makes the narrow banner fit on all manner of displays. However, the maximum size on the TV setting leaves a huge amount of space above and below the strip that is visible.

5. **Click the Adjust the Crop button.**

   A nested rectangle appears. Drag the crop handles to shrink or expand the photo to fit the size, or drag the image so that the most important part fits into the horizontal stripe that is featured on desktop and mobile sites.

6. **Click the Select button when the image looks the way you want it to.**

   Your new banner appears on your YouTube channel, as shown in Figure 7-14.

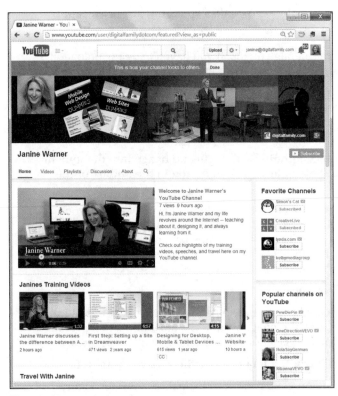

Figure 7-13

Figure 7-14

tip

Test to see how well you centered the crucial content in your design by clicking and dragging the browser window to resize it. You should see the pixels on the sides of your cover art image gradually get clipped off and reappear as you drag the window back and forth. If you really want to test things, try accessing your YouTube page on a smartphone, a tablet, or even on a device enhanced with Google TV to get the full effect.

Setting links from your channel to your other sites

After your main channel art is created and uploaded to your satisfaction, start customizing some of the other settings on your YouTube channel.

First, take a look at the links that can appear over your banner image. You can choose to have as many or as few appear as you want, assuming that you have established profiles on these other social media sites, or that you have your own custom-built site.

remember

Linking from your YouTube videos to these profiles can help drive traffic to your other profiles. This can also be a great SEO device to help your site rank higher in search engine results. Most search engines value *inbound* links — that is, sites that link to yours — and a link from a site as popular as YouTube to your website can really give you a boost.

1. **Log in to your Google account and navigate to** www.youtube.com.

2. **Hover your pointer over your channel art and click the Edit button that appears in the upper-right corner of your channel art image (it looks like a little pencil).**

   The edit drop-down panel appears.

3. **Click Edit Links.**

   The Customised Links window opens, as shown in Figure 7-15.

4. **Fill in the fields with the URLs of your website or your social media profiles.**

   You can choose to display up to four social media sites, such as Facebook, Twitter, and Google+, on your channel art image.

5. **Click Done when you have the links set the way you like.**

   The links will appear as little icons on your channel art.

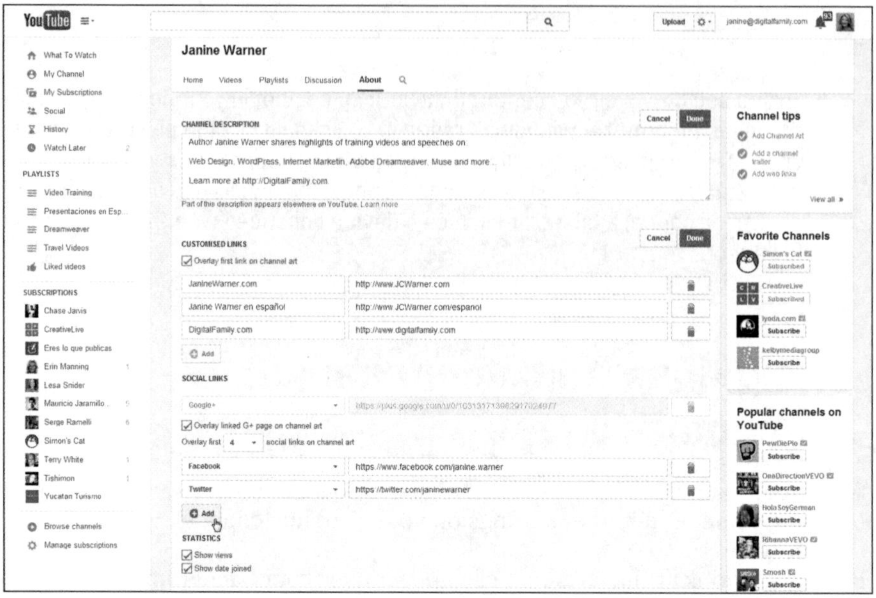

Figure 7-15

Activating Other Account Features

One of the benefits of attracting subscribers is that after you pass the 100-user threshold, your account will be enabled for live video streaming. That means that you can use Google's entire infrastructure to broadcast and record live video.

Check the Account Features section of your home page to check whether you've met the criteria. If you have, all you need to do is click the Enable button.

Here are some of the other features that you can activate on your YouTube channel. Figure 7-16 shows off several of these features.

Annotations: Once the sole province of snarky "Pop-up Video" wannabes, these little messages that you can set to appear during the playback of your video can now be used to insert hyperlinks to an online store (yours or another's, such as Amazon, where you might have your merchandise for sale).

Transcripts: Unlike Annotations, Transcripts simply contain the text of what is said in the video. They are automatically timed using speech-recognition technology.

Playlist: If you have a list of videos that you want your viewers to watch — say, "The Worm-Eating Fernbird Parts 1–20" — you can put these related videos into a playlist. YouTube will then automatically show your viewers the next video in the series when they come to the end of the one that they're watching. To enable this function, mark your playlist as a Series when you are setting it up.

Figure 7-16

▶ **YouTube Analytics:** Much as Google Analytics has become the default tool for small and beginner webmasters to measure and understand what visitors come to their sites, what they do, and how long they stick around, YouTube Analytics will help you figure out who your real viewers are, what they like, and which parts of what videos they are really watching.

▶ **Google+:** As we mention earlier, the integration between YouTube and Google+ is ongoing. Each month seems to bring a new feature designed to make the creations, comments, likes, and dislikes expressed on one Google platform show up on the other.

Crafting a Custom Thumbnail for Your Videos

One of the best tools you can use to customize your YouTube profile and entice casual passersby into clicking and watching your videos is using a high-quality, custom thumbnail image.

This image can make all the difference — and all too often, the freeze-frame that YouTube chooses to represent the content in your video is blurry, poorly lit, or shows a person with his or her face contorted into the least flattering expression ever.

tip

You need a verified YouTube account in good standing to be trusted to upload a custom thumbnail image.

We suggest that you take matters into your own hands by exporting a frame from your video and then taking that still image into a photo editor for further enhancement. Or you can start from scratch and create your own image that you think will best capture the essence of your video and lure viewers into clicking to watch.

YouTube does have some technical guidelines for what kind of image you are allowed to use (besides the obvious ones written in its Community Guidelines, which ban explicit nudity, obscenity, violence, or spam):

 The image should be less than 2MB.

 The image should be fairly high resolution. YouTube suggests using an image that's 1280 x 720 px (not quite full-HD).

 Use acceptable web formats, such as PNG, JPG, GIF, or even the venerable BMP.

After you create your custom thumbnail image, replace the thumbnail image that YouTube selected for you (or that you picked from the gallery of possibilities when you uploaded the video in the first place). This is a fairly simple process, but you may need to check the final effect a couple of times because as part of the post-upload process, YouTube automatically resizes the thumbnail image to appear in a wide variety of circumstances and resolutions, such as on a smartphone or tablet.

remember

These thumbnails are tiny, so if you create an image with a lot of text or fine details, these are going to be blurry or completely lost when the image is shrunk to fit these spaces.

1. **Log in to your YouTube channel.**

2. **Click the down arrow next to your profile photo in the upper right.**

   The YouTube account management settings drop-down menu appears.

3. **Click the Video Manager link.**

   A page opens, containing all the videos that you have uploaded. You can view them as a grid of thumbnails or in a list, where you can also see when they were uploaded, how many times they have been viewed, and other information. (See Figure 7-17.)

4. **Click the Customised Thumbnail button.**

   The Upload Custom Thumbnail window opens.

5. **Choose the image that you want to use and then click OK.**

   Your custom thumbnail image is uploaded.

6. **Click the Save Changes button.**

   Your custom thumbnail image replaces the current still frame.

remember

If you haven't verified your YouTube account, this button won't appear. Find out how to verify your YouTube account at `https://www.youtube.com/verify`.

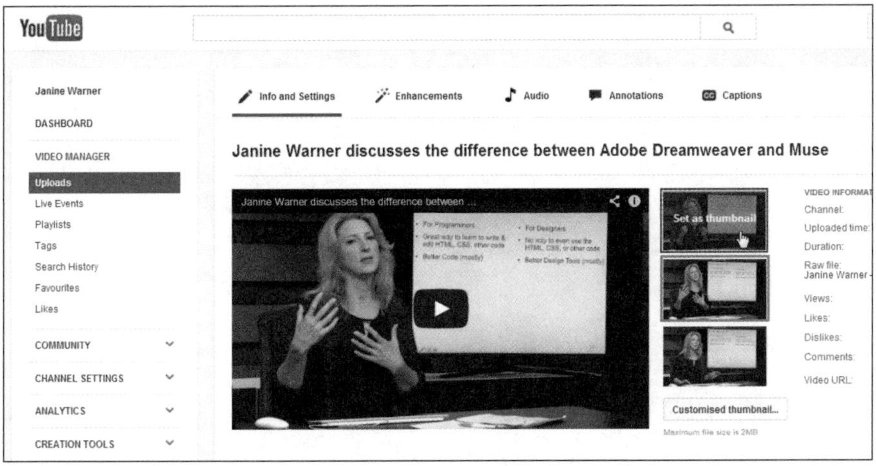
Janine Warner
DASHBOARD
VIDEO MANAGER
Uploads
Live Events
Playlists
Tags
Search History
Favourites
Likes
COMMUNITY
CHANNEL SETTINGS
ANALYTICS
CREATION TOOLS
Info and Settings
Enhancements
Audio
Annotations
Captions
Janine Warner discusses the difference between Adobe Dreamweaver and Muse
Janine Warner discusses the difference between ...
Set as thumbnail
Customised thumbnail...
Maximum file size is 2MB
Channel:
Uploaded time:
Duration:
Raw file:
Views:
Likes:
Dislikes:
Comments:
Video URL:

Figure 7-17

Part III

Extending Your Social Reach

Chapter 8: Review the most professional of the social media sites, LinkedIn, and find tips for how to design a profile that can help boost your career.

Chapter 9: Delve into Google's social media site, Google+ and see how to create a great profile.

Chapter 10: See show you how to use the highly visual Pinterest to set up boards

Chapter 11: Check out Flickr, the online photo-hosting site.

Visit www.dummies.com/extras/socialmediadesign for ideas on how to make your social media content easy to share.

Indiana University-Purdue University at

Indianapolis, Indiana Area

Home   Notables

Explore Careers of 43,322+ Alumni

Where they work ▸

IUPUI	974
Indiana University Health	521
Eli Lilly and Company	502

more ▸

What they do ▸

Operations

Healthcare Services

Sales

General Information

Indiana University-Purdue University Indianapolis, one of the top 15 "up-and-c

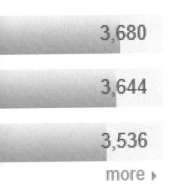

I'm

Who yo

20 first-

1,264 s

Notable

3,680

3,644

3,536

more ▸

American

CHAPTER 8

Upscaling Your LinkedIn Profile

In This Chapter

- Make the right introduction on LinkedIn.

- The right introduction includes a profile, bio, and photo.

- You can then enhance and edit your profile.

Å   Skills & Expertise

Most endorsed for...

81	Web Design	
77	Dreamweaver	
74	Content Strategy	
66	WordPress	
50	Wordpress	
47	Online Marketing	
40	Multimedia	
37	Social Media	
28	Interaction Design	
28	Digital Marketing	

Janine also knows about...

25 Adobe Creative Suite	21 Graphic Design	21 New Media	19 CSS
17 Published Author	13 Publishing	12 Mobile Applications	11 Digital Media
10 Training	10 Photoshop	10 Video	9 Mobile Design	User Experience
9 Digital Photography	9 User Interface Design	See 25+ >

inkedIn is the social platform that, above all other platforms, is used primarily for professional reasons. Because LinkedIn has limited options for images, you will have fewer design opportunities, but that doesn't mean that your design is not a factor in people's first impression of your profile.

At the top of every LinkedIn profile, you're limited to placing only one small image. Thus, any successful profile starts with a great photo that makes your face easy to recognize, as Dana Underwood did in his profile (shown in Figure 8-1). Because LinkedIn is a professional networking site, your profile image should err on the side of professional. This is not the time to share your fun selfie from last weekend or share your artistic side. Further down the page, you are allowed to add examples of your work, which provides additional opportunities to add visual elements to your profile.

In this chapter, we explore the opportunities for enhancing your LinkedIn design. We also provide tips for creating great content, including how to write your own biography and how to request testimonials.

tip

If you're looking for advice on how use LinkedIn, pick up a copy of *LinkedIn For Dummies*, by Joel Elad.

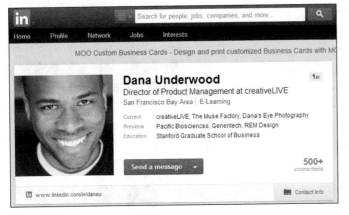

Figure 8-1

Dana Underwood (www.danaseye.com)

Introducing Yourself on LinkedIn

Design your LinkedIn profile as if you were giving a virtual job interview. Consider the perspective of the people you want to attract, and make sure every aspect of your profile is designed to make a good impression on your most important professional audience. See Figure 8-2 for a complete LinkedIn profile.

Most social media experts agree that successful LinkedIn profiles include

- ▶ A great profile photo
- ▶ A succinct "Professional Headline" next to your photo
- ▶ An interesting and well-written biography in the Summary section
- ▶ A carefully curated work history in the Experience section
- ▶ A list of keywords representing your skills and expertise
- ▶ University and other training in the Education section
- ▶ Testimonials and endorsements from colleagues, clients, and employers in the Recommendations section
- ▶ Examples of your work in the form of written materials, video clips, or links to other websites (see Figure 8-3)

Profile photo   Professional headline   A curated work history and education

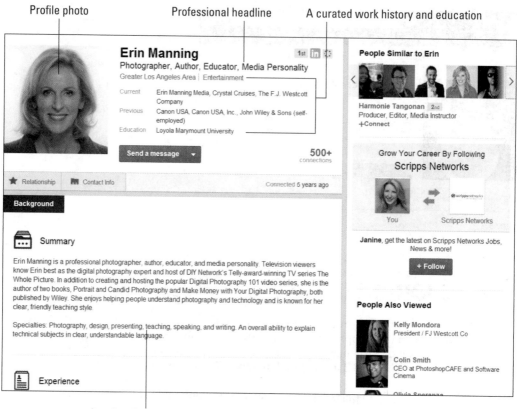

A well-written biography

Figure 8-2

Erin Manning (`http://erinmanning.com`)

tip

Adding examples of your work in the form of images, videos, or documents can dramatically enhance your profile. Look for the Get Discovered field, such as the one shown in Figure 8-3, at the end of the Summary and Education sections.

USING LINKEDIN AS A SEARCH TOOL

LinkedIn is a great place to introduce yourself, network, and job hunt in the professional world — and it's also a great place to search for other people. And because LinkedIn works on smartphones, tablets, and computers, use it as a resource for researching colleagues, potential clients, employees, and more. Here are a few great ways to use LinkedIn as a search tool:

- At a conference or an event, use your laptop, tablet, or smartphone to search for potential contacts.

- Search for people you've met.

- Keep up with your friends and colleagues as they change jobs or take on new projects.

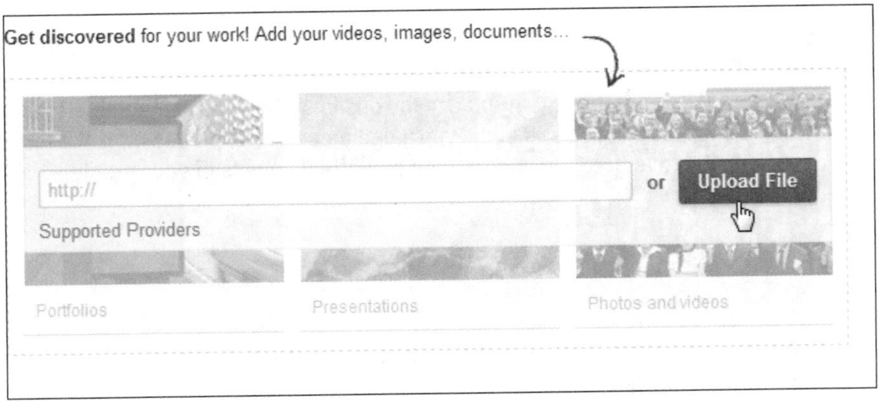

Figure 8-3

Creating a LinkedIn Profile

Start by designing your LinkedIn profile based on the audience you want to reach and the skills and experience you most want to be known for in your professional life. The first step is to create a profile.

1. **Open LinkedIn.com in your favorite web browser.**

   If you're not already logged into an account on LinkedIn, the LinkedIn registration page opens.

2. **Enter your full name, e-mail address, and a password.**

3. **Click the Join Now button.**

   The Grow Your Network on LinkedIn page opens with your e-mail address in the address field.

   Simultaneously, LinkedIn sends an e-mail with a confirmation link to the e-mail account you enter in the registration form in Step 2.

4. **Open the confirmation message from LinkedIn.**

   The message will have the subject line, *Action Required: Please Confirm Your LinkedIn Account.*

5. **Click the Confirm Your Email Address button in the e-mail confirmation message.**

   The Grow Your Network on LinkedIn page opens.

6. **Click the Continue button or click the Skip This Step link.**

   - *Continue:* Click the Continue button, and LinkedIn searches your e-mail contacts for potential connections on LinkedIn and then gives you the option of inviting any or all the people in the search results.

   - *Skip This Step:* Click the Skip this Step link to continue building your profile.

remember

Although LinkedIn doesn't offer as many design options as some of the other social media sites featured in this book, you'll find a number of places on LinkedIn where you can improve both the appearance and effectiveness of your profile.

tip

We recommend you opt for Skip This Step when you're first creating a LinkedIn profile. You can invite new contacts any time after you have a profile on LinkedIn. We find it more effective to send invitations after you add more information to your profile.

7. **Click the profile icon at the top-right corner of the LinkedIn page to open your profile page, as shown in Figure 8-4.**

   Your profile page opens.

Figure 8-4

8. **Click the Edit Profile button, as shown in Figure 8-5.**

   The profile page changes to reveal a variety of editing options, including adding past work positions and education.

Figure 8-5

9. **Click any of the pencil icons or the Edit buttons and fill in your professional information, as shown in Figure 8-6.**

   You can add as many past jobs, places of education, and other details as you choose.

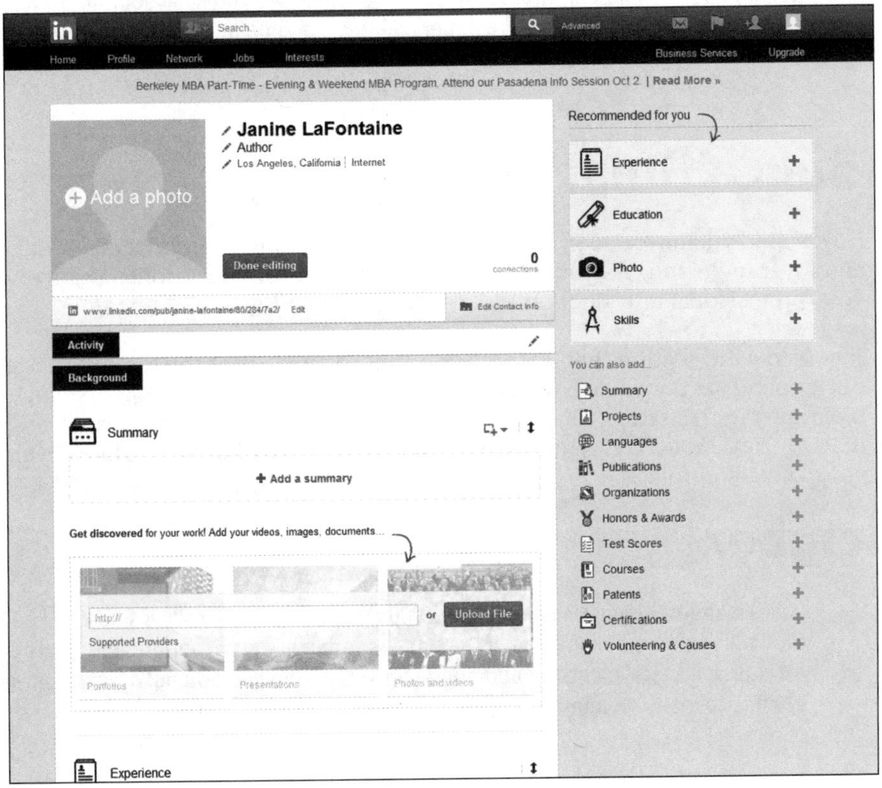

Figure 8-6

10. **Click the Done Editing button, at the top of the page, when you're finished adding new information.**

    You can always go back and add, edit, or remove information later, as shown in Figure 8-7.

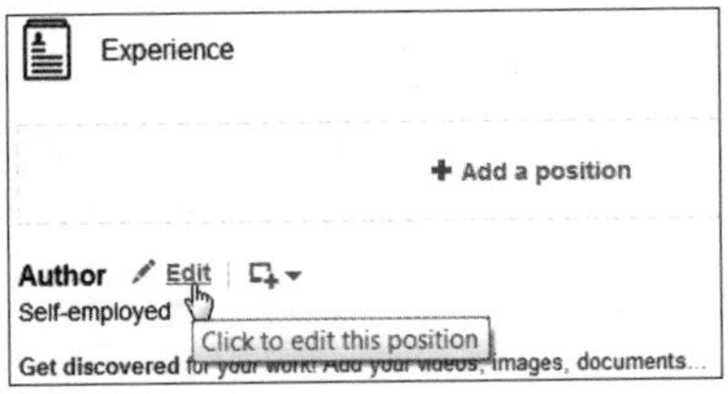

Figure 8-7

In the sections that follow, find tips and suggestions for how to make the most of the various sections in your LinkedIn profile.

remember

LinkedIn is designed for professional connections. As you fill in your information, treat it like you would treat a resume, taking care to be accurate and to focus on your accomplishments and skills.

Writing a Great Biography

How would you introduce yourself if you were meeting a potential client or an employer in person? As you develop the biography for your profile, think of it as your professional introduction.

Just below the section that features your photo and title at the top of the page is the Background section, which includes your profile Summary. Most people include a biography in this space. As noted earlier, you can go back to your profile and edit it at any time. You may want to write a short biography in this section as you build your LinkedIn profile.

remember

Your LinkedIn Summary is limited to 2,000 characters. Generally it's best to keep your Summary brief, highlighting just the best aspects of your experience. Be sure to focus on your skills as well as the audience you serve. Spelling counts! This is your first chance to make an impression, so edit your biography carefully.

You can write your biography in the first or third person. (You can find a mix of the two styles throughout LinkedIn.) In general, a first-person biography will be perceived as more friendly, and a third-person biography is more formal. For example:

▶ **First person:** "I attended American University from 1995 to 1999."

▶ **Third person:** "Amy attended American University from 1995 to 1999."

Most writers will tell you that the hardest thing they've ever written is their own biography. It's a challenge for most us to find the right balance between making a good first impression and not feeling like we're bragging or sharing too much or too little information.

Here are a few tips for writing a great biography:

 Review the information you've shared on other social media platforms to ensure consistent messaging.

 Lead with the most important information first.

Consider what you want to be known for now and in the future, more so than what you have done.

Describe yourself in the way you wish to be perceived.

Above all, be accurate.

warning

If you get caught lying in your biography or on your resume, people won't trust you.

Putting Your Best Face Forward

LinkedIn allows only one small image at the top of your profile. If you're like most professionals, you want to upload a photo of yourself dressed as you would for a job interview or a business meeting. For many, that means a business suit (or at least a clean shirt). Professor Alexander Randall opted for formal shot of himself in a tux with a microphone (see Figure 8-8), as is fitting for his profession in the communication world.

Figure 8-8
Permission: Dr. Alexander Randall, 5th, Professor of Digital Media Communication, University of the Virgin Islands

If you use your image on other social media platforms, be sure that your LinkedIn photo is recognizable as being associated with those other platforms.

warning

Here are two important reasons why you need an appropriate LinkedIn photo:

- Many people won't connect with other LinkedIn users who don't include a photo because it makes it harder to confirm that they're connecting to the right person.

- If you don't include an image in your LinkedIn profile, you will be represented by a generic-looking gray silhouette avatar, as shown in the bottom right of Figure 8-9.

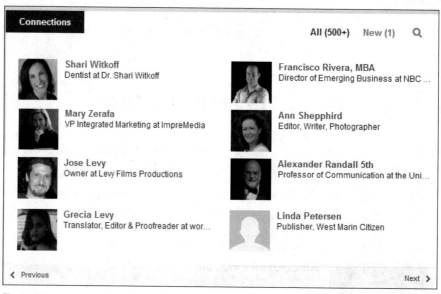

Figure 8-9

Sizing your profile photo

LinkedIn officially states that you can upload an image up to 4MB in size, but what really matters are the dimensions of the image. The current design works best if you upload an image that is a perfect square, at 200 pixels x 200 pixels.

If your image isn't square, you can crop it after you upload it, but you'll have more control over how you size and crop your image if you prepare it first in a photo-editing program like Adobe Photoshop before uploading it.

tip

If you upload an image smaller than the recommended size, LinkedIn adds a light gray box around your image, as shown in Figure 8-10.

Figure 8-10

Changing your profile photo

You can change your profile photo at any time. If you change your hairstyle, or your photo gets outdated, replace it with an image that will help people recognize you if they meet you in person.

tip

If you created a LinkedIn profile very long ago, you may want to replace the small photo that LinkedIn used to require with a larger image that better fills the space.

Follow these steps to change your profile photo.

1. **With your account open, click the Edit Profile button in the top section of the page.**

   The Edit button, including the camera icon shown in Figure 8-11, appears on the page.

2. **Click the camera icon, as shown in Figure 8-11.**

   The Upload a Photo page opens.

Figure 8-11

3. Click the Browse button.

The Choose File to Upload dialog box opens.

4. Browse to and choose the photo you want to use as your profile image and then click Open.

The Choose File to Upload dialog box closes.

5. Click the Upload Photo button.

The image is uploaded to LinkedIn and displays in a preview window, as shown in Figure 8-12.

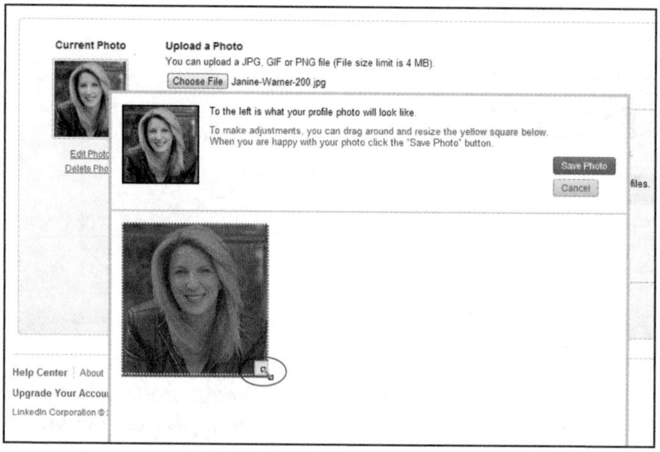

Figure 8-12

6. Click and drag the yellow square, as shown in Figure 8-12, to adjust the crop on your photo.

The image will appear in LinkedIn as it appears in the cropped area in the preview.

7. Click the Save Photo button.

The image appears in LinkedIn as it appears in the cropped preview window.

8. Click the Save button.

The Upload a Photo page closes, and the profile page appears in the browser window.

9. Click the Done Editing button, at the top of the page, to save your changes and apply them to your profile.

remember

You can always go back to change or adjust the photo again by clicking the Edit Profile option and repeating Steps 2 through 9.

Enhancing Your LinkedIn Profile

As you go through the various sections on LinkedIn, it can seem overwhelming. You can spend considerable time filling in all your past work history, accomplishments, and awards, as well as requesting reviews and sending out invitations.

Start with the most important information: your current position and your most recent, or most notable, accomplishments. As you do, here are a few suggestions about filling in the various sections of your profile on LinkedIn.

remember

You can always come back and add more details by clicking Edit Profile as outlined earlier in this chapter.

Adding examples of your work

The most important thing to keep in mind as you design your profile is who you want to reach on LinkedIn, and what you want them to do as a result. Are you looking for a steady fulltime job as an accountant, or do you want to be a freelance creative director?

tip

Consider what you want to be known for and let that guide the way your write your biography and choose the projects you include as examples of your work.

- If you're a designer or photographer, upload a few of your best photographs or images that demonstrate your design talents.
- If you're a public speaker or television personality, like Zain Meghji (shown in Figure 8-13), including a video of a recent speech or appearance lets visitors see you in action.
- If you're an author or a consultant seeking media attention, including a video of an interview can demonstrate that you're media savvy.

To add videos, images, or other documents to your LinkedIn Summary, click the Upload File button or add the URL of the file while editing your profile. Be sure that your file is within the 200K limit imposed by LinkedIn.

Figure 8-13

Zain Meghji (`www.zainmeghji.com`)

Key positions (but not necessarily all)

You can list the company (or companies) you work for now as well as those in your professional past. If any of those companies have websites, you can link to them from your profile to include additional information and greater credibility.

Adding each place you've worked to the Experience section takes time, and the options for positioning multiple jobs are limited. For example, if you have more than one current position, the two titles will be separated by a comma, but you can't put them on separate lines to make it clear they are both current positions.

remember

Make sure you include at least enough detail to reinforce the information you include in the Summary section.

On LinkedIn, job and educational listings are posted in reverse chronological order, so pay special attention to the dates you include when you add a new position.

Accomplishments and awards

If you've been voted the best sales representative in your region, by all means let people know. If you've won a literary award, a scholarship, or anything else that helps build your credibility and expertise, include it in your profile. LinkedIn provides you with a place to add this type of information in the Honors & Awards section of your profile. To add notable achievements, simply click the Edit button next to this section while editing your profile.

Recommendations: References build credibility

LinkedIn offers a number of ways to endorse people for specific skills as well as write testimonials. Including testimonials from employers, colleagues, and clients is one of the best ways to build credibility and improve the chance that someone else will hire you based on what they find on LinkedIn.

In addition to recommendations, you can give and receive endorsements for specific skills. When people endorse you, their profile photos appear next to the skill that they have endorsed you for. In Figure 8-14, you see the endorsements that have been made to date for Janine Warner, one of the co-authors of this book.

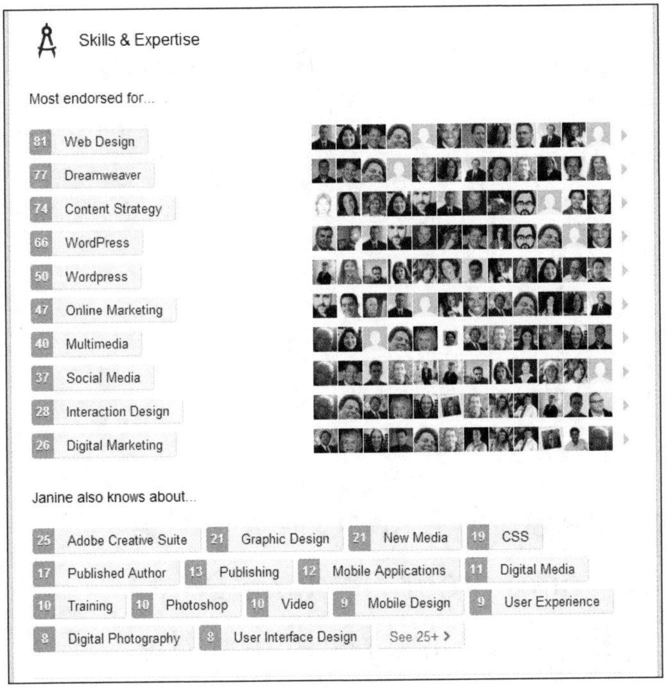

Figure 8-14

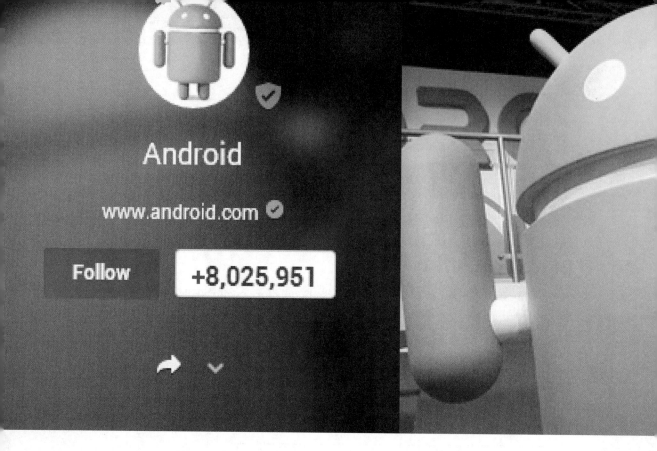

Android

www.android.com ✓

Follow   +8,025,951

About   **Posts**   Photo

Android
Shared publicly - Feb 4, 2014

Ha

Just can't wait until Valentine's Day? Shoppers in the
San Francisco Bay Area can also order Nexus 5 Bright
Red with Google Shopping Express and receive it the
same day.

CHAPTER 9

Generating a Google+ Profile

In This Chapter

- Start by understanding how Google+ fits in with other Google sites.

- Get inspired by other Google+ designs.

- Create your own Google+ profile!

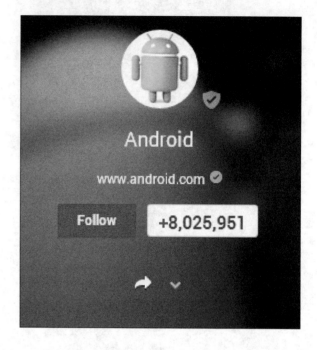

It took Google, the Internet behemoth, a couple of tries before getting the hang of creating a social media site. There were Google Wave, Google Buzz, Bebo, and many other experimental social media sites that died quiet deaths on the testing servers in Silicon Valley.

But out of all that has come Google+, which is starting to get traction; see Figure 9-1 for a look-see at a Google+ site. Sure, it doesn't have the billion users that Facebook (the global phenomenon and market leader) has, nor does it have the flash and dazzle of some of the newer entrants, such as Pinterest or RebelMouse. What Google+ does have, though, is the considerable technological edge that comes with being part of the unquestioned leader in organizing the collected knowledge of all of humanity.

If you want to improve your SEO (search engine optimization) hits, Google+ has much to offer. One of the most popular features Google+ has rolled out is Google Hangouts, where you can conduct virtual teleconferences, share screens, take turns speaking, and collaborate on linked Google Docs.

Google has also carefully started to link and merge all its online properties; the videos you watch on YouTube, the calls you make on Google Voice, and the spreadsheets and documents you create in Google Docs are all accessible and linked to your Google+ account. And if you use Gmail, you can use the same login across all your Google services.

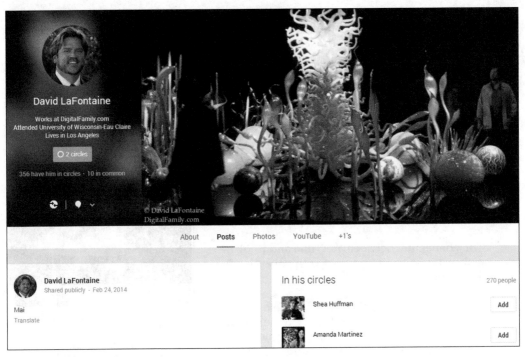

Figure 9-1

Google+ page of David LaFontaine (www.davidlafontaine.com)

Creating One Design, Multiple Platforms

Sure, the Google+ environment is still fairly nerd-heavy. Users tend to be the types of contrarians who stop following their favorite rock band the minute all their friends start Liking it on Facebook, too. And there is a sizable Google+ loyalist contingent of folks fleeing the incessant notifications from Facebook friends as to how many virtual cows have been virtually milked this afternoon.

The math geeks at Google brought in some design professionals and actually started incorporating what they say into the overall design scheme. Before this, Google was clueless about design — it famously tested 41 different shades of blue to figure out what to use on a toolbar.

If you've already checked out Chapter 7 (which covers YouTube), you'll notice a similarity to the design layouts that are allowed for Google+. This isn't an accident.

In April 2011, Google launched "Project Kennedy," aimed at streamlining the design sense of all Google products so that as users clicked from Gmail to Google Docs to Google Play to YouTube, they got the same look and feel. The fonts and typography were streamlined, the pages started getting more white space so they didn't feel so crowded, and the images started getting bigger. In fact, Google's social media profiles allow you to use the largest images of any of the sites we've looked at when researching this book.

The design effort came because all the different divisions within Google finally started talking with each other, and they realized that if they broke things down into basic units called "cards," those cards could then be shared from one platform to another.

Thus, Liking a video on YouTube, such as the NASA video shown in Figure 9-2, causes a "card" to appear on your Google+ profile that includes thumbnails of other Google+ users who have Liked or commented on the video. Other Google+ users can vote using the buttons to give you a "+1" to a post (which will translate into a "thumbs-up" on your YouTube profile). Of course, users can also give a "–1" and vote a post down.

Figure 9-2

The connection between YouTube and Google+ makes it easy to share a post with your friends across multiple sites.

On a large computer display, the Google+ layout is three cards wide. That is, underneath the banner image, three posts appear side by side. The layout is one or two cards wide on a mobile phone or tablet display (respectively). For posts from people that you pay particular attention to or that contain the type of content that Google's algorithms determine you are likely to respond to, the layout shifts to a card that takes up all three columns (see Figure 9-3).

Unlike Facebook, for example, where there is just the wide single column running down the page, the Google+ layout allows viewers to more quickly scan the content available for them. Another differentiator for Google+ is that animated GIFs are allowed. (We recommend several apps that you can use to create an animated GIF in Chapter 12; Tumblr is another service that allows animated GIFs.)

The cross-platform movement also extends to the popular blogging platforms of Typepad and WordPress, via the Author Attribution function. When you use your Google+ account to log in to your blog, your posts automatically link to your Google+ profiles.

But this isn't just a one-way street. Open the drop-down menu in the upper-right corner of a Google+ post, and you can grab a snippet of code that allows you to embed the post into your own blog or website, with all the same functionality (share, Like, comment) of the original Google+ post preserved. If you're a more advanced user, check out *Google+ Ripples,* which is a tracking and analytics tool to allow you to see how popular and viral a post has been (see Figure 9-4).

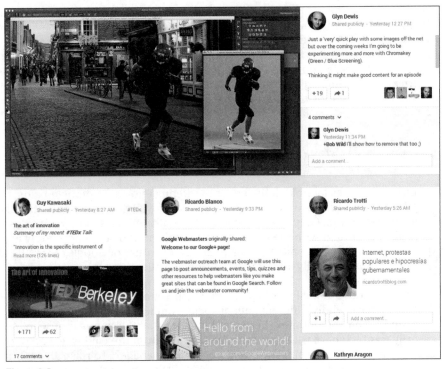

Figure 9-3

Primary post and photo by Glyn Dewis, http://glyndewis.com

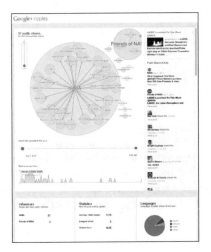

Figure 9-4

As you can see, the analytics not only show who has been sharing and reacting to the NASA post about the launch of the Lunar Atmosphere and Dust Environment Explorer (LADEE) probe, but it breaks down the number of shares on a timeline, how many times per hour the post is shared, and what languages it is shared in. If you want to track your social media marketing campaigns, this is a gold mine of information — which, given that Google supports all its products by making it easy for people and brands to advertise, makes sense to use.

Managing Your Google+ Circles

When Google+ was launched, the entire marketing effort was modeled after the way that Apple has managed to create such fanatical loyalty amongst both its adherents and detractors. Only a select few were initially invited to create profiles and start playing around with the interfaces and tools in Google+. These early adopters quickly realized that the most radically different feature of Google+ was that all your friends are automatically added to what Google called *Circles*.

Unlike every other social media platform at the time, Google+ seemed to recognize that we all have wildly different sets of social contacts that we interact with in our daily lives — and sometimes there are things we share with one group but don't necessarily want to share with another. The pictures from the wild weekend party with college buddies aren't things we want corporate managers to raise an eyebrow over, while the latest technological advances are of little interest to family members who just want to coo over cute videos of their grandchildren.

With Circles, you can set how much access to your life and your updates you grant to the contacts in your social life — and this allows you a shortcut to checking in on what's happening in these various aspects of your life. You can switch from checking in with your artsy friends to see what they think of the latest music video, over to a Circle devoted to political activists.

tip

Your Google+ account comes equipped with default Circles to allow you to sort and organize your contacts and connections: Friends, Family, and Acquaintances. However, you can create as many new Circles as you want to define your relationships. And you can add someone to more than one Circle. For example, your sister can be in both the default Family Circle and your custom-created Circle of "People I grew up with" that also includes your grade school classmates. The default Circles always stay at the top of your list, but after that, they are sorted alphabetically.

Google+ also empowers users to organize themselves into communities. Your Circles always remain private to you (unlike, say, Twitter, where if you add someone to a list entitled "People I Despise," they are notified). On Google+, Circles are always private, but Communities are both open to the public and visible to everyone. (See Google Hangout Communities in Figure 9-5.) As you can see, there are thousands of communities, catering to every conceivable interest.

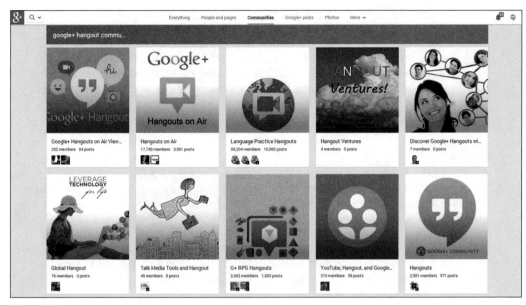

Figure 9-5

If you find a community that particularly appeals to you, you can add every person there to your Circles. You can search for them by browsing through the All Communities tab or see what Google+ thinks you may be interested in by clicking Recommended for You. Some communities are closed, and you must ask and be approved to join.

Reviewing Google+ Profile Designs

Google has sought to differentiate itself from most other social media platforms by allowing you full rein to "go big" with the banner image for your profile. This increase in the amount of screen real estate is both a blessing and a curse. Some major brands and design professionals have reacted to this by producing beautiful visuals, but others have struggled with adapting lower-resolution images to this expanded space (with predictably blurry and grainy results).

A Google+ design update at the end of 2013 changed the layout of the Google+ cover photo. The cover photo is now partially obstructed by an overlay, blurring the portion of the image behind the overlay. This overlay contains page information such as page name and related hyperlink. The cover photo dimensions are 2120 x 1192 px, which is an aspect ratio of 16:9.

tip

> For the best results, start with a clear, high-resolution image. We suggest using a photo taken with a modern digital camera, a collage of lower-resolution images that you created in an image-editing program, or a scalable vector graphics illustration that won't distort when blown up to full size.

NASA

You'd expect NASA to be particularly well suited for such a nerdy social media platform as Google+ — and you'd be right! The space agency regularly updates its profile with stunning panoramic photos that take advantage of the extra display space that Google+ gives its viewers.

A rocket launch is just one of the images that NASA regularly updates; the images of Earth from space, astronauts out on spacewalks, or intergalactic quasars are changed regularly to reflect the latest achievements. See Figure 9-6.

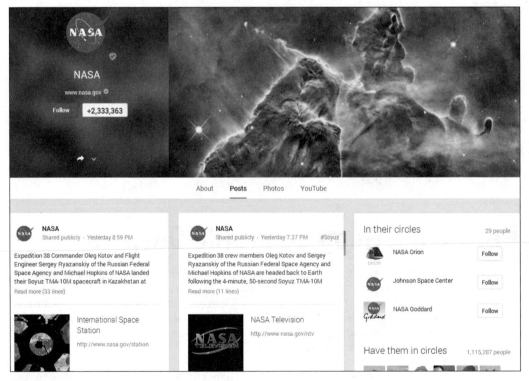

Figure 9-6

remember

remember

If you're working in a field that lends itself to creating good visuals, changing the banner image whenever you have something new or momentous happen helps to keep your visitors coming back.

Notice how the designers have cleverly used a PNG version of the NASA logo with a transparent layer so that the red "swoosh" appears to continue off of the blue circle of the logo. This is a great example of how to make your brand's logo stand out on your Google+ profile.

Firefox

This header perfectly captures the can-do optimism and playful spirit of the team behind Mozilla Firefox. Ever since *People* magazine became famous for capturing celebrities on the rebound in mid-leap, photographers around the world have copied and parodied the style.

Getting an entire group to jump in sync like this requires a lot of patience, many takes, and comfortable shoes because you're not going to get it right the first time. If you're thinking about producing your own banner image that features you (or pets or inanimate objects) frozen in mid-air, you will need a steady hand on the camera and a really fast shutter speed to capture the image without motion blur.

Also note how the Firefox logo in Figure 9-7 fits perfectly into the circle that Google+ allocates for your profile photo.

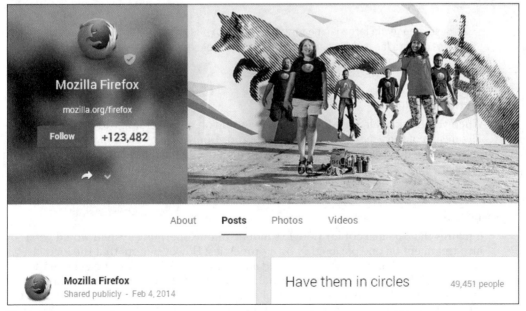

Figure 9-7

Cadbury

It stands to reason that Cadbury, the maker of delicious chocolates, would feature its products. But rather than going for a crowded, busy image that features all of its brands, Cadbury UK instead chose to keep the image simple showing only mouth-watering treats and the Cadbury logo, as seen in Figure 9-8.

Figure 9-8

remember

Even though the large image format can tempt you to cram in too much, sometimes less is more (as in this case), and a close-up shot can tell a more tantalizing story.

American Airlines

When you think of air travel, you think of jetting off into exciting, wide-open spaces. The design of the American Airlines banner for Google+ takes advantage of this underlying feeling, and the image of one of its jets climbing into an endless blue sky gives an optimistic, energizing feel. The design is simple, focusing on the red, white, and blue colors and basic logo, as shown in Figure 9-9.

Android

It figures that the mascot for Google's mobile phone operating system would get a nice treatment on one of Google's own properties. However, note that the logo in Figure 9-10 also has a somewhat rushed and perfunctory feel. Yes, the echo in the little circle of the main image is nice, but the designers had an opportunity here to do more. It doesn't help that the lighting and shading on the profile photo of the robot are pretty much exactly the same as on the robot in the main banner.

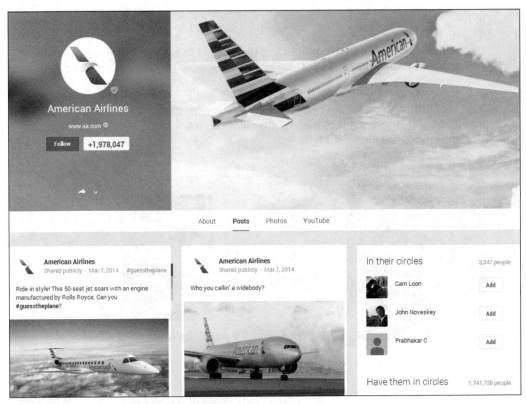

Figure 9-9

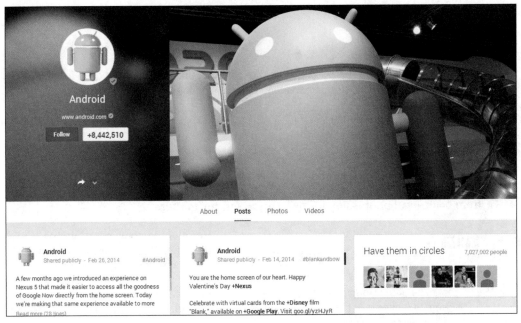

Figure 9-10

Flipboard

The tablet app Flipboard uses a nice, textured background and a rose in a vase (note the subtle shadow cast down and to the right on it) to give visitors to its Google+ profile the soothing feeling of sitting down at a table with a linen tablecloth to read a few good magazines.

Experts at Photoshop would notice that the image in the center of the tablet looks just a little off-kilter, and that it has probably been layered in — but at a glance, this design works. (See Figure 9-11.)

Figure 9-11

remember

If you're going to create a collage, make sure that the images you choose for the lower portion of the design can stand up to having their details overshadowed by the Google+ interface.

Rachel Brenke

Rachel Brenke is a photographer and an attorney who uses her social media profiles to showcase her specialized talent for helping creative professionals with everything from basic legal permission forms to more serious matters.

warning

The small profile photo is displayed in the left side of the Google+ cover area — you want to make sure that the larger image leaves space for the smaller one.

Her inviting pose in her photos gives her Google+ profile a warm and friendly feeling, as shown in Figure 9-12. Note the creative touch in how Rachel uses the same image, in color in the smaller version, and in black and white in the larger one.

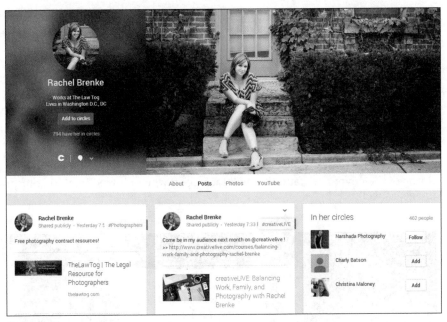

Figure 9-12

Rachel Brenke, business consultant and photographer (`http://rachelbrenke.com`)

Creating a Great Google+ Profile

The broad canvas that Google+ provides you comes with quite a few quirks, which have led to a great deal of disagreement with designers.

Google+ includes a large space at the top of each profile for a big image — or collage of images — but Google also resizes your image for best display across computers, tablets, and smartphones as well as Google TV and other large displays.

Because your profile and cover images are used in so many sizes, there are a dizzying array of specifications, or "safe zones," that you need to consider when you're creating a profile that will work no matter where it appears.

remember

Because social media sites, like Google+, change their design so frequently, you may need to adjust the instructions in this book based on Google's latest guidelines.

Setting your cover photo size

Google+ is arguably the best site for displaying big images in cover designs, providing far more real estate for users to add an image at the top of each profile than Facebook or Twitter.

Choosing the best size for your cover photo has gotten more complicated now that Google+ has cut the available space at the top of each profile page by splitting the cover area into two parts:

▶ **Right side:** This section — two thirds of the design — holds the image you upload.

▶ **Left side:** This smaller section (one-third) holds the profile photo and text.

Behind the text and profile photo in the left third, Google+ automatically generates a copy of your cover image with very a strong blur effect (see Figure 9-13). To take best advantage of the space, you want to upload an image that looks good in just two thirds of the cover area, and that will look good when blurred behind your profile image, as well.

Figure 9-13

Janine Warner (https://plus.google.com/+JanineWarner)

To take best advantage of the limited options on Google+, keep these image parameters in mind when you design your profile and cover images:

▶ Google+ uses the responsive design approach to adjust the size of images to best fit the display of large and small screens.

▶ The maximum size of the cover area is 2120 x 1192 px.

▶ The minimum size of the cover area is 480 x 270 px.

In general, use images that are a little larger than Google recommends because you're given the option to crop, as you upload it. That way, cutting a little off the image is relatively easy as you position and crop the image to best fit the space.

tip

For the latest on Google changes, consult the latest notifications at `https://support.google.com/plus`.

Changing your cover photo

With your new Google+ banner created, you have to upload it to your profile. If you haven't been careful creating this image, you may need to resize it and drag it around a bit for it to achieve the effect you're looking for.

1. **Log in to your Google+ profile.**

2. **Mouse over the Home menu on the left side.**

   The fly-out menu with options to navigate around Google+ appears.

3. **Click Profile.**

   Your Google+ profile page opens. If you haven't already configured a banner image, you'll see a placeholder.

4. **Roll your cursor over the cover image until the Change Cover button appears (as shown in Figure 9-14) and then click it.**

   The cover art window appears. At the top, you can choose from the following options:

Figure 9-14

Janine Warner

- *Gallery:* Google has a gallery of high-resolution images that you can choose from.

- *Upload:* Upload a picture from your computer.

- *Albums:* If you've created any photo albums in Google+, you can choose from them. If you have set your mobile phone to sync photos to an online service, such as Picasa, they may well show up here.

- *Cover Photos:* Bring back any of the cover photos you've used in the past.

warning

If the photo you selected is too small, you get an error message and will be prompted to try again.

5. **Choose your image and adjust the size and position.**

   A box within a box appears, where you can crop and size the image for your profile, as shown in Figure 9-15.

Figure 9-15
Janine Warner

6. **Click Select Cover Photo to complete the process.**

   Your new Google+ banner appears atop your profile, as shown in Figure 9-16.

Figure 9-16
Janine Warner

remember

If you browse Google+ profiles, you may notice that there are still many sites with banner images that are very wide in relation to their height. As Google+ makes changes to the design, it's easy to look outdated. Cover images that were created when Google+ had a more restrictive image format and may not look quite right in the new space.

Sizing your profile photo

Pay close attention to your profile image because it's featured heavily in the latest Google+ redesign. In addition to appearing in the top left of your cover design, your profile image appears anywhere you post, or you're reposted, on Google. Your profile image will also be used if you participate in Google Hangouts or other Google+ related services.

remember

You need to upload a JPEG, GIF, or simple PNG file. Layered PNG files or Photoshop PSD files aren't compatible for Google+, and trying to upload an image in one of these formats will result in an error message.

To upload and edit a profile photo, follow these steps:

1. **Sign into your Google account.**

2. **Place your cursor over your profile picture and click the camera icon, as shown in Figure 9-17.**

3. **To add or change your profile image, select from the following options:**

   • Upload a New Photo

   • Choose a Photo from One of Your Albums

   • Take a New Picture

4. **Crop and edit your photo with the tools provided by Google.**

5. **Select Set As Profile Photo to save changes.**

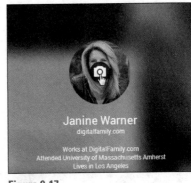

Figure 9-17
Janine Warner

tip

To create a collage by extracting and arranging photos on our template, see Chapter 3.

Sea creatures
Janine Warner

7 Pins

Follow

The Internet is made of
Janine Warner

1

Follow

Books I've written...
Janine Warner

DO-IT-YOURSELF

Web Sites
FOR
DUMMIES

All things geek
Janine Warner

The most beautiful virus
your computer can catch

Dress up any screen
with these scientific
wallpaper images

xvivo

Places I've visited
Janine Warner

Follow

Inspirations
Janine Warner

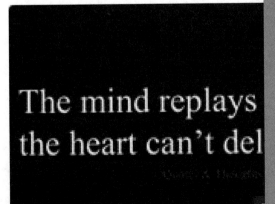

The mind replays
the heart can't del

CHAPTER 10

Setting Up Pinterest Boards

In This Chapter

- Create and edit your profile.

- Post images to Pinterest.

- Create interesting Pinterest boards.

P interest is a highly visual site that burst onto the social media scene and became the fastest growing social site in 2012. Especially popular among designers, artists, fashionistas, and other creative types, Pinterest makes it easy to "pin" and share images and video in collections called *boards,* as shown in Figure 10-1.

tip

If you're looking for advice on how use Pinterest, consult *Pinterest For Dummies,* by Kelby Carr, who also wrote *Pinterest Marketing For Dummies.*

One of the simplest social media sites to use, Pinterest is designed to make sharing and organizing images easy. You are a bit limited in design options when creating your profile, but how you set up and share images gives you almost infinite possibilities when it comes to creating the overall look of your Pinterest pages. This ease of use and invitation to creativity make Pinterest an appealing platform for the casual user and the marketer alike, with everyone from home businesses to large brands jumping on the Pinterest bandwagon to promote their products.

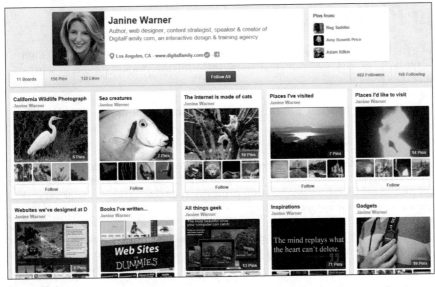

Figure 10-1

Janine Warner

PINTEREST IS PERFECT FOR MOBILE

With a modular design made up of small boxes, Pinterest is highly mobile-friendly, meaning that the site works well on small and large screens. Most other social media sites came out with mobile versions or mobile websites after they launched, but from Day 1, Pinterest has worked well on mobile devices — in large part because of the modular style of Pinterest.

Each "board" (read all about those later in this chapter) is a separate box, and those boxes can be aligned side by side or stacked one on top of each other. That makes the design ideal for large and small computer screens.

As you see in this figure, even on a small smartphone screen, Pinterest looks great.

Inspiring Pinterest Profiles

Pinterest is a highly image-focused social media site, so it's a great place for designers, photographers, artists, interior designers, fashionistas, and anyone else who cares what things look like.

Here are a few Pinterest Profiles and Business Pages that we admire.

Erika Barker

In her Pinterest profile, Erika Barker describes herself as a New York fashion and portrait photographer, veteran combat photojournalist, visual storyteller, Photoshop warrior, and public relations ninja. Creative professionals like Erika are well served on this highly visual social media website.

On her Pinterest pages, she shares her amazing portraits and other images, as shown in Figure 10-2, and she links to her main website at www.erikabarker.com.

Figure 10-2
Erika Barker (http://erikabarker.com/)

Karen Nace Willmore

Photographer Karen Nace has set up a Pinterest board to showcase her African wildlife photography, as shown in Figure 10-3. To view more of Karen's photographs from all over the world, visit her website at www.karennace.com.

tip

Some Pinterest users focus on a specialty or category, such as animals; others post a more varied collection of images. You can set up as many boards as you like on Pinterest and use them to organize your own images or images that you get from the web.

Figure 10-3

Karen Nace (www.karennace.com)

Melanie Duncan

Melanie Duncan describes herself in her Pinterest profile as a Serial Entrepreneuress, business mentor, and style lover, as shown in Figure 10-4. She teaches courses in how to use Pinterest more successfully, and she's active across many social media sites, with more than 100,000 Likes on Facebook and multiple websites, including www.melanieduncan.com.

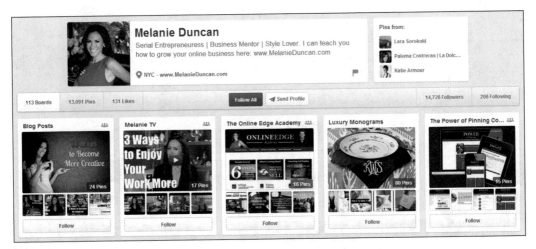

Figure 10-4

Melanie Duncan (www.melanieduncan.com)

Diana Barbatti

Beautiful family portraits adorn the pages of photographer Diana Barbatti's Pinterest profile, as shown in Figure 10-5. Showcasing boards that follow her passion for fashion, interior design, and great imagery, Diana uses Pinterest to invite friends and potential photography clients to her website at `http://dianabarbatti.com`.

Figure 10-5

Diana Barbatti (`http://dianabarbatti.com`)

Kelly Vorves

San Francisco–based photographer Kelly Vorves has lots of great images to share on Pinterest, as shown in Figure 10-6. She showcases her portraits and other photographs, as well as pins about fashion and her other passions. She also runs a website at `http://kellyvorves.photoshelter.com/archive`.

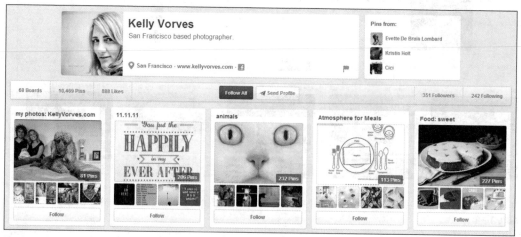

Figure 10-6

Kelly Vorves (`http://kellyvorves.photoshelter.com/archive`)

Creating and Editing Your Pinterest Profile

Although Pinterest doesn't offer as many design options as some of the other social media sites featured in this book, you can edit your profile after you create it.

Follow these instructions to create a profile on Pinterest:

1. **Browse to Pinterest (www.pinterest.com) in your favorite web browser.**

   If you don't already have an account on Pinterest, you have two options: sign up with your Facebook account or through e-mail.

   The Follow 5 Boards to Get Started window opens.

2. **Choose a category from the left site of the Follow 5 Boards to Get Started window, as shown in Figure 10-7.**

   All the boards in that category displayed on the right of the window in Figure 10-7.

   tip

   You can select as many boards as you like, but Pinterest requires that you start with at least five.

3. **Click the red Follow button to select a board, as shown in Figure 10-7.**

Figure 10-7

4. **Click the red Follow button to select at least four more boards and then click the Next button at the top of the window.**

   The main Pinterest page opens with your selected boards displayed and also an overlay that offers a guided tour.

tip

For a guided tour of Pinterest, click the red Take a Look Around button.

5. **Confirm your account by clicking the link in an e-mail message from Pinterest (sent to the e-mail address you entered when you registered).**

Whether you just created a new account or you want to edit your profile in an existing account, click the small pencil icon (bottom right of your profile window), as shown in Figure 10-8. The rest is easy:

Search
Pinterest
Janine Warner
Author, web designer, content strategist, speaker & creator of DigitalFamily.com, an interactive design & training agency
Los Angeles, CA · www.digitalfamily.com
Edit your profile.

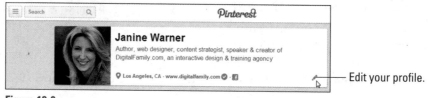

Figure 10-8

1. **Fill in or edit the fields as desired in the Edit Profile dialog box, as shown in Figure 10-9.**
2. **Click the Save Profile button to save the changes and close the dialog box.**

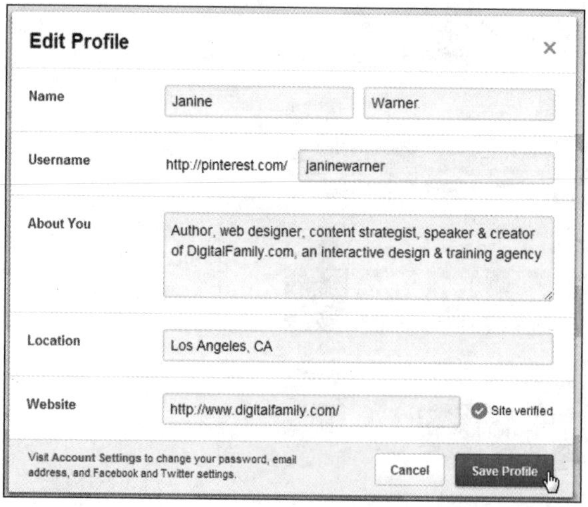
Edit Profile
Name
Janine
Warner
Username
http://pinterest.com/
janinewarner
About You
Author, web designer, content strategist, speaker & creator of DigitalFamily.com, an interactive design & training agency
Location
Los Angeles, CA
Website
http://www.digitalfamily.com/
Site verified
Visit Account Settings to change your password, email address, and Facebook and Twitter settings.
Cancel
Save Profile

Figure 10-9

remember

Pinterest, like other social media websites, changes its design and features on a regular basis. As a result, Pinterest may have changed some features and interface design since we wrote this book.

Creating Pinterest Pins and Boards

After you create an account on Pinterest, you can add pins and create boards.

tip

Posting a pin is "pinning."

▶ **Pin:** Any image or video that you post (or pin) to Pinterest

▶ **Boards:** Collections of pins and videos

In Figure 10-10, you see a Sea Creatures board, with six pins, each of which is a photo of an aquatic animal.

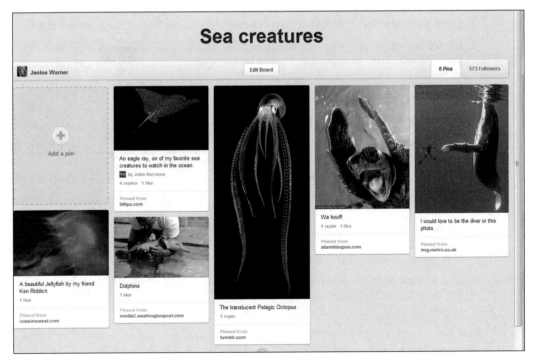

Figure 10-10

Pinning images and videos on Pinterest

You can pin images and videos to Pinterest by uploading them from a computer, or you can add images that already appear on a web page by entering the URL. Many websites also include a Pinterest "share" button that makes it easy to pin an image from the website you're viewing to any of your Pinterest boards. You can also add a Pinterest button to your favorite web browser's toolbar, allowing you to pin an image from the website you're currently browsing.

Each board on your Pinterest page needs to be named, which you can usually do around a theme. Create board names that correspond with search terms other users might use to find those images. For example, if you're creating a board with Halloween costume pins, name your board Halloween Costume Ideas or something more specific, such as Halloween Costumes for Girls or Disney Inspired Halloween Costumes.

Pinterest is an incredibly visual platform. Choose the most visually appealing pin for your board's cover image. You want the cover image to convey the content of the rest of the board. We explain how to choose a cover image later in this section. Then take some time to rearrange the pins in a visually appealing manner, paying attention to the size of the pins as well as the content in the images.

Here are the steps to pin an image or a video to Pinterest (after you have an account created):

1. **Open Pinterest in your favorite web browser and log in to your user account.**

2. **Click the red plus (+) sign just to the left of your Profile icon, as shown in Figure 10-11.**

   A drop-down menu opens with options for how to add a pin, as shown in Figure 10-11.

3. **Choose to do one of the following:**

   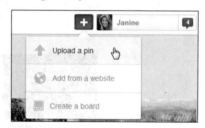

   Figure 10-11

   • *Upload a Pin:* This allows you to upload an image or video from your computer.

   • *Add from a Website:* This option allows you to type a web address and select an image from that site.

   • *Create a Board:* Choose this option to create your board before adding pins. This is not required to begin pinning. You can name your boards as you pin if you wish.

   When you select the option to upload a pin from your computer, the Add a Pin from Your Computer dialog box opens, as shown in Figure 10-12.

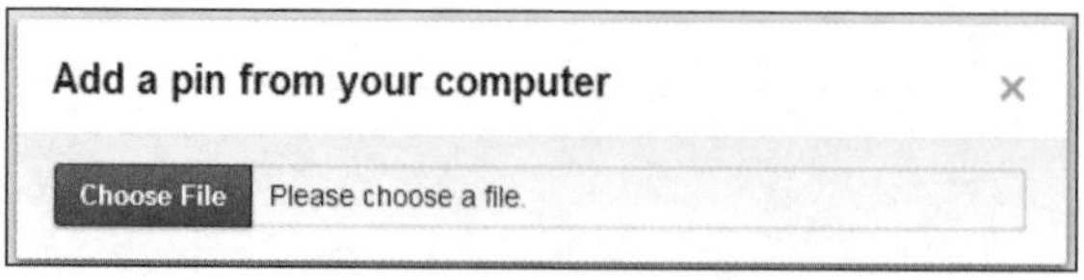

Figure 10-12

4. **Click the Choose File button to browse to and select an image or a video from your hard drive.**

   The Upload a Pin dialog box opens.

5. **Click the Create a Board button to add the pin, or choose any existing board, as shown in Figure 10-13.**

tip

When you pin something, you're prompted to include it on a board.

For this example, we opted to pin the new image to the existing Sea Creatures board.

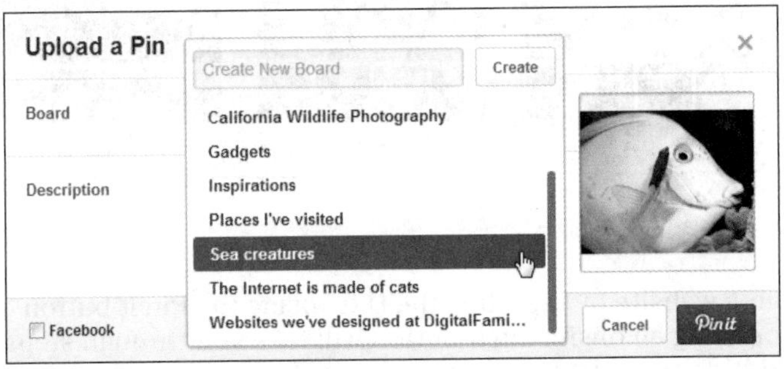

Figure 10-13

6. **Write a description or include a message with the pin, as shown in Figure 10-14.**

   This step is required.

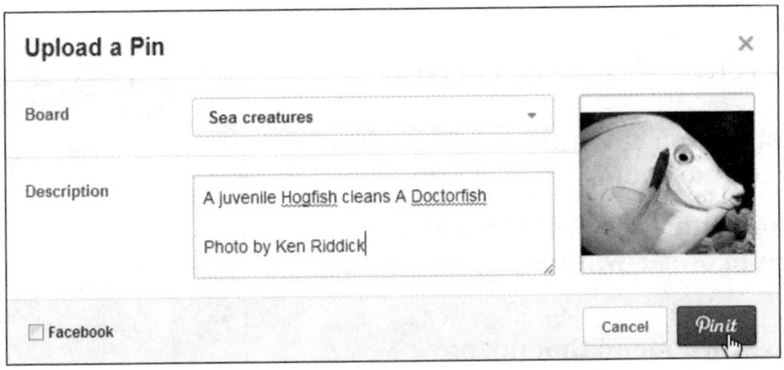

Figure 10-14

7. **Click the red Pin It button.**

   The image is added to the specified board in your profile, as shown in Figure 10-15.

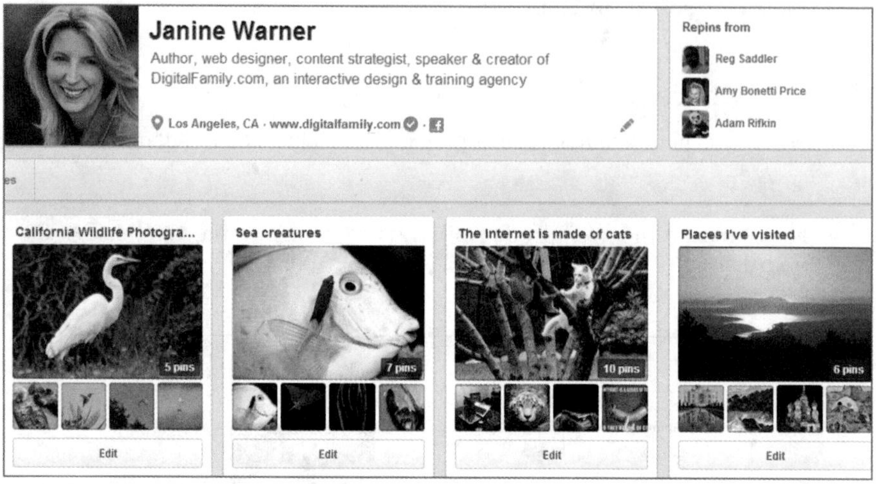

Janine Warner

Author, web designer, content strategist, speaker & creator of DigitalFamily.com, an interactive design & training agency

Los Angeles, CA · www.digitalfamily.com

Repins from

Reg Saddler

Amy Bonetti Price

Adam Rifkin

California Wildlife Photogra...   5 pins   Edit

Sea creatures   7 pins   Edit

The Internet is made of cats   10 pins   Edit

Places I've visited   6 pins   Edit

Figure 10-15

Pinning content from a website by inputting the URL, using the Pin It button on your browser's toolbar, or using an onsite Pin It button will take you through steps. You have to add a description to each image you pin as well as either add that pin to an existing board or create a new board on which to place the pin.

Creating Pinterest boards

With your profile set, you can create as many boards (collections of pins) as you like. Boards are quite handy for organizing your pins. And you can name your boards anything you like!

Here are the steps to create a board on Pinterest:

1. **Open Pinterest in your favorite web browser and log in to your user account.**

2. **Click the button with your profile name at the top right of the browser window, as shown in Figure 10-16.**

3. **From the drop-down menu that opens (see Figure 10-16), choose Your Boards.**

   Your main profile page opens, showcasing all your boards.

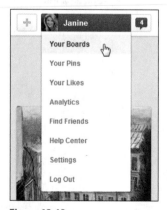

Janine

Your Boards

Your Pins

Your Likes

Analytics

Find Friends

Help Center

Settings

Log Out

Figure 10-16

4. **Click the plus (+) sign in the middle of the gray board that reads Create a Board, as shown in Figure 10-17.**

California Wildlife Photogra...

Create a board

5 pins

Edit

Figure 10-17

The Create a Board dialog box opens, as shown in Figure 10-18.

5. **Enter a title (name) and description and then choose a category, as shown in Figure 10-18.**

Create a Board

Name*	Tech Gadgets
Description	My favorite technical gadgets and accessories
Category	Geek
Secret	No

Cancel   Create Board

Figure 10-18

tip

You have the option to keep your Pinterest board set as secret, meaning that other users cannot see it. This is great if you're working on a collection you'd like to keep to yourself, such as a list of gift ideas.

These categories help users search for the pins that interest them most. Some of the most popular categories include DIY, crafts, and recipe-related categories. Although there may be many pins competing for attention in these popular categories, there are also millions of users searching for this content!

POPULAR PINTEREST BOARDS

Although you can create a board on any topic, common board types tend to attract a following faster. Here are some of the most popular board names on Pinterest:

- Inspiration
- Recipes
- DIY
- Fashion

- Travel
- Quotes
- Design

6. **Click the red Create Board button.**

   The new board is created, as shown in Figure 10-19, and we used the name *Tech Gadgets.*

7. **Populate your new board. Click the plus (+) sign above the text Add a Pin, as shown in Figure 10-19, and follow the instructions in the previous exercise to pin images and videos to the board.**

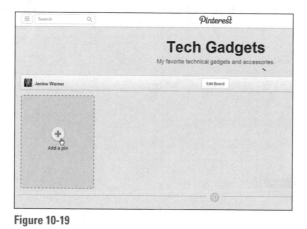

Figure 10-19

Editing a Pinterest board

Every Pinterest board has a *cover image,* the featured image that introduces your board to other users. You can change the cover image and order of Pinterest boards after you create them. This makes it easy to organize and change the overall design of your profile page.

Here's how to change a board's cover image:

1. **Open Pinterest in your favorite web browser and log in to your user account.**

2. **Click the button with your profile name at the top right of the browser window.**

3. **From the drop-down menu that opens, choose Your Boards.**

    Your main profile page opens with all your boards.

4. **Roll your cursor over the board you want to edit.**

5. **Click the Change Cover button that appears; see Figure 10-20.**

Figure 10-20

The Change Board Cover dialog box opens, as shown in Figure 10-21.

6. **Click the right or left arrows in the Change Board Cover window until you find the pin (the image or video) that you want to use as the cover of your board.**

7. **Click the red Save Changes button to select the new cover.**

    The Board Cover dialog box closes, and the new cover is displayed on the board in your main profile, as shown in Figure 10-22.

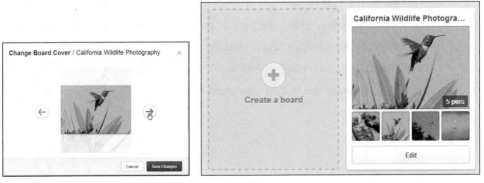

Figure 10-21   Figure 10-22

tip

Your cover image should not only properly represent the rest of the pins in that board but also work well with the rest of the cover images on your Pinterest page.

Feeling creative? You can create cover images that will grab users' attention while still explaining the content of your board.

Remember that you have the ability to upload images from your computer, not just pin existing images from around the web. Have fun with your cover images!

Changing the order of Pinterest boards

You can rearrange the order of your Pinterest boards on your profile page to reflect their importance or to better illustrate your passions. Many users also rearrange their boards to keep up with the calendar. For example, in January you may not want your first board to be Halloween Costume Ideas. One of the beautiful things about Pinterest is that you have the option to slide that Halloween board down to the bottom of your page and then bring it back to the top come October.

tip

The first couple of rows on your Pinterest page are prime real estate. This is a user's first opportunity to get to know who you are as a pinner. Not only do you want to arrange your boards in a visually pleasing way, but you also want to show the pinning world what matters most to you via your pins.

Take some time to play around with the order of the boards on your page, and don't be afraid to go back and rearrange if you find that some of your best content is being ignored.

Here's how to change the order of your boards on Pinterest:

1. **Open Pinterest in your favorite web browser and log in to your user account.**

2. **Click the button with your profile name at the top right of the browser window.**

3. **From the drop-down menu that opens, choose Your Boards.**

   Your main profile page opens with all your boards.

4. **Click to select the board you want to move.**

5. **Drag the selected board to a new location, as shown in Figure 10-23.**

   The boards adjust to make room for the board you moved, as shown in Figure 10-23.

Figure 10-23

ATTRACTING MEN AND WOMEN ON PINTEREST

Since it launched, Pinterest has been used by more women than men, but that doesn't mean it's not an effective way to reach both genders. Early studies show that Pinterest drives more people to make purchases than many of the other social media sites combined, and that goes for men and women.

To attract both genders, consider posting images of products that appeal to both men and women, and add boards that are of general interest to your most important target audience.

Janine Warner

janinewarner

Photostream **Sets** Favorites

From the river, Moscow, Russia
12 photos

Moscow, Russia
33 photos

Cold War Museum, Moscow,...
83 photos

Egrets at Audubon Canyon Ranch
7 photos

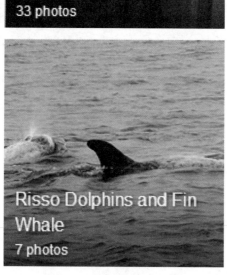
Risso Dolphins and Fin Whale
7 photos

Gray Wolf
7 photos

Hummingbird & Racoon

Golden Gate Bridge

Janine's Videos

CHAPTER 11

Creating a Flickr Presence

In This Chapter

- Upload a buddy (profile) icon to Flickr.

- Create a customized cover image for your Flickr page.

The photo-sharing service Flickr has been around for more than a decade (an eternity in Internet years). Although newer photo-sharing services (such as Instagram) have gotten more attention in recent years, the addition of a number of new features is making Flickr relevant again, including a redesign of the entire Flickr experience and adding a free terabyte (TB) of online storage space for each user.

Among the design options (shown in Figure 11-1), Flickr offers you a large profile photo (a *buddy icon*) and a customizable cover image at the top of your profile. A photostream also streams your photos as well as those of your Flickr friends, depending on which page you're viewing.

Flickr's changed design options have met with mixed reviews. Some users seem pleased with the new options, especially the increased hard drive space, and many people have found creative ways to decorate their profiles.

on the web

We created a template you can use for your Flickr cover image. You can download it at www.digitalfamily.com/social.

But because the site is already filled with photographs, many users have complained that a cover photo is unnecessary and that there should be a way to remove it. In this chapter, you find a variety of design ideas for Flickr, including a workaround that essentially makes the cover image disappear.

remember

Cover photos appear in your photostream.

Buddy icon   Cover image   Photostream

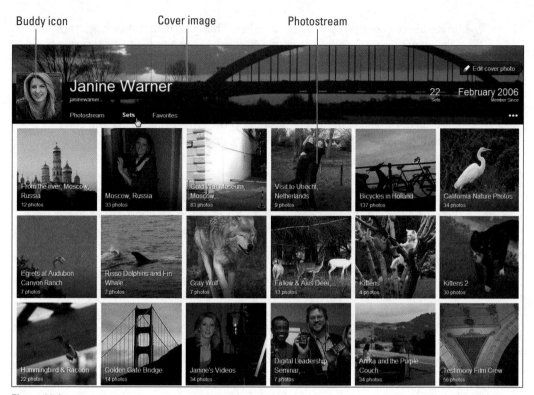

Figure 11-1

Janine Warner

Designing a Flickr Cover Photo

A big change to Flickr is the customizable cover photo at the top of every profile. In this section, you find the specifications and instructions for creating and uploading a cover image, as well as a few cover image designs to inspire you. Here are some of the specifications for your Flickr cover photo:

▶ The cover photo is a thin horizontal format. The crop ratio of the image is about 7:1. Based on our testing, you'll have best results if the area you want to display is 2048 pixels (px) x 342 px.

▶ The cover photo must be uploaded to Flickr before you can select it.

tip

To ensure that your cover photo looks good when displayed full-width in a large browser window as well as when it's cropped to fit in a smaller window, click and drag the edge of your browser window to make it smaller after you insert your cover photo.

▶ Cover photos are visible to all Flickr users. That means that the image you select can't have privacy restrictions enabled. For example, if you choose an image for which you set the privacy settings to Only Me, the image won't display in the cover image area.

▶ Flickr uses a responsive design, which means that the images in the display area are reduced in size when the browser becomes smaller, such as when a profile is viewed on a mobile phone. On the smallest screens, the sides of your cover photo are cropped when your profile is displayed.

Inspiring cover photos

Although the space for a Flickr cover photo is (as of this writing) not as big as the cover photos that you can use on Facebook or Google+, you still have ample opportunity to show off your creativity and design sense. Here are a few examples of cover photo designs to get your creative juices flowing.

Olga Egoraeva

Photographer, author, writer, and editor-in-chief at *Best* magazine, Olga Egoraeva shares her fashion photography in her profile on Flickr (see Figure 11-2). Olga uses a relatively simple background for her banner but opted for the doubled profile photo, which is a Flickr feature that makes it easy to add to a profile image.

Figure 11-2
Olga Egoraeva (`http://olgaegoraeva.wix.com/folio`)

Travis Nep Smith

For his banner image, web designer Travis Nep Smith also selected the double-profile image from Flickr, but he used his cat instead of his own image (see Figure 11-3). In general, we recommend that you use a profile photo that shows your face to make it easy to recognize you, and that you use the same or similar images across all your social sites.

Figure 11-3
Travis Smith (`www.hopstudios.com`)

However, Flickr is by far one of the least formal of the social media sites. If you're using Flickr just to share a few photos with friends and you're not concerned about building a big following or using the site to showcase your work to potential clients or employers, you can definitely get away with using a pet photo for your Flickr profile image — as Travis has done.

Lesa Snider

Lesa Snider is a photographer, creativeLIVE instructor, and author of *Photoshop: The Missing Manual* (O'Reilly). Lesa has lots of great images to share on Flickr, as shown in Figure 11-4.

Lesa (often called "Photo Lesa") showcases her travel photos and takes advantage of the large amount of storage space available on Flickr. To see more of Lesa's photos or learn more about her work, visit `http://photolesa.com`.

Figure 11-4
Lesa Snider (`http://photolesa.com`)

David LaFontaine

Author David (Dave) LaFontaine combined three nature photos to create his banner image for Flickr (see Figure 11-5). You find instructions for creating a composite image with Photoshop later in this chapter.

Dave started using Flickr years ago, but like so many others, he'd drifted away from the photo-focused social media site until Flickr started offering 1TB of free storage space to each user. Dave takes advantage of Flickr's ample storage to back up images as well as share large collections of images with friends.

Figure 11-5
David LaFontaine

Using a simple background

Even if you don't have lots of great images for your banner, it's easy to dress up your Flickr banner with a basic background. When you set up a profile with Flickr, you can choose from any of the default images as a way to get started.

To keep things interesting, author Janine Warner changes her banner image regularly. The following sections show off a few different approaches to creating a background and how to work around the inherent design elements in Flickr.

remember

Because social media sites (like Flickr), change their design so frequently, you may need to adjust the instructions in this book based on their latest guidelines.

Choosing a pattern or an abstract image

You don't have to use photographs in your cover image. Indeed, some of the nicest cover photos are made up of a simple gradient, pattern, or abstract image, such as the one shown in Figure 11-6.

Figure 11-6
Janine Warner

Designing a filmstrip

One way to fit photographs into the long, narrow space provided by Flickr for the cover image is to create a filmstrip composite that showcases multiple images one after another, like the one shown in Figure 11-7. We show you how to create a filmstrip later in this chapter.

Figure 11-7
Janine Warner

Making your cover photo disappear

Although there is no way to completely delete the Flickr cover, here's a nifty work-around. Upload a plain white image that fits the space, and — *ta-dah!* — the cover image all but disappears.

remember

Substituting even a pure white image as a mask won't look completely white, as you see in the cover image shown in Figure 11-8. That's because Flickr places a gray gradient over the bottom of the image, which darkens any image you use as your cover. Flickr does this to ensure the white text with your name is readable against the image.

Any image you upload as your cover will appear darker than it actually is because of the overlay gradient that Flickr adds.

Figure 11-8
Janine Warner

Settling for Flickr's cover photos

Even if you've never added a cover photo to your profile, there will be an image inserted in this space because Flickr automatically adds an image by default. There seem to be at least a few different images Flickr uses, including a photograph of fall leaves, as well as the colorful doors shown in the cover image in Figure 11-9.

Figure 11-9
Janine Warner

tip

See how the buddy icon in this figure is too small. This is what can happen if you haven't updated your photo in a while.

Changing a Flickr cover image

There are many wonderful ways to design a Flickr cover image. We give you some inspiration in the beginning of this chapter, but now it's time to create your own.

remember

As of this writing, you can't select one of the default Flickr cover images. And if you replace the image that Flickr applies to your profile with your own image, you can't change back to the Flickr image.

To make it easier for you to resize and position your cover image, we created a template you can download from our website in three popular formats — JPEG, TIFF, and PSD — for your convenience. Any of these will work with the steps that follow.

To use our template to design a Flickr cover image, follow these instructions.

1. **Open the Flickr-template file in an image-editing program.**

   The template file opens, and you can see the guides we included to help you adjust your design to fit Flickr's limited space (see Figure 11-10).

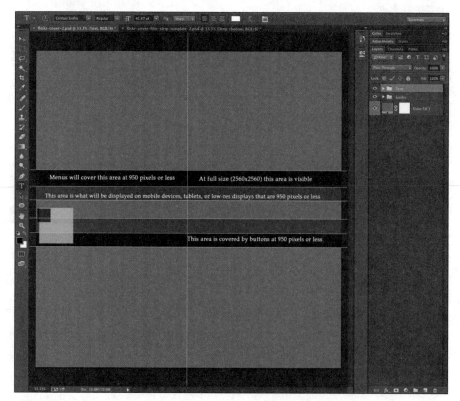

Figure 11-10

2. **Choose an image (or more) that you want to use in the cover image in your design.**

   We suggest you start with photos taken with a fairly high-resolution camera so that the image is at least 2560 px wide — or that you use line art, drawings, or other images large enough to fill the space without having to enlarge them in an image editor.

remember

Most cameras today produce images with a much higher resolution. For example, the camera in the iPhone 5 produces images that are 3264 x 2448 px.

3. **Insert the image(s) into the template.**

   You can use a number of different methods to insert images. We suggest the following:

   a. Choose File⇨Place.

   The Place File window opens.

   b. Navigate to where your images are stored.

   c. Click to select the image(s) you want to work with.

   If you want to create a collage or composite image for your Flickr cover image, select multiple images.

   d. Click the Place button.

   The image is imported into the template. Or, if you chose more than one image, they're all there on their own layers, as shown in Figure 11-11. In this example, we're using three images to create the radically horizontal image called for in Flickr's design.

GOING WITH FLICKR PRO

If you don't mind seeing an ad every now and then, the free level of service on Flickr is probably more than enough for you. But if you want to make your Flickr experience ad free, you can upgrade to a Flickr Pro account for $50 a year. To upgrade your account, go to `www.flickr.com/account/upgrade`. Your account renews automatically every year.

Note: You still get the same 1TB of storage as you did with a free account, so think carefully about whether $50 a year is worth going ad free.

If you need more storage, you can sign up for a Doublr account — for $500 a year — which gets you 2TB of storage. But if you need more than 1TB of space (an equivalent of 538,000 photos), then maybe it's time to start rethinking what you need on Flickr.

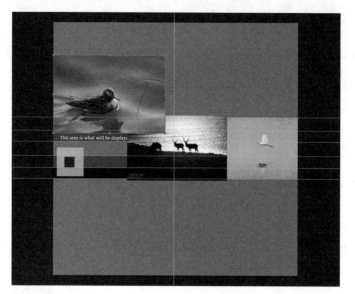

Figure 11-11
David LaFontaine

4. **Arrange the imported photo(s).**

Now you can resize your images and click and drag to move them around the template, as shown in Figure 11-12.

Figure 11-12
David LaFontaine

tip

The cyan guides on our template that help you align your elements won't be saved with the final image.

5. **When you're satisfied with how your design looks, turn off all the template layers (including the profile photo) so that just the images you want in the banner are visible.**

To turn layers on and off in Photoshop, click the eye icon just to the left of each layer, as shown in Figure 11-13.

Figure 11-13

6. **Choose File⇨Save As. Save your custom cover image in a web-compatible format.**

You need to save your cover image in JPG, GIF, or PNG file format to upload it to Flickr.

Now upload the photo to Flickr and turn it into your cover image:

1. **Open a browser and log in to your Flickr account.**

2. **Mouse over the Edit button on the menu bar underneath your account name.**

3. **Click the Edit Cover Photo button that appears in the upper-right corner of your Flickr cover image.**

In the Choose Cover Photo window that opens, you can choose from existing images or upload the new custom image that you just created in the preceding steps.

4. **Click the Upload a Photo button.**

5. **Upload your photo with one of these methods:**

   - Drag and drop your images into this window.

   - Click Choose Photos and Videos and then navigate to where you have your custom cover image stored on your hard drive.

6. **Click the Upload 1 Photo button in the upper-right corner of the upload window.**

   Your custom cover image will be uploaded into your photostream. Don't worry about the blank spaces above and below that image. You'll take care of those in Step 9.

7. **Click again on Edit Cover Photo.**

   The Choose Cover Photo window opens again.

8. **Double-click the image that you just uploaded into your photostream.**

   Your custom cover image is loaded into the space on your profile page. A window over the page directs you to drag the image to set the position (see Figure 11-14).

Figure 11-14
David LaFontaine

9. **Click and drag the image until you're pleased with the way it appears.**

   You should be able to arrange the photo in your cover image window so that it displays without any of the background layer color showing through.

10. **Click Save.**

    Your new cover image is saved and becomes visible at the top of your photostream, as shown in Figure 11-15.

tip

If you're having trouble with too much or too little of your desired images fitting into the allotted space, go back to Steps 2–6 in the preceding step list and adjust the size and spacing of the images in your design.

Figure 11-15
David LaFontaine

Setting Your Flickr Buddy Icon

After you've tackled the challenge of creating a Flickr cover image, you're ready to take a look at the profile photo, also known as the *buddy icon*.

Adding a buddy icon

Whether you're creating a profile for the first time or you haven't updated your profile in a while, the first thing you should do is choose a photo to serve as your buddy icon.

The buddy icon, as shown in Figure 11-16, appears at the lower-left corner of the cover image. The buddy icon is visible when you view your photostream as well as when you view Flickr with the image sets selected, which is what you see in Figure 11-16.

Buddy icon

Figure 11-16
Janine Warner

To upload your buddy icon, log in to your account and click the You link. Then click the initial placeholder or your existing buddy icon.

If Flickr believes your existing buddy icon is too small (as shown in Figure 11-17), rolling your cursor over the icon reveals the message Upload a bigger, better photo. Please. If your existing buddy icon is the correct size, the message reads Change your Buddy Icon.

Figure 11-17
Janine Warner

When the Your Account/Your Buddy Icon page opens, as shown in Figure 11-18, you have two options from where to select your buddy icon image: your hard drive or your Flickr photos.

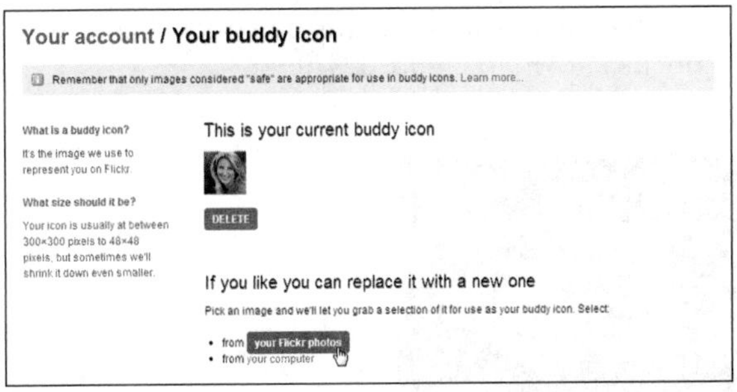

Your account / Your buddy icon

Remember that only images considered "safe" are appropriate for use in buddy icons. Learn more.

What is a buddy icon?

It's the image we use to represent you on Flickr.

This is your current buddy icon

What size should it be?

Your icon is usually at between 300×300 pixels to 48×48 pixels, but sometimes we'll shrink it down even smaller.

DELETE

If you like you can replace it with a new one

Pick an image and we'll let you grab a selection of it for use as your buddy icon. Select:

- from your Flickr photos
- from your computer

Figure 11-18

To upload a photo from your hard drive, follow these steps:

1. **Click the Your Computer link, which is displayed just below the blue Your Flickr Photos button.**

   The Edit Your Profile/Your Buddy Icon/Upload page opens.

2. **Click the Browse button.**

   The Choose File to Upload dialog box opens, displaying the contents of your hard drive.

3. **Navigate to find the image you want to use, click to select it, and then click Open.**

   The Choose File to Upload dialog box closes, and you return to the Edit Your Profile/Your Buddy Icon/Upload page.

4. **Click the Upload button.**

   The image is uploaded and becomes visible in the Edit Your Profile/Your Buddy Icon page, shown in Figure 11-19.

Edit your profile / Your buddy icon

To the left is what your buddy icon will look like. You can drag around and resize the square below to get it just how you like it. When you are happy with your icon, click the pink button to the right.

☒ constrain selection to square

MAKE THE ICON

CANCEL

Figure 11-19

5. **Click and drag the cropping area around the larger thumbnail image to specify how the image should be cropped**

6. **Click the pink Make the Icon button to save the selected image as your buddy icon.**

   You return to your main profile page, where the image you selected is displayed as your buddy icon, as shown in Figure 11-20.

Figure 11-20
Janine Warner

To use an image already uploaded to Flickr, follow these steps:

1. **Click the blue Your Flickr Photos button (refer to Figure 11-18).**

   The Edit Your Profile/Your Buddy Icon/Choose page opens, displaying thumbnail versions of all images you've uploaded to Flickr, as shown in Figure 11-21.

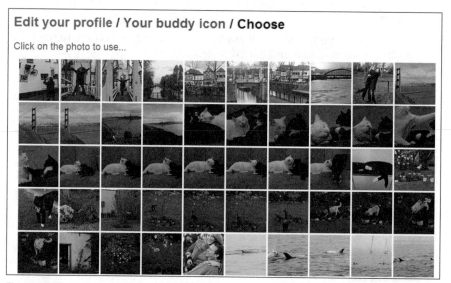

Figure 11-21
Janine Warner

2. **Double-click to select any thumbnail image.**

   The selected image opens in the Edit Your Profile/Your Buddy Icon page, as shown in Figure 11-22.

3. **Click and drag the cropping area around the larger thumbnail image to specify how the image should be cropped.**

4. **Click the pink Make the Icon button to save the selected image as your buddy icon.**

   The Your Account/Your Buddy Icon page closes, and you return to your main profile page, where the image you selected is displayed as your new buddy icon, as shown in Figure 11-23.

Figure 11-22
Janine Warner

Figure 11-23
Janine Warner

Changing buddy icons in Flickr sets

Unlike many other social media sites, the buddy icon, which acts as your profile image, changes when you select a specific set of images within that Flickr profile. This is very similar to the cover photo on a Pinterest board. The image that's selected as the main image in each set takes the place of the buddy icon when that set is selected. In Figure 11-24, the set named California Nature Photos is selected, and a photo of an egret is displayed as the buddy icon because we chose that image as the buddy icon for that set.

Figure 11-24

Janine Warner (`http://jcwarner.com`)

To create a set, go to your Flickr account and follow these steps:

1. **Select Sets from the horizontal navigation bar.**

2. **Click the Create Your First Set Now button.**

3. **Drag images from your Flickr content from the photostream at the bottom and drop them into the set.**

4. **Name your set in the left sidebar and (optional) add a description.**

5. **Click Save.**

tip

To remove content, drag it back to your photostream below the set.

To specify the buddy icon for each set, select the set and then click the Edit button at the top of the window area. Then click and drag the image you want into the thumbnail space at the left of the window, as shown in Figure 11-25.

Figure 11-25

tip

You have to get the image exactly over the thumbnail area to change the icon.

After you see your selected image replace the existing icon image, click Save. The icon is changed, as you see in Figure 11-26.

Figure 11-26
Janine Warner (http://jcwarner.com)

remember

A set's buddy icon is also used as the main photo displayed for the set when all sets are viewed together.

TAGS, SETS, AND COLLECTIONS

Part of the fun of Flickr is that it appeals to the urge to impose order on the chaos of our photo collections. Who hasn't rummaged through a shoebox full of snapshots or paged through stacks of photo albums, wishing there were a better way to find great photos.

The organizing tools in Flickr (located at www.flickr.com/photos/organize) allow you to do powerful things to your collection (especially if you're something of a digital packrat). The default interface shows you sets of photos in the main window, and a filmstrip underneath, where you can see your individual photos and then drag and drop them into new sets or collections.

To best take advantage of all these ways of finding, organizing, and sharing your photos, you will need to understand some of these tools.

Tags are the keywords that you typed in when you uploaded your photos. (You did take the time to carefully choose these words, didn't you?) These help you and others find your photos when you search for them. The more keywords you have that describe a photo, the better the chance you will have to find it.

Sets are small collections of photos, organized under a topic, date, or other data. This can be the day you shot it ("Thanksgiving 2013"), the place you shot it, or a description ("Beautiful Sunsets"). You can choose to add photos to multiple sets when you're uploading them, or you can add them to sets afterward.

Collections are basically sets made up of sets. They allow you to organize your photos by date ("Photos from 2014") or by another topic ("Vacation Snapshots"). You can also drag individual photos into a collection from the filmstrip at the bottom of the Organizer screen.

After you create a collection, you can create a pretty mosaic of the collection that you can then share or embed on your website or blog. You can change the order of the photos in the mosaic by clicking and dragging them around, or you can drag photos from the filmstrip at the bottom of the screen into the mosaic.

Think of a collection as a way for you to further organize your photos. By putting multiple sets into a collection, you ensure that when you go looking for just the right shot for your social media profile design, you will be able to browse efficiently, rather than having to click . . . and click . . . and click to scroll through an endless undifferentiated mass of images.

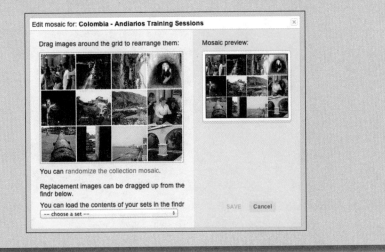

Part IV

Integrating Your Social Networks

Chapter 12: Check out Tumblr, a microblogging site where you can post short sentences, photos, or videos in one place.

Chapter 13: Discover how to use RebelMouse to display your latest posts and images from all your social sites in one page design.

Visit www.dummies.com/extras/ socialmediadesign for a gallery of the designs shown off in this book.

WolframAlpha computational...
knowledge engine

pi curve

≡ Examples ⚄ Random

Input interpretation:

pi curve (popular curve)

Plot:

(plotted for t from 0 to 2π)

⟳ Enable interactivity

Associated character:

π

Equations:

Parametric equations:

$$x(t) = \frac{17}{31}\sin\left(\frac{235}{57} - 32\,t\right) + \frac{19}{17}\sin\left(\frac{192}{55} - 30\,t\right) + \frac{47}{32}\sin\left(\frac{69}{25} - 29\,t\right) + \frac{35}{26}\sin\left(\frac{75}{34} - 27\right)$$

Guess what day it is?

http://wolfr.am/1fXuMDW

⬧ TAGGED   WolframAlpha , wolframfunfacts , math , piday ,
gettingdownonpiday , wootwoot

🕓   2 days a

♥ 96 NOTES   💬 0 COMMENTS   🔗 PERMALINK   🐦 Tweet ⟨0⟩   f Lik

Compiling a Tumblr Page

The Official Tumblr of

WolframAlp

What would you like to know about?

MAKING THE WORLD'S
KNOWLEDGE COMPUTABL

Welcome to the official Wolfram|Alp

Tumblr! Follow us to get tips, fun facts

the latest news about Wolfram|Alpha s

to your Dashboard.

CONNECT

In This Chapter

● Look at successful Tumblr designs before creating your own design.

● Use a custom background on Tumblr that reflects you.

● Create and upload an animated GIF for extra interest.

T he microblogging site Tumblr has traveled an unlikely path to prominence amongst social media junkies. It was launched in February 2007 as a way to allow users to quickly and easily post and share short sentences, photos, or videos that were found on the web.

Since then, it has evolved into a more sophisticated platform, but one with a quirky ethos all its own. Tumblr blogs are kind of a hybrid of a full-fledged blog, Twitter, and Flickr stream — that is, a place where you can post short, funny, or heartfelt phrases, accompanied by attention-grabbing photos.

Tumblr shot to prominence in 2011, when it was used by the Occupy Wall Street movement as a way to organize protest rallies. Since then, the site has almost single-handedly revived the animated GIF as an art form.

When it comes to design, most Tumblr users content themselves with choosing from the vast library of free themes available from Tumblr or third-party designers. This chapter shows you how to go beyond the themes and create a design that works for you, as shown in Figure 12-1.

Figure 12-1

When Is Tumblr Right for You?

Tumblr blogs tend to be narrowly focused on a single subject or thought, although some celebrities have adopted Tumblr to advertise their co-branded merchandise or post publicity materials from their latest stroll down an A-list red carpet event. Still, this is not the platform for long-form meditations on being and nothingness, nor for 10,000 word posts on the migration patterns of the Arctic tern.

technical stuff

The name *Tumblr* comes from the term "tumblelog," which is how tech geeks describe a blog where the owner posts only short sentences or photos.

This is also known as *microblogging,* which is a much briefer form of traditional blogging. Tumblr is best understood as a way for you to give a little more information to your friends and followers than Twitter allows, but without having to go through the more formal and thorough process of publishing to the web required by many blogging software platforms.

Tumblr is a very visual platform, and Tumblr recently opened its platform to allow designers to add more custom touches to their themes. You can now trick out your Tumblr page with drop-down lists or jQuery plugins to make pages automatically resize themselves for tablets and mobile devices.

With the full spectrum of HTML and CSS tools coming into play to allow you to customize your Tumblr blog, the platform is starting to look more and more like traditional blogging — only shorter, which is probably the intent.

So, although we encourage you to customize your Tumblr page to your heart's content, teaching you the required HTML and CSS skills would take the rest of this book. If you don't know the first thing about custom-coding a web page but still want to learn how to take complete control of the design of your Tumblr blog, check out co-author Janine Warner's *Web Sites Do-It-Yourself For Dummies* or *Beginning HTML5 & CSS3 For Dummies,* by Ed Tittel and Chris Minnick.

tip

> If you're feeling a little overwhelmed by all the choices, a good course of action might be to download and install a custom theme and then add a few flourishes here and there, such as changing the font, banner, or color scheme.

We start with a look at some of the more innovative and eye-catching designs to give you an idea of what's possible, and then show you some basic instructions on how to personalize your Tumblr page as well as produce animated GIFs (a lesson that might come in handy to generate content for some of the other social media platforms as well).

Comparing Inspiring Tumblr Designs

The typical Tumblr blog used to be just a long, centered stream of photos with a few snippets of text sprinkled throughout — and many Tumblr blogs still retain that basic look. However, the trend in the last few years has been to try to break out of that rigid vertical format, taking advantage of HTML5 and CSS3 features being built into modern web browsers. Some web designers are creating eye-pleasing designs that invite you to click content; others seem to have gone a little overboard with all the freedom.

YAHOO! TAKES OVER TUMBLR

Amidst a general outcry from dedicated users, the Tumblr site was sold in June 2013 to Yahoo! for $1.1 billion. Yahoo! CEO Marissa Mayer took the unusual step of publicly promising "not to screw it up," a crucial step in retaining the dedicated core of users, long accustomed to seeing big corporations suck the life out of social media sites after acquiring them (such as when Rupert Murdoch's News Corp bought Myspace).

Cory Doctorow

http://mostlysignssomeportents.tumblr.com

Quirky science fiction author Cory Doctorow (perhaps better known as one of the founding bloggers of BoingBoing) uses his "Mostly Signs, Some Portents" Tumblr blog as a place to post "Things Cory Doctorow saw." The banner for the site gives you a pretty clear idea of what you're in for: elaborately decorated tennis shoes, funky space aliens, snack cakes, and a photo of the author seemingly being attacked by a hideous green monster hand (or perhaps just getting a scalp massage). See Figure 12-2. Doctorow uses a diverse collage of images to reflect the eclectic nature of his postings, and to reveal his somewhat absurdist sense of humor in his Tumblr design.

Figure 12-2

Cory Doctorow (http://mostlysignssomeportents.tumblr.com)

Coca-Cola

```
http://coca-cola.tumblr.com
```

Coca-Cola brings eye-catching action to its Tumblr with animated gifs, running contests inviting people to send in their own short animated sequences. Running contests on social sites, like Tumblr, is a great way to engage site visitors and can help you populate your Tumblr blog with content while rewarding your most loyal customers and turning them into fans. The responsive web design techniques used here allow the Tumblr blog to fit the width of the user's screen, whether a standard display (Figure 12-3) or an ultra-wide display (Figure 12-4).

Figure 12-3

Figure 12-4

Wolfram|Alpha

```
http://wolframalpha.tumblr.com
```

The scientific "answer engine" Wolfram|Alpha uses subtle pastel graphics on its Tumblr blog (see Figure 12-5). The sprockets, gears and connecting belts are all echoes of the company's logo. The understated graphics work well as a design cue for the delicate and intricate calculations that you can do using Wolfram|Alpha.

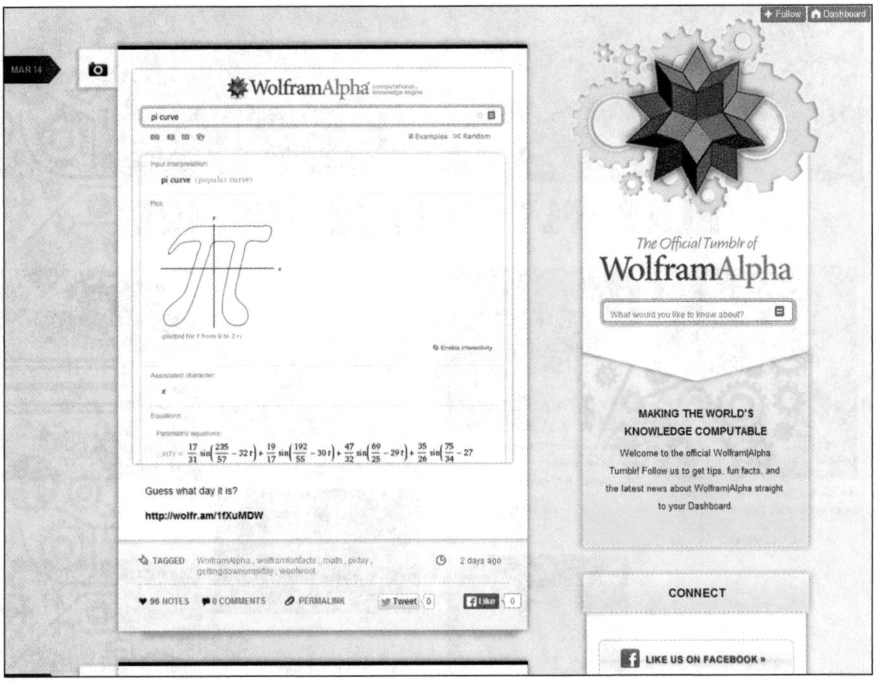

Figure 12-5

The company's posts are illustrations of how you can use Wolfram|Alpha's combination of search and scientific computational abilities to figure out things, like how far from Earth the Rosetta spacecraft has traveled while on its way to land on comet 67P/Churyumov-Gerasimenko . . . or how long it would take to travel from Los Angeles to New York if you were riding a cheetah at full sprint the entire way. (Answers: 499 million miles and 33 hours, respectively, although the poor cheetah would be pretty tuckered out by the time you got there.)

Red Bull

`http://redbull.tumblr.com/tagged/create`

This energy drink company has become a leader in digital media. Red Bull's Tumblr page is a place for the company to promote the extreme sports, aggressive, can-do type of content that fits with its corporate image of being the drink of choice for people who do crazy-cool stuff (see Figure 12-6).

Figure 12-6

Red Bull has created a page with four big navigation tabs — Play, Fly, Create, and Inspire — each leading to a subpage of its Tumblr site. The gritty black-and-white design fits with this page; it looks like it's been banged around a bit but is still standing. The simple design doesn't take away from the colorful animated GIFs that are the main content on this page.

warning

Using an infinite scroll the way Red Bull does in its design can provide a great, seemingly never-ending experience to some users, but older web browsers can sometimes freeze or crash when trying to load the additional content.

RadioLab

    http://wnycradiolab.tumblr.com

The stories that come out of Radiolab are broadcast on NPR stations around the world, but sometimes there is an aspect to the story that is best told with images.

The clean, stripped-down design on New York City's RadioLab Tumblr blog (see Figure 12-7) puts the emphasis on the images. Radiolab, hosted by Jad Abumrad and Robert Krulwich, also produces a popular podcast.

Figure 12-7

Their well-designed Tumblr blog mixes short posts, quotes, and images that illustrate many of the same topics that the two cover in their podcast and radio show. The two have attracted a strong following by asking provocative questions and exploring quirky science and technology.

Today's Document

    http://todaysdocument.tumblr.com/

Each day at the Today's Document Tumblr (shown in Figure 12-8), you'll find an image, a video, or an animated GIF featuring some notable event that took place on the same day in history. According to the About page on the site, Today's Document started as a small feature on the Archives.gov website several years ago as a way to highlight interesting documents from the National Archives.

tip

The use of Tumblr to showcase and share the most popular or most frequently requested documents demonstrates how well Tumblr can serve as a complement to a much larger website, such as the one at Archives.org.

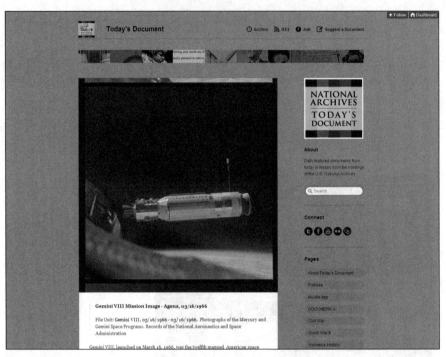

Figure 12-8

Changing the Background on Tumblr

One of the quickest ways to improve your Tumblr blog from the often–generic-looking start themes is to upload your own background image and use it to give individuality and character to your site.

tip

Most modern computers have displays at least 1000 pixels (px) wide, if not wider. For more onscreen resolutions, see Chapter 2. If you have a blog about photography or graphic design, you can probably assume that most of your audience will have big computer monitors that can display a background image in full HD resolution: that is, 1920 x 1080 px.

However, to reach the widest possible audience, experiment with your background images to make sure that you aren't overwhelming the capabilities of your users' computers.

Before you begin, do these two small things:

 Open a text editor.

 Have your replacement image of appropriate height and width already uploaded to your Tumblr blog or somewhere online.

on the web

For more in-depth instructions on how to custom-code your own Tumblr theme, check out the tutorials at `http://buildthemes.tumblr.com`.

Your image should have a height of at least 700 pixels and a width between 1400 and 1600 pixels. Your image should be a PNG file.

1. **Log in to your Tumblr site.**

2. **Click the Customize link in the upper-right corner.**

   The Customization panel opens, and most of the page is taken over by a live preview of the changes you're making to your Tumblr blog.

 tip

You can also change the title and description of this blog from this panel (see Figure 12-9).

Figure 12-9

3. **Click the Edit HTML button in the left column.**

   A code window appears, as shown in Figure 12-10.

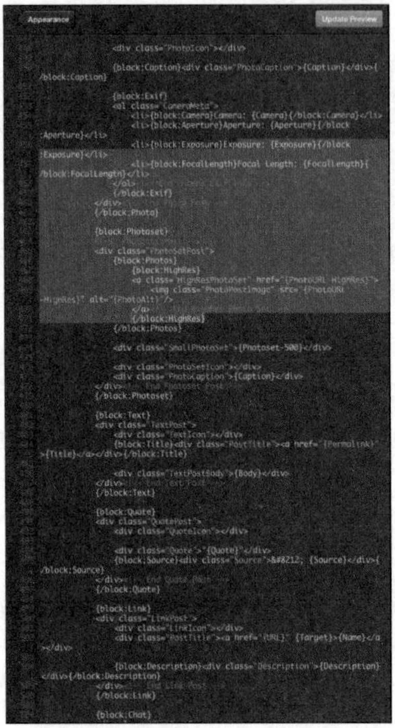

Figure 12-10

4. **Click anywhere in the left side-bar, in the HTML and CSS code.**

5. **Copy the HTML code.**

   Yes, the sheer amount of code that appears here is a little intimidating, but you're changing only a very small part of it.

6. **Paste the code into a text editor (Ctrl+V/⌘+V) so that you can safely edit the code outside the HTML page.**

remember

Select all the code (Ctrl+A/Windows or ⌘+A/Mac) and then copy the code (Ctrl+C/⌘+C).

warning

We recommend using a simple text editor, such as WordPad for a Windows PC or TextWrangler on a Mac. You *can* use a word-processing program like Word or Pages, but you may get unwanted formatting codes mixed in with your HTML unless you're very careful.

7. **Search the code (Ctrl+F/⌘+F) for the** `background:` **line.**

   You can also scroll through the code, looking for the section that starts with the `body {` tag. In our example, that looks like this:

   ```
   html, body {background: {color:Background}; height: 100%; color: rgb(82,82,82);
               font-family: Helvetica, Arial, Sans-Serif;}
   ```

8. **Change the HTML code after** `body` **to insert your new image.**

   Insert the URL link to the image in brackets after the `{color:Background}` tag so that it reads something like this:

   ```
   html, body {background: {color:Background}
               url('{http://farm8.staticflickr.com/7161/6789596839_b4a61cf2fc_b.jpg:
               Background}'); height: 100%; color: rgb(82,82,82); font-family: Helvetica,
               Arial, Sans-Serif;}
   ```

9. **Click the Update Preview button (upper right; refer to Figure 12-10) to check whether the image is showing on your Tumblr blog the way you want.**

remember

If you make an error that really messes up how your Tumblr blog looks, just cut and paste the original code that you saved into your text editor window back into the Customization panel and start all over again.

Making an Animated GIF for Tumblr

Another way to add a little spice is to use an animated GIF on your Tumblr blog.

As of this writing, the Tumblr policy is that the size limit for an animated GIF is 1MB and that pictures must be smaller than 500 x 750 px, or they will be automatically scaled down.

tip

When you choose a video clip to convert to an animated GIF, select a clip that contains motion and what landmark photojournalist Henri Cartier-Bresson pioneered as "The Decisive Moment."

Think of the moment when the sprinter crosses the finish line, the waiter drops the tray loaded with full champagne glasses, or the baby turns his heads and smiles. A loop of your roommate staring out the window moodily may seem like it conveys existential angst, but you can do the same thing with a still photo, so why bother with an animation?

OR SO THEY SAY . . .

The Tumblr rules for animated GIF specs are subject to change without much notice. For years, there was a 500KB cap on GIFs, but in January 2012, that limit was raised to 1MB. Since then, there has been much disagreement. Although the official Tumblr policy states that the size limit for animated GIFs is still 1MB, many people claim that in practice, the real limit is 1.5MB, while other users report that they have uploaded and played animated GIFs up to 2MB.

Additionally, GIFs larger than 500 px wide are blocked or banned, or they break the basic Tumblr themes. As we mention earlier, the official documentation states that pictures must be smaller than 500 x 750 px.

If you have Photoshop, it's a great choice for creating animated GIFs. If you don't have Photoshop, or if you want to have a program that streamlines and simplifies the process of creating an animated GIF, a lot of choices are on the market. Some are free, but the most popular and useful solutions usually cost $10 or so. If you're really looking to crank out animated GIFs quickly and frequently, it might be worthwhile to test some of these standalone products.

There is a lot of trial and error involved when using a high-powered program like Photoshop to create an animated GIF. Photoshop allows you to exert control over every pixel in every image in your animation. The tradeoff with that is that you have to manually make a lot of choices yourself.

The following programs can automate those choices or make adjustments more intuitive:

▶ **GIF Brewery** (Mac)

http://gifbrewery.com

Available from the Mac App Store, this program enables you to quickly achieve sophisticated effects, such as changing the cropping to zoom in, setting a custom number of loops, and applying color correction.

▶ **GifBoom** (iOS and Android)

http://gifboom.com

This app for both Android and iOS devices allows you to create simple animated GIFs while away from your computer. You can even add voice and music backgrounds and send your creation as a private message. GifBoom also has a popular online gallery where users can share and vote on each other's creations.

tip

By no means is this list all-inclusive. A casual Google search turns up at least 24 programs promising to make creating animated GIFs easier, and you can probably find dozens more. Given the exploding popularity of the animated GIF, developers and coders are likely launching new software programs every week.

▶ **Imgflip** (online app, platform agnostic)

`http://imgflip.com/gifgenerator`

This nifty online app allows you to take your own videos, as well as videos from YouTube, Vimeo, or other online video hosting sites, and convert them to an animated GIF. Imgflip is free to try, but if you want to use larger video files (bigger than 35MB), you have to upgrade to the Pro version for $9.95 per month.

▶ **GifCam** (Windows)

`http://blog.bahraniapps.com`

Unlike many of the other programs, GifCam works by allowing you to draw a box around the video that you want to turn into an animated GIF on your screen, and then recording a snippet of that video and converting — *transcoding,* in tech speak — it. You can also do simple drawings using some of the tools in GifCam. It's free to use, but the developers ask that you donate a few dollars if you like using it.

Francis Pisani

Francis Pisani
@francispisani

Artists Continually Try New I
It's much harder in business f
good reasons. The price is less
innovation buff.ly/1f15l07

9 Dec 2013

www.innovationexcellence....

Francis Pisani
@francispisani

Software Is
Reorganizing the World /&
gives birth to reverse
diasporas: start distributed
then gather. Read.
buff.ly/IixjcX

27 Nov 2013

Enter Email | Get Alerts

Francis Pisani
@francispisani

Drones or robots? How do you want your pizza delivered? You may have the choice... one day
buff.ly/1jCNT5F

9 Dec 2013

bits.blogs.nytimes.com

Tweet

Francis Pisani
@francispisani

How Cities Are Using Data To Save Lives @anya1anya /with data driven policy making & putting outcomes first
buff.ly/18rAzyY

29 Nov 2013

www.fastcoexist.com

CHAPTER 13

Aggregating Profiles with a RebelMouse Page

In This Chapter

- Bring your social designs together in RebelMouse.

- Understand your RebelMouse design options.

- Customize your layout, theme, and navigation bar.

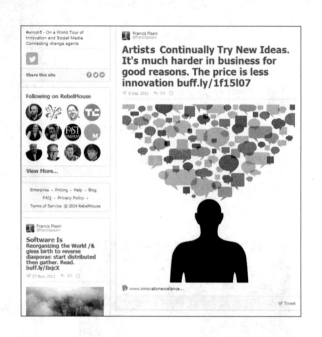

The growth of social media sites — as demonstrated by all the sites that have sprung up in the past couple of years and that we cover in this book — has resulted in tech startups launching new sites dedicated to increasingly narrow niches. So what's the problem? Well, the issue with the ever-growing number of social media sites means that folks are finding it difficult to keep track of what they're saying to whom and where.

The solution? Into this void step the social media aggregators, such as RebelMouse and About.me. With these sites, you can pick and choose the best of your tweets, Facebook posts, Tumblr shares, and YouTube videos, mix them all up, and spin them into your very own social media mash-up mix.

Like a dub-step mix that brings in snippets from old Western movies, a Jamaican reggae rhythm track, a blistering heavy-metal guitar solo, and lyrics from bleak Russian poetry, sites like RebelMouse enable you to create a fascinating web page by assembling snippets from all the things you love into a digital collage — a "social front page."

RebelMouse excels at this mix of personal and professional although it takes a bit of thought and experimentation to get things right. News organizations and journalists have even started to use RebelMouse to cover breaking news that surfaces on social media, such as what Andy Carvin (see Figure 13-1) does where he shares a mix of news and private moments from his life.

Figure 13-1
Andy Carvin (www.andycarvin.com)

There are a lot of social media aggregators; About.me and RebelMouse are just two of them. Search online for *social media aggregators* to find more choices.

In this chapter, we demonstrate the best way to set up your own RebelMouse page and also show you how the available design choices can help you express your individuality.

Checking Out What You Can Do on RebelMouse

The following sections show off a few RebelMouse pages that display various content in a variety of ways.

General Electric

Corporations — such as GE — use the RebelMouse to create pages that bring in photos, videos, blog posts, Vines, tweets, and other content that GE generates through its social-media marketing campaigns (see Figure 13-2).

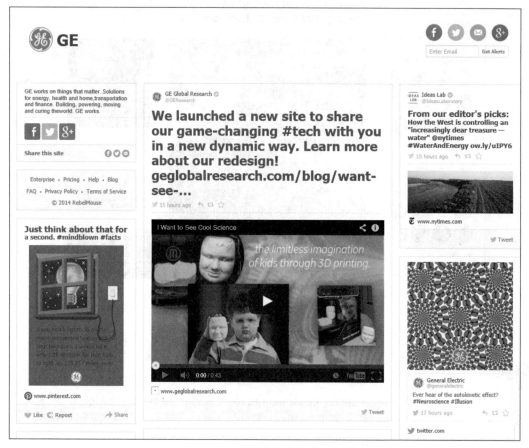

Figure 13-2

Francis Pisani

Writers and journalists are often active social media participants, and you'll find many of them on RebelMouse. Francis Pisani, whose work is regularly published in leading international newspapers, including *Le Monde* in France and *El País* in Spain, uses RebelMouse (see Figure 13-3) to aggregate his social media posts, which makes it easy to keep up with all his latest research.

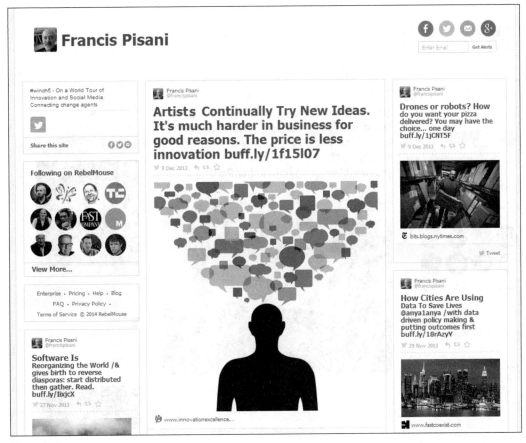

Figure 13-3

Francis Pisani (http://francispisani.net)

Travis Smith

Travis Smith, president of the Hop Studios web design firm, uses social media to stay in touch with friends as well as promote his business. Travis posts a nice mix of funny, as well as informative, posts on a variety of social media sites. Visit his RebelMouse page, shown in Figure 13-4, to see his Facebook, Google+, Twitter, and Instagram updates all in one place.

Figure 13-4

Travis F. Smith (www.hopstudios.com)

Marsha Collier

Author Marsha Collier is active on all the top social media websites, which makes RebelMouse an ideal place to find her latest tips and tricks (see Figure 13-5). Best known for her books on eBay, including *eBay For Dummies,* Marsha is the author of 48 books, and her use of social media provides a great model for how to promote books (or any other products) by becoming a great source of information for your target audience.

Figure 13-5

Marsha Collier (www.rebelmouse.com/marshacollier)

RebelMouse

It should come as no surprise that RebelMouse has its own RebelMouse page (www.rebelmouse.com/RebelMouse; see Figure 13-6). The central post in Figure 13-6 highlights the company's extraordinary growth and some of its most recent successes, including hosting the Winter Olympics hub for United Airlines.

Figure 13-6

DECIDING WHETHER TO UPGRADE

At the top of every RebelMouse page is a Power Your Site button, which urges you to upgrade to a paid level of service, starting at $500 per month. So, if you can use RebelMouse for free, why bother to pay to upgrade? Isn't that like paying to use Facebook or Twitter?

Well, sort of — but not really.

Many users like having a social-aggregation engine like RebelMouse, but they prefer to have the results of all their online activity appear on their own website. That way, the content and the resulting page traffic are completely under their control — and that means ponying up for the upgrade.

Paying for one of the upgrade options allows you to at least

- Use enhanced branding control.
- Access enhanced analytics.
- Process your feed faster.
- Add additional admins.
- Receive priority e-mail support.

Assembling the Content for Your RebelMouse Page

After signing up for an account, the next step for any proud user of RebelMouse is to start choosing the social media feeds that you want to show up on your page. Most of this process is pretty self-explanatory, but we want to point out some little features that can make all the difference.

To begin with, you can import content from 25 different social media feeds, including

▶ Your personal profiles

▶ Content from employees, co-workers, or people you admire and think are clever

▶ Searches or filters to the feeds that you add

tip

Here's an example. Say your page just happens to be devoted to assembling all the things that make teenage girls scream. You add a feed from the music site Pitchfork but filter it so that only news items about Justin Bieber show up.

warning

If you bring in content from other users and then use the professional level of RebelMouse to embed it onto your own site where you're attempting to monetize the site via advertising or other e-commerce, you should — at the very least — ask permission from the other users whose feeds you're using.

In a bit, we discuss tips and instructions for the most prominent social media sites that you're allowed to bring into RebelMouse. However, because the social web is constantly evolving and changing, there may be new sites that we didn't cover, or maybe some established sites (like Myspace) no longer appear.

But first, here's how to access the page where you can set up your feeds:

1. **Create or log in to your RebelMouse account.**

2. **Click the link to open your dashboard.**

   Look for the link next to the gear icon at the top right of the page.

   From your RebelMouse dashboard page that opens, you can control the design, the feeds, and the type of e-mail notifications you receive; check your site statistics; and access Goodies (such as buttons showing the militant blue mouse logo).

3. **Click the Content & Feeds tab.**

   The Total Feeds page opens, as shown in Figure 13-7. The numbers in the parentheses below the tabs show you how many feeds you've added to your RebelMouse page (of the max of 25).

4. **In the text fields next to the social media sites on this page, enter the URL or other information you need to add a feed from that social site to your RebelMouse page.**

   The process for each site works differently, depending on the security settings of the social media site. Some sites allow you to access a feed merely by typing the name of the person or hashtag. Others require you to sign in. Keep reading to see how different sites handle this.

Twitter

You can bring in tweets by

▶ Connecting your Twitter account by authorizing RebelMouse to import your tweets or publish tweets to your profile

▶ Entering a user's *handle* — the `@TheirName` that they use

▶ Adding a hashtag (#) for a keyword or subject that you want to feature on your page.

▶ Adding a Twitter list, such as a collection of only your closest friends

Figure 13-7

David LaFontaine (www.rebelmouse.com/davelafontaine)

For each Twitter feed that you add, you can choose the following options:

 Post tweets and retweets.

 Post only tweets but not retweets.

 Post tweets and retweets to the Drafts folder, which allows you to publish manually later

 Save tweets to the Drafts folder and ignore retweets.

 Add a filter that uses Twitter's advanced search capabilities, such as choosing to add only tweets with an exact phrase — say, "social media design for dummies" — by adding the quote marks around the phrase.

on the web

For more on Twitter's advanced search, see https://twitter.com/ search-advanced.

Facebook

After you authorize RebelMouse to access your Facebook Profile, you can choose to bring in content from your main Profile, or you can choose to feature content from a Facebook Group or Page.

From the Facebook drop-down menu, you can

▶ Choose from Pages you've created.

▶ Check for new Facebook Pages.

▶ Turn off the feed from Facebook altogether.

Instagram

The process for adding the trippy photos from Instagram users closely resembles that for adding tweets. You can

▶ **Connect your Instagram profile to bring in all your photos.**

RebelMouse will put your photos into the Drafts folder so you can choose which ones you want to share and optionally write a more complete description.

▶ **Use a hashtag (#) to bring in photos around a subject that you're interested in.**

▶ **Bring in photos from another user. Just type his or her username.**

▶ **Use the same type of advanced search features found on Twitter to filter the photos, such as a minus sign to exclude certain terms.**

For example: You love photos of food, but you're a vegetarian, so you add the filter **"food –meat"** so you don't get photos of steaks.

Google+

You can connect your Google+ page and also add content from any feed by adding that URL to any Google+ page.

The only options as of this writing are to

▶ Immediately publish content from a Google+ feed to your RebelMouse page.

▶ Hold it in your Drafts folder for your editing and approval.

Flickr

Just click the Sign In with Flickr button on the Content & Feeds tab and complete the login process. RebelMouse says that it will publish only those images marked Public to your profile, meaning that photos marked as Private or only for family and friends should not show up on your RebelMouse page.

StockTwits

The social network for wanna-be Wall Street moguls, StockTwits is itself a kind of aggregator for short Twitter-like messages about investing and the stock market. Click the Sign In with StockTwits button to authorize RebelMouse to bring in your StockTwit feed, complete with charts, graphs, and videos (if any) that you post there.

LinkedIn

Like StockTwits, the professional connection site LinkedIn allows you to bring in only your own feed. Click the Sign In with LinkedIn button and authorize RebelMouse to bring in your professional updates and shares.

YouTube

Adding videos from YouTube to your page is more like importing from Twitter or Google+. Just type the username of a channel that you like (your own or someone else's) and then click the Add button. You can open the drop-down menu to control whether new videos are automatically added to your RebelMouse page, or saved into your Drafts folder for you to review, edit, and approve.

Tumblr

The process for adding posts from a Tumblr blog is also quite open. Just type the username for a Tumblr blog that you like and then click the Add button.

RSS

Ever since Google got rid of Google Reader, the world of RSS readers has been in a state of flux. However, every blog worth its digital salt should have an RSS feed that allows you to bring in posts and content. At the time of this writing, RebelMouse does sport an Import Google Reader button.

As we said, though, given that Google Reader no longer exists, clicking this button opens a window directing you to create an archive of your Google Reader data. Ignore this. Instead, visit blogs that you like or want to feature, click that RSS feed button, and copy and paste the URL into the field here.

remember

You are allowed a total of 25 feeds. If you choose too many blogs to add here (a not-unlikely occurrence, given statistics showing that people's RSS readers are crammed with more than 30 blogs), you won't be able to add content from your social media profiles.

Pinterest

You can add all your Pinterest boards or just a few. To add all your boards, just type your username in the field and then click the Add button. To add only one board, type your username/name of the board — for example, `davelafontaine/the-way-the-future-was` — to limit the content to only the pins you have on that board.

Just think about that for a second. #mindblown #facts

www.pinterest.com

♥ Like Repost   Share

Customizing Your RebelMouse Page Design

When it was first launched, RebelMouse offered only a few simple tools to customize the look and feel of a site. RebelMouse has rolled out features that now allow you to change how your page looks:

⏵ Width and number of columns on your page

⏵ Fonts in the headlines and posts

⏵ Custom header (a feature that had previously been confined only to premium users)

In a nutshell, first choose your layout and font and then set your theme. Then you can customize a navigation bar and create a custom banner.

Choosing a page layout

When it comes to page layout, you have two basic decisions to make. Click the Design tab to see your options:

⏵ The layout of your page

⏵ Whether to enable the Giant Splash

Five basic designs

You can choose from five basic designs as well as more than 20 headline and description text font combinations (see Figure 13-8). To choose a column layout or font combination you like, simply click the graphic that you like and then click the Return to Front Page link below the name of your RebelMouse site on the top of the page.

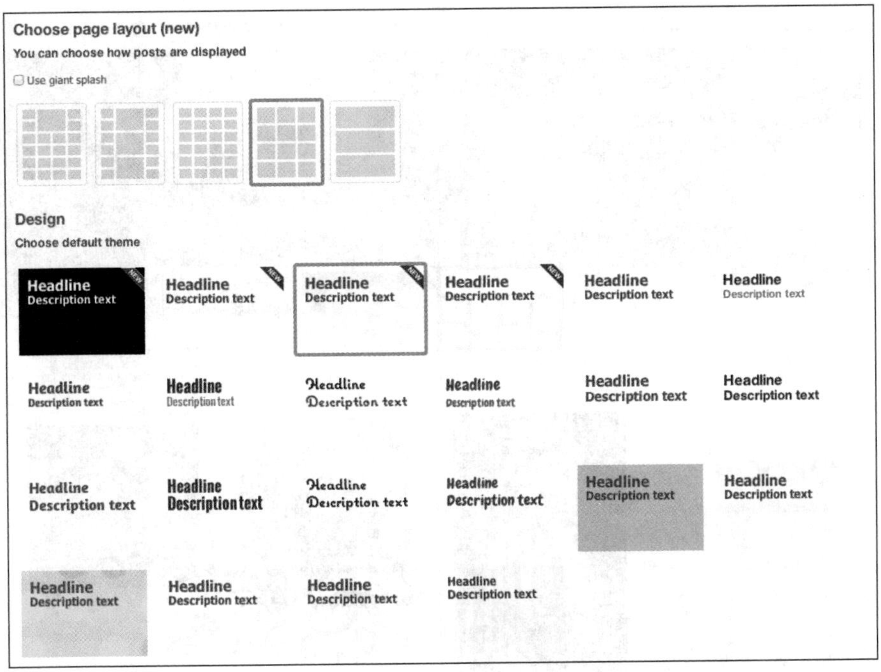

Figure 13-8

remember

Don't worry — the changes are nondestructive. If you're not pleased with the effect, just return to the Design tab in your dashboard and click a different graphic layout.

For anyone who has played with layout options on a traditional blogging platform, the grids at the top of this panel will be familiar. However, if all this looks new, we explain the differences and why you might want to choose one layout preset over the others.

Now see how the content-dense four-column layout looks in Figure 13-9. You might like this layout if you have a lot of activity on the various social media platforms and want to keep as much of the recent photos and posts "above the fold" on your RebelMouse page as possible.

tip

Note that the photos are pretty much thumbnail-sized, and there is a lot more text on the page than with some of the other layouts. If you tend to be more of a writer than a photographer, this layout could be perfect for you.

Figure 13-9

David LaFontaine (www.rebelmouse.com/davelafontaine)

Last, there is the full-column width layout (the last one on the right in Figure 13-8), where each of your posts takes up the entire column. In the right hands, with the right sort of curation and monitoring of feeds, this can be a truly powerful layout.

However, as shown in Figure 13-10, when you take the content that fits into the other layouts and give it the entire column, only a few items can be seen at a time. Also, note that the text descriptions that appear besides the thumbnails in the four-column layout are pretty much absent here. All you get is the headline (blown up to very large size) and maybe a few words as a caption.

Figure 13-10

David LaFontaine (www.rebelmouse.com/davelafontaine)

remember

And, like when using Giant Splash, vertical photos waste a lot of space on either side of the content. We talk about Giant Splash in the next section.

If you're a photographer, an artist, or someone who posts a lot of horizontal images without much text accompaniment, this single-column layout could be perfect for you. You'll just have to carefully monitor and control the content that makes it into your RebelMouse page to ensure that your posts are making the best use of the entire column.

The Giant Splash

Notice the Use Giant Splash check box. If you enable this option, you'll notice that the five basic layouts suddenly sport a big pink bar on top of them (see Figure 13-11).

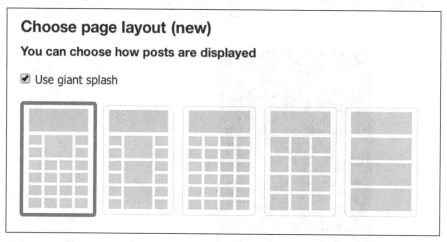

Choose page layout (new)

You can choose how posts are displayed

☑ Use giant splash

Figure 13-11

Enabling Giant Splash changes the size of the most recent item posted to your RebelMouse site, making it take over the entire width of the page. You would use this option if you want to really make an impact with your most recent post (such as having a compelling photo of yourself sitting in the Iron Throne from *Game of Thrones,* as shown in Figure 13-12) and you want to really set it off from the rest of your content.

Here's what happens. In Figure 13-9, the photo is the featured content, and the other posts fit in nicely around it. In Figure 13-12, the post has been expanded until it takes over the entire horizontal space.

So here's where you need to think about enabling Giant Splash or not as well as your post choices. You can readily see the design problem because the photo is vertical, and thus you have a lot of wasted space on the margins. Of course, if you were using a horizontal photo, you wouldn't have this problem.

Figure 13-12

Author David LaFontaine (www.rebelmouse.com/davelafontaine/)

Here's another negative result from using this particular layout with Giant Splash enabled: The new vertical photo also pushes down the RebelMouse buttons and other content on the left side.

SO, CAN WE SPLASH IN THE POOL OR NOT?

Our advice is that you carefully test how using Giant Splash works with your content. If you have something special that you really want to feature on your RebelMouse page for a short defined period of time, this may make a lot of sense for you. However, leaving the Giant Splash option turned on all the time runs the risk that you will forget that it's there, and any users that come to your RebelMouse page might find themselves confronted with the somewhat awkward layout scenario we demonstrate here.

Themes: Fonts and colors

After you choose your layout type, pick your default font and the color scheme for your RebelMouse page. Beneath the column layout picker are the available headline font and descriptive text choices; refer to Figure 13-8.

RebelMouse constantly adds to these choices by installing new font and color combinations. We can't possibly predict which combination you will find most pleasing or appropriate for your RebelMouse page. We can only say that picking just the right font is a subject that designers can spend days or weeks agonizing over.

A good general guideline is that for a personal site or for a site dedicated to art, design, or photography, you can get away with using a more ornate or decorative font. However, if you're trying to promote a more restrained or professional image, you would probably do best to stick to one of the simpler font and color combinations.

Create your own custom theme

Beneath the array of font styles is the option that will allow you to take complete control over colors, fonts, and styles on your RebelMouse page. Click the box with a plus sign in it to open window containing all the CSS code for your page, as shown in Figure 13-13.

Create your own custom theme

+

Create new custom theme   Save

```
68        font: bold 15px/21px Tahoma,sans-serif;
69    }
70 -  /* Change Twitter header */
71 -  .author-head .user .name  {
72        color: #5C5C5C;
73        font: 11px/10px Tahoma,sans-serif;
74    }
75 -  .author-head .user .name .screen {
76        color: #898989;
77        font: 10px/12px Tahoma,sans-serif;
78    }
79 -  .widget:hover .widget-details .widget-date, .widget:hover .user .name .screen {
80        color: #505050;
81    }
82 -  .widget-details .widget-date {
83        color: #898989;
84    }
85
```

Figure 13-13

If you know CSS, you can tinker in RebelMouse to use fonts and colors different than the limited selection of the theme options that RebelMouse offers. Remember to click Save when you're done. You can always consult *HTML, XHTML & CSS For Dummies* by Ed Tittel and Jeff Noble.

warning

If you've never worked with CSS before, we suggest that you leave these options alone.

Editing the RebelMouse navigation bar

When you first create your RebelMouse site, a few navigation tabs are created automatically for you. All users will receive the Drafts and Home tabs, but RebelMouse may create additional tabs based on the social media accounts you've connected to your RebelMouse account and the content on those platforms. However, you can add, subtract, or customize those tabs to spotlight content. You can also choose to make the tabs private. The Drafts tab is private by default.

To edit your navigation bar, follow these steps:

1. **Log in to your RebelMouse account.**

2. **Locate the small pencil icon to the far right of your navigation bar. Click the icon to edit your navigation bar.**

   The Edit RebelMouse Navigation window opens, as shown in Figure 13-14.

3. **Click any field under the Page Title heading and enter the text you want on your navigation buttons.**

   You can add buttons to the bar to lead your users to more narrowly defined content and topics on your site — say, a collection of all the posts across all your feeds that mention dolphins, or a page dedicated to all your Instagram photos.

   tip

   You cannot change the names on the two default buttons on your navigation bar: Drafts and Home.

4. **Under Page Type, open the drop-down list and choose the type of page you want the navigation button to open.**

   You can choose from a sub-page on your RebelMouse site, link to someone else's RebelMouse site, or even link to any other URL.

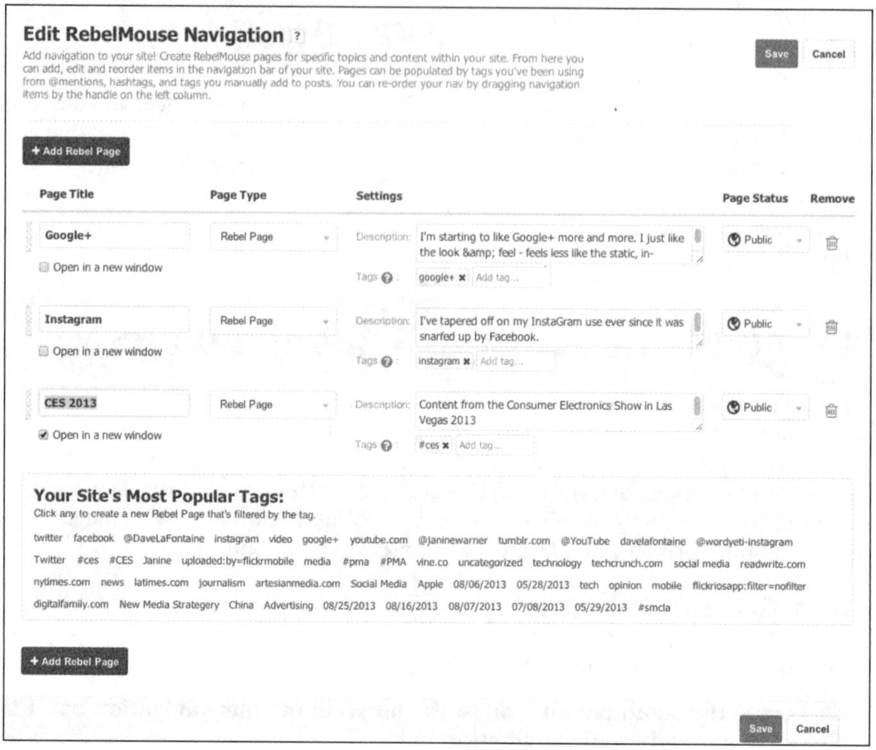

Edit RebelMouse Navigation ?

Add navigation to your site! Create RebelMouse pages for specific topics and content within your site. From here you can add, edit and reorder items in the navigation bar of your site. Pages can be populated by tags you've been using from @mentions, hashtags, and tags you manually add to posts. You can re-order your nav by dragging navigation items by the handle on the left column.

Save   Cancel

+ Add Rebel Page

Page Title	Page Type	Settings		Page Status	Remove
Google+ ☐ Open in a new window	Rebel Page ▾	Description:	I'm starting to like Google+ more and more. I just like the look & feel - feels less like the static, in-	⊙ Public ▾	🗑
		Tags ❓ :	google+ ✕ Add tag...		
Instagram ☐ Open in a new window	Rebel Page ▾	Description:	I've tapered off on my InstaGram use ever since it was snarfed up by Facebook.	⊙ Public ▾	🗑
		Tags ❓ :	instagram ✕ Add tag...		
CES 2013 ☑ Open in a new window	Rebel Page ▾	Description:	Content from the Consumer Electronics Show in Las Vegas 2013	⊙ Public ▾	🗑
		Tags ❓ :	#ces ✕ Add tag...		

Your Site's Most Popular Tags:

Click any to create a new Rebel Page that's filtered by the tag.

twitter   facebook   @DaveLaFontaine   instagram   video   google+   youtube.com   @Janinewarner   tumblr.com   @YouTube   davelafontaine   @wordyeti-instagram   Twitter   #ces   #CES   Janine   uploaded:by=flickrmobile   media   #pma   #PMA   vine.co   uncategorized   technology   techcrunch.com   social media   readwrite.com   nytimes.com   news   latimes.com   journalism   artesianmedia.com   Social Media   Apple   08/06/2013   05/28/2013   tech   opinion   mobile   flickriosapp:filter=nofilter   digitalfamily.com   New Media Strategery   China   Advertising   08/25/2013   08/16/2013   08/07/2013   07/08/2013   05/29/2013   #smcla

+ Add Rebel Page

Save   Cancel

Figure 13-14

5. **Under Settings, add a short sentence telling your users what they will find if they click this button.**

6. **Click the Add Tag box and add tags to filter the content.**

   For example, if you add the tag *YouTube.com,* then any content that comes from YouTube (such as videos that you post or Like) or any content that mentions YouTube will wind up on this sub-page on your custom RebelMouse page.

7. **Click Save.**

remember

The Description box won't appear if you're linking to an external URL.

tip

Not sure what tabs to add to your navigation? Choose from the tags that RebelMouse indicates are among the most popular for your site.

Creating a custom header image

Now available to all RebelMouse users, you can create a custom header image. By default, your header is just your profile picture and your site name. The header width is 1043 px, but images that are at least 600 px are acceptable. The minimum image height is 187 px.

remember

The tools for uploading and sizing your image are fairly user-friendly, with ample opportunity to crop and resize your photo after you upload it.

To create a custom header, follow these steps:

1. **Log in to your RebelMouse account.**

2. **On the front page, roll your cursor over the header image.**

   A small Edit Header Image button (it also bears a pencil icon) appears next to your profile photo and the name of your RebelMouse page.

3. **Click the button to edit your header image.**

   The header creation window opens, offering you three choices:

   - Use just your site name and profile photo (or avatar).

   - Add a logo.

   - Add a large header image.

   We concentrate on the latter option because it offers the most flexibility and greatest visual impact.

4. **Select the Add Large Header Image radio button.**

   A panel opens where you can upload and do basic sizing on your chosen image.

5. **Navigate to and upload your image.**

   - *For an image stored on a device (your computer, a thumb drive, and so on):* Click Upload an Image, navigate to where your image is located, and then click Open.

   - *For an image from another social media site or that appears elsewhere on the web:* Click Upload from URL and then enter the URL of the photo that you wish to use.

   The photo you choose appears in the central panel.

warning

A smaller-resolution image may look pixelated or distorted when viewed full-size in the header.

6. **Click and drag the handles at the corner of the screen to crop and choose the area of your photo that you want to appear in your header.**

   - *Width:* RebelMouse suggests that a header image be at least 1043 pixels (px) wide, but images of only 600 px will also work.

   - *Height:* The minimum recommended height is 187 px. However, we have found that the RebelMouse design will accommodate images that are much larger in height. Just drag the sizing handles to expand the working area to include the areas you want to appear, as shown in Figure 13-15.

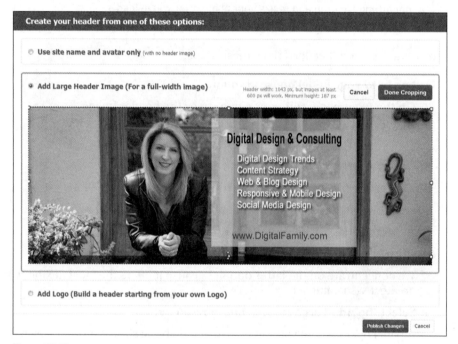

Figure 13-15

7. **Click the Done Cropping button.**

   Your header image will appear as your site visitors will see it. If you don't like how it appears, click the Recrop button in the upper right and repeat the process.

8. **You can now choose whether you want the name of your site and your avatar (basically, your portrait photo) to appear on the final RebelMouse header.**

   If the image you chose for your RebelMouse site already includes the site name and identifying information, you can choose to omit these two items. Otherwise, they will show up by default.

9. **(Optional) From the Site Title field (you may need to scroll down to see it), change the title of your site.**

10. **(Optional) Open the Text Color drop-down list to change the color of the text.**

tip

Try to choose a contrasting text color. That is, if you have a photo with a dark area in the upper-left corner, where your avatar and site title appear, choose a light color so that it shows up better (and vice versa).

11. **Click the Publish Changes button (lower right) to see your creation.**

    Your new RebelMouse header appears at the top of your page, as shown in Figure 13-16.

Figure 13-16

Janine Warner (`www.rebelmouse.com/janinewarner`)

You are at the center of your network. Your connections can introduce you to 13,993,000+ professionals — here's how your network breaks down:

Your Connections Your trusted friends and colleagues	1,346
Two degrees away Friends of friends; each connected to one of your connections	758,200+
Three degrees away Reach these users through a friend and one of their friends	13,233,500+

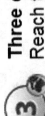

Part V

The Part of Tens

Chapter 14: Find a collection of social media management tools, which can help you manage multiple accounts, find friends, and make new connections.

Chapter 15: Harness the power of social media analytics tools, which offer a powerful way to measure the success of your social networking activities.

Chapter 16: Read ten tips for social media engagement to help you build stronger relationships online.

Visit www.dummies.com/extras/socialmediadesign for an additional list of social media tools.

Dave LaFont

Dave LaFontaine is friends & family(e

Photostream   Sets   Fa

David LaFontaine

Ten Social Media Management Tools

With so many social media platforms on your docket, managing your brand's content can become overwhelming. To tackle that program, what you need is a social media management tool, and many are available to help you get control over your little piece of real estate on the Internet. Social media management tools range from free to pricey, and each one offers a variety of features to help you save time while being social.

Planning Ahead with HootSuite

`http://hootsuite.com`

HootSuite (see Figure 14-1) makes it easy to manage multiple profiles across multiple social media sites such as Twitter, Facebook, Google+, LinkedIn, Foursquare, WordPress, Myspace, and mixi. Sign up for a free account with HootSuite and connect it with your social media accounts for an efficient interface for all your social media management, monitoring, and analytics. For example, use HootSuite to organize your friends and followers, and also monitor keywords as well as individuals. Upgrade to HootSuite Pro, which offers enhanced analytics and the ability to link additional social media accounts.

Figure 14-1

tip

HootSuite also enables you to preschedule posts to multiple social media sites and run powerful searches to see what topics are trending.

Keeping in Touch with Nimble

www.nimble.com

Nimble is a social media tool that makes it possible to manage your e-mail, contacts, social media messages, and more all in one central dashboard. The company was founded by the developer of one of the most successful customer relationship management (CRM) tools, GoldRush, and is designed to bring a sales management focus to social media.

With Nimble, you can integrate your contacts and then read, write, and organize all your communications across Gmail, Facebook, Twitter, LinkedIn, and more in one program. For example, when you get an e-mail from someone, you can quickly see that person's latest Facebook updates, check for any direct messages on Twitter, and view her latest job title on LinkedIn, all within the same program.

Nimble allows you to try it for free for 14 days, but then the cost moving forward is $15 per month.

Managing Social Sites with Sprout Social

http://sproutsocial.com

You can use Sprout Social to manage multiple social media accounts from one program. Use it to coordinate your social media activities and then to review the results. This tool handles both management and analytics.

tip

Manage multiple social media accounts with Sprout Social.

Using Sprout Social, you can track conversations, follow specific keywords, and assign tasks to different team members.

Sprout Social offers a few plans, each of them available through a free trial. The three plans are

▶ **Standard:** This plan includes basic Sprout Social tools for up to 10 profiles. It costs users $39 per month.

▶ **Deluxe:** Deluxe users may include up to 20 profiles and receive enhanced reporting. This plan is $59 per month.

▶ **Premium:** This option allows users to manage up to 50 profiles while receiving enhanced reporting and training. It costs $99 per month.

Sharing Is Easy with AddThis

`www.addthis.com`

Visit any well-designed website, and you're likely to find a row of links to the most popular social media sites. You can link from a website to your own page on Facebook, Twitter, or other social sites and invite your visitors to Like or follow your profiles. You can also set up links that make it possible for your visitors to share on their social site pages what they find on your site.

That's where AddThis comes in. After you register for this free online service, you can use the service to add social media icons to your website or blog. Simply choose the size and design of the social media icons you want to use, copy and paste a little code from the AddThis site onto your site or blog, and you're done. When visitors to your site click one of the icons, they are walked through the process of sharing content and links to your site on their social media profiles.

tip

Simply copy and paste a little code into any website, such as the DigitalFamily.com site shown in Figure 14-2, and you can share any article or blog post on your website.

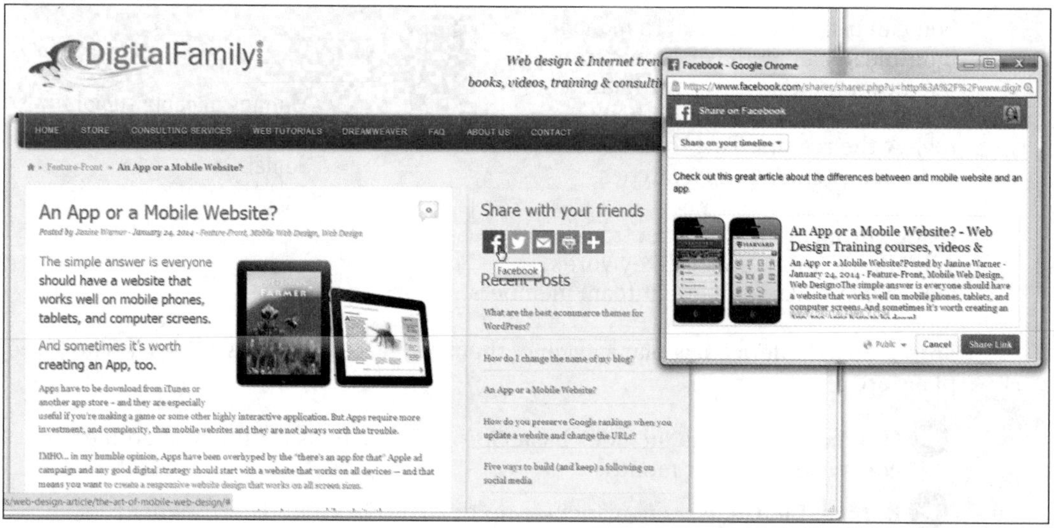

Figure 14-2

Using bitly to Shorten URLs

```
https://bitly.com
```

bitly is an online service that you can use to create shortened versions of any URL. For example, this URL

```
www.wowthisisanincredblylongurlwithseveralnumberstoboot.com
```

becomes

```
www.ashortURL.com
```

tip

> Using fewer characters in a web address is especially useful if you're posting to Twitter, where you can use only 140 characters, and you don't want a long URL to take up too many characters in your post.

If you take the time to set up an account on bitly (it's free), the service also tracks how many people click each link you post, which can help you determine which links are most successful, who in your audience is responding, where they are located, and even the best time of day to post social media updates. In Figure 14-3, you see the stats on a specific Facebook post.

Figure 14-3

Although signing up for an account does give you access to great tracking features, you aren't required to join to use the platform. Brands may also choose to upgrade their free accounts and work directly with bitly on a fee-based plan.

Using SharedBy for More than Short URLs

www.sharedby.co

Use SharedBy to shorten URLs so you share them more efficiently on social media sites. Additionally, SharedBy adds an extra feature to URL shortening by building in a special bar that appears across the top of the screen when someone follows one of your SharedBy Links from Twitter, Facebook, or another social site.

The SharedBy bar appears at the very top of the screen. The bar can include your name, business name, links to your social media sites, and of course, a link to SharedBy.

Shared by ACME Inc.   Check out the latest ACME apps

SharedBy offers a free account but also allows users to upgrade for $7 a month. This upgrade gives you access to an unlimited analytics history as well as bitly integration.

Cleaning Up Twitter Followers

www.justunfollow.com

JustUnFollow, a Twitter service, can help you manage the people you follow as well as those who follow you back. What makes the service different is that it can also help you manage some of the common problems with Twitter followers.

After you sign up with JustUnFollow, you can use it to identify anyone who has followed you — and then, after you followed them back, "unfollowed" you. Unfortunately, this is a relatively common practice on Twitter.

warning

Many people follow thousands of others just to drive up their own list of followers, but then unfollow people who follow them back so that they don't have to follow as many people in return.

JustUnFollow also gives you lists of people you follow who are not active on Twitter as well as people you have followed who have never followed you back. This allows you to unfollow people who aren't following you back, which prevents your following to follower ratio from becoming unbalanced. This is a free service.

Identifying the Fakers on Twitter

`http://fakers.statuspeople.com`

You might not realize this, but a lot of the "people" on Twitter aren't really people at all. Twitter is now home to a growing number of *fake followers,* which are accounts created by one person trying to appear to be more influential or who may be selling followers to others on the service.

If you're wondering whether all those followers your friends claim to have are real or not, you can use Fake Follow to check whether your followers, or anyone else's, are using fake accounts. This tool offers a free level and premium levels of service.

Growing Your Audience with Wildfire

`www.wildfireapp.com`

Run by Google, Wildfire is best known for helping manage social media promotions and giveaways, a great way to boost your followers and build your network — legitimately.

Wildfire is a comprehensive promotional service used by big brands as well as large nonprofit organizations. Visit the website to explore the services Wildfire offers.

Creating Contests, Coupons, and Quizzes with AgoraPulse

`www.agorapulse.com`

The AgoraPulse Facebook management and analytics tool is for advanced users who want to build apps for friends or customers to use. You can use AgoraPulse to create quizzes, sweepstakes, photo contests, coupons, and more.

The AgoraPulse services starts at $29 per month and can handle large accounts with highly complex needs. The Medium price package at $99 per month is deemed the best value by AgoraPulse, but the company is also willing to work with you to create a custom price based on the number of platforms you need to manage and the number of fans on those platforms.

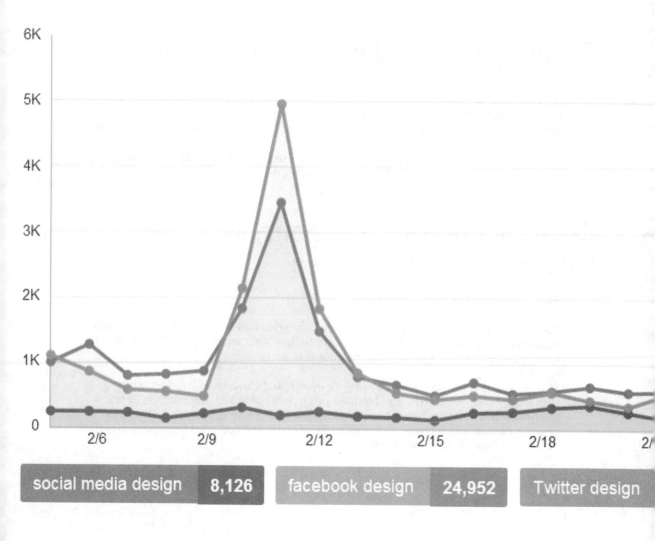

Tweets per day: social media design

Twitter design

February 5th — March 7th

social media design	8,126	facebook design	24,952	Twitter design

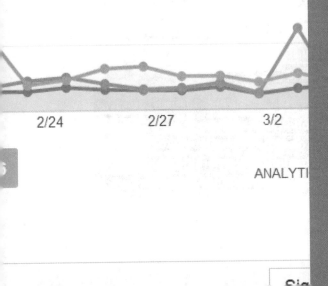

Search | Advanced search

acebook design,

2/24   2/27   3/2

ANALYTI

easuring influence on social media is a big business. Smart companies are using social networking sites to identify influencers, generate sales, and measure sentiment. If you're looking for ways to search for names, brands, or keywords being mentioned on social sites, the ten services in this chapter will not only help you identify where those names are shared but also help make the results more relevant. Many of these services produce sophisticated analytics and reports, and the best ones charge big fees to do so. Which ones you use should depend on your budget, your needs, and your preferences for how they search and generate information.

Getting a Global View with Trendsmap

`http://trendsmap.com`

Visit Trendsmap anytime day or night, and you'll see the most important keywords being shared on Twitter around the globe. This highly visual site displays a map, overlaid with the current most popular keywords on Twitter. As you scroll around the map onscreen, as shown in Figure 15-1, you see the keywords over the United States at the time this screenshot was captured. You can change the screen view on Trendsmap and see the trending keywords change while you move around the globe.

Figure 15-1

This real-time view of the Twitter-verse is quite a wonder to behold when you consider that it offers a glimpse of what's on the minds of millions of people all over the world.

Pricing for Trendsmap varies based on the specific services engaged. Free trials are available.

tip

Use Trendsmap to get an idea of local passions and region-specific issues, as well as follow big news stories, natural disasters, and events.

Measuring Your Klout Score

`http://klout.com`

The Klout web service, shown in Figure 15-2, assigns every social media user a score between 1 and 100 that purports to show how influential you are.

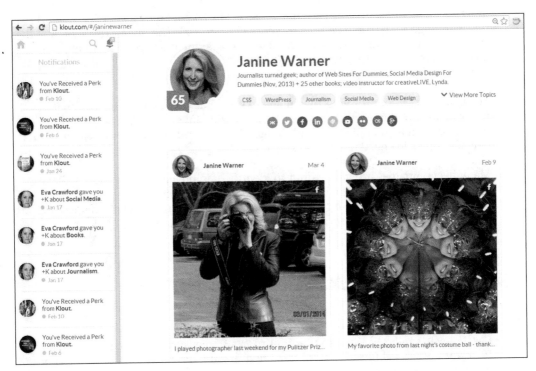

Figure 15-2

remember

> Klout scores are based on how many connections you have, how many sites you use, how often you post on social media sites, and perhaps most importantly, how often your comments are Liked and shared by others.

At the time this book was written, Klout connected to the following social media platforms:

- Twitter
- Facebook
- Facebook Page
- Cinch
- Instagram
- Google+
- LinkedIn
- Foursquare
- YouTube
- tumblr
- Blogger
- WordPress.com
- Last.fm
- Flickr
- Yammer

Most social media users have a Klout score below 20, and only a very few celebrities with huge social media following score close to 100. The higher the scores of the people who Like, comment on, or share your posts, the more your score increases, so connecting with others with high Klout scores is a good way to keep your own score elevated.

You can search Klout for your own name to see what your score is or search for other people to identify their ranks. Klout also identifies specialties among users, which makes it a good place to find thought leaders and anyone with influence on specific topics in social media.

Many big companies are using Klout to identify opinion leaders who they believe may be especially valuable when it comes to promoting their products or brands because they represent a large following. As a result, Klout users with high scores are awarded prizes from sponsors hoping to win their favor.

Earning Deals with PeerIndex

www.peerindex.com

PeerIndex is similar to Klout in that it purports to measure influence. However, PeerIndex offers a different way of ranking users and uses a system of rewards based on offering product discounts than prizes.

You can log in to PeerIndex by connecting through Facebook or Twitter and immediately see what your current ranking is on a scale of 1 to 100. Based on your score and areas of interest or influence, PeerIndex then produces a list of products and services you can buy at a discount.

tip

Especially popular among the fashion conscious, PeerIndex is based in Europe, and product prices are listed in euros.

Trading Favors at Empire Avenue

http://empireavenue.com

Although Empire Avenue is yet another site designed to help rank social media users, it's quite different from PeerIndex or Klout. Empire Avenue, shown in Figure 15-3, functions like a social stock market, where participants use virtual currency to buy and sell shares in each other's profiles.

Using the site is like playing a big online game, and active players can dramatically affect each other's valuations while building connections. It is free to create an Empire Avenue profile.

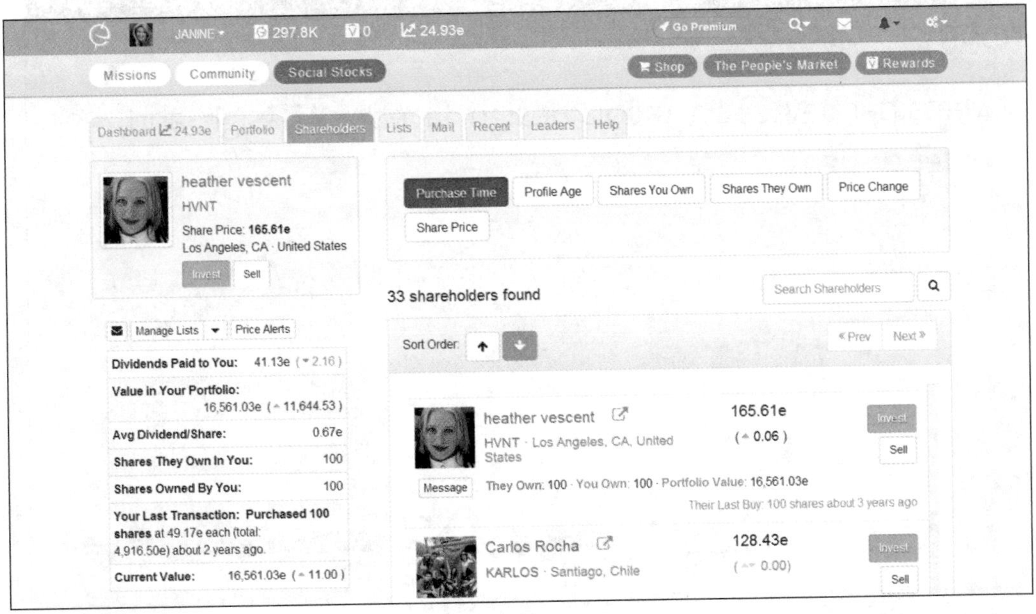

Figure 15-3

Exploring Social Media with Topsy

www.topsy.com

Topsy is a search engine, similar to Google or Bing, except that it searches social media sites, including YouTube, Twitter, and Facebook. Enter a name, keyword, or phrase, and Topsy crawls through the social sites you've selected, looking for matches.

You can use Topsy to compare trending search times, as shown in Figure 15-4. Search for competing terms to find out whether people are talking about you, your brand, your business, or any person or topic you find interesting.

tip

Topsy offers a free search and a professional level of service that is more advanced (for a fee). This site can be especially useful if you're trying to build your network around a specialty and you want to identify other people who are sharing information on that topic.

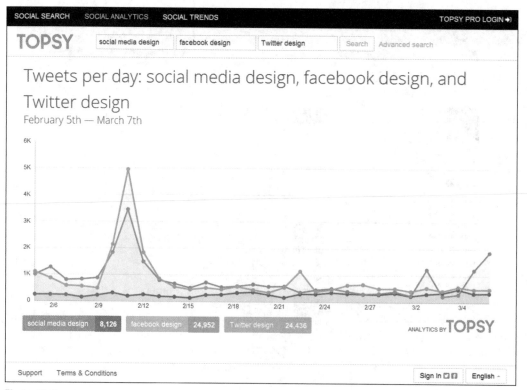

Figure 15-4

Studying Metrics with Radian6

```
www.salesforcemarketingcloud.com/products/
            social-media-listening
```

At the top of the heap of social media metrics tools, you'll find Radian6, now owned by Salesforce. Radian6 is one of the most advanced — and expensive — ways to track keywords, identify opinion leaders, and explore social media in depth.

Big companies spend thousands of dollars per month to use Radian6 to track what people are saying about brands online and even to help target followers with specific demographics. This is a powerful tool — with high price tags to match.

tip

Radian6 is a powerful addition to Salesforce. If you just want to study social media activity, you can purchase Radian6 separately.

Enjoying the View with uberVU

```
www.ubervu.com
```

You can use uberVU to follow keywords over time, study audience engagement, and schedule and market posts through a sophisticated online dashboard.

Although uberVU isn't as expensive as Radian6, it is a professional tool that starts at $499 per month. If you're working for a large or medium-sized business, the quality of leads this program can generate — as well as its ability to measure your impact on social media — may be well worth the price.

Checking Facebook Engagement

```
www.edgerankchecker.com
```

The EdgeRank Checker online tool is specifically designed to monitor and assess social media interactions on Facebook. Use EdgeRank Checker to compare the popularity of posts and help you determine what kinds of posts are most likely to gain attention and rank high on Facebook.

Measuring Social Sentiment

www.rs.peoplebrowsr.com

Enter any name into PeopleBrowsr, shown in Figure 15-5, and you'll get an in-depth look at online activity related to that name over a period of up to 1,000 days.

Figure 15-5

Full use of the service requires a subscription, but the first nine searches are free.

You can search for a person's name, brand name, or other keywords. PeopleBrowsr not only lists matches, but it also displays who mentioned the name and how often it was shared, Liked, or retweeted. The service also identifies the locations where the name is most frequently mentioned, what communities may be sharing the name, and whether the sentiment expressed is primarily negative or positive.

Reporting Results with Viralheat

www.viralheat.com

Viralheat offers a suite of tools for social media marketing, monitoring, and analytics. The price is lower than uberVU or Radian6, but this is still a professional set of tools you can use to manage small to large business accounts online.

Like other tools of its kind, you can use Viralheat to identify sales leads, measure sentiment, and produce a variety of reports.

CHAPTER 16

Ten Ways to Build Social Media Engagement

esigning a beautiful social media profile is a great way to introduce yourself online, but when it comes to building real connections, how you engage with people is at least, if not more, important. Numerous books have been written about social media engagement, but we'd be remiss if we didn't at least include our top ten tips for building quality connections online.

Liking, Sharing, Retweeting, and Commenting

Sharing a post is the highest compliment you can give on Facebook. Similarly, retweeting is the highest praise on Twitter. Taking the time to read what other people have to say and share comments and posts that you think will be of interest to your followers is one of the most powerful and effective ways to build engagement on social media. Adding a thoughtful comment on someone else's posts is also an effective way to show support and build your own reputation on Facebook.

If you like a post, but don't want to rebroadcast it to your audience, here are the ways to show your appreciation on the top social media sites.

Facebook:

Twitter:

Janine Warner shared a link.
April 11 near Los Angeles

Getting excited about my Web Design with WordPress course for creativeLIVE April 29 + 30. You can register for free to watch the course live, or order the video by visiting http://www.creativelive.com/courses/wordpress-101-janine-warner

Wordpress 101 with Janine Warner
www.creativelive.com

You don't need to be a geek or spend a fortune to create a great website or blog. With WordPress and this two-day workshop with "techy translator" Janine Warner, who specializes in making web

Like · Comment · Promote · Share   12 11 1

DaveLaFontaine @DaveLaFontaine
"Anytime you meet a cartooning hero, it's always a huge disappointment," Harkham
Expand   ← Reply ⇄ Retweet ★ Favorite ••• More

Email Tweet

Embed Tweet

- **Like:** Publicly note your approval.

- **Comment:** Add a text message below the post.

- **Promote:** (Only available on your own posts.) Share a post more publicly — for a fee.

- **Share:** Add a post to your timeline or send a post to someone else's timeline or in a private message.

- **Reply:** Send a public reply to the person who posted the tweet.

- **Retweet:** Share the message posted by another person with all of your followers.

- **Favorite:** Indicate that you like a tweet and save it in your Favorites list (accessible from your profile page).

- **More:** Open a drop-down list where you can choose to e-mail the tweet or to embed it. Choosing the Embed Tweet option opens a dialog box with code you can copy and then paste into a webpage, blog, or anywhere else on the web.

Google+:

Pinterest:

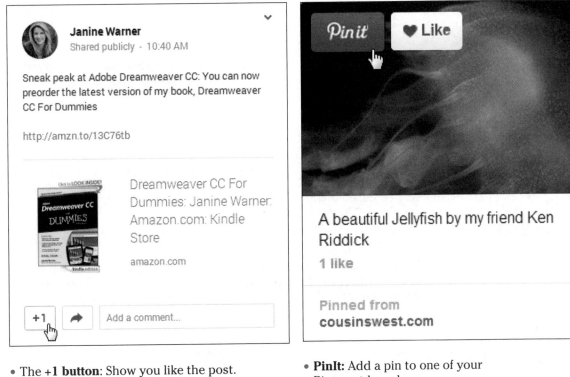

- The **+1 button**: Show you like the post.
- The **right-curved arrow:** Share it with people in your Circles or enter a comment in the comment field.

- **PinIt:** Add a pin to one of your Pinterest boards.
- **Like:** Publicly note your approval.

tip

You can also add a comment to the bottom of most things posted on Pinterest.

Social Media Is Like a Party

Too many people dive into social media and start broadcasting posts without ever taking the time to review what others have to say. You wouldn't walk into a party, jump into the middle of a group of people having a conversation, interrupt them to talk only about you, and then leave before anyone else could get a word in edgewise.

Okay, maybe you've seen other people that do that, but *you* wouldn't be so rude at a party. If you're socially aware enough to let your friends get a word in edgewise at a party, carry those same good habits into the virtual world of social media.

Think of your participation on Facebook, Twitter, Pinterest, and all social networking sites like participating in a party, and you'll be well on your way to building good relationships.

tip

Telling great stories is fun and can make you the life of the party, but if you never listen to what anyone else has to say, pretty soon you're going to lose your own audience.

Posting Photos

Clearly the most popular activity on Facebook, Pinterest, Google+, and many other social networking sites is checking out other people's photos and then sharing, Liking, or commenting on them.

tip

Posts with eye-catching images, such as the post shown in Figure 16-1 from Facebook that includes an image author Janine Warner captured on a trip to Abu Dhabi, are significantly more likely to get attention — and get shared, Liked, or retweeted.

Janine Warner
February 10

Going through photos from my trip to Abu Dhabi last week. The WSA mobile conference was great, but visiting the Grand Mosque was one of the highlights.

Like · Comment · Promote · Share   27 4

Figure 16-1

Sharing Videos

Most social media sites make it as easy to share videos as photos. Video is a powerful medium. If you're sharing ideas, concepts, and anything that requires a demonstration, finding or creating a video to include with your post can add impact and improve engagement. Figure 16-2 shows an example of a Facebook post that includes a video from the Twitter video service, Vine.

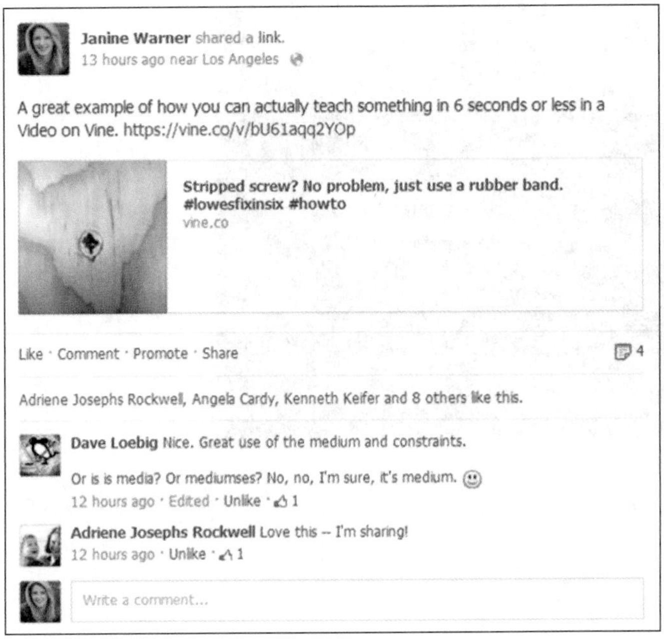

Janine Warner shared a link.
13 hours ago near Los Angeles

A great example of how you can actually teach something in 6 seconds or less in a Video on Vine. https://vine.co/v/bU61aqq2YOp

Stripped screw? No problem, just use a rubber band.
#lowesfixinsix #howto
vine.co

Like · Comment · Promote · Share   4

Adriene Josephs Rockwell, Angela Cardy, Kenneth Keifer and 8 others like this.

Dave Loebig Nice. Great use of the medium and constraints.
Or is is media? Or mediumses? No, no, I'm sure, it's medium.
12 hours ago · Edited · Unlike · 1

Adriene Josephs Rockwell Love this — I'm sharing!
12 hours ago · Unlike · 1

Write a comment...

Figure 16-2

Informing with Infographics

Creating and sharing infographics is a popular way to build engagement. An infographic, like the one shown in Figure 16-3, can garner more attention than using simple images or text updates.

tip

A growing number of websites (such as SingleHop.com, which made the infographic shown in Figure 16-3) create infographics and encourage visitors to share them on social media as a way to drive traffic to their websites.

Figure 16-3

Introducing Your Friends

Although you can introduce and recommend friends on all social networks, LinkedIn is often considered the most valuable place to help make connections. As shown in Figure 16-4, you can review how many connections you have on LinkedIn and how those connections link you to others.

Figure 16-4

Asking Questions

A great way to invite people to engage with you in social media is to ask a question. Many people feel more comfortable answering a question than simply commenting on a post, and questions can also bring out people's natural desire to help.

tip

That doesn't mean you should ask a question just to elicit a response or that you should ask a question in every post you make, but questions often bring greater engagement.

If you're using Facebook, Twitter, or another social media site for business, you can use questions to better understand your customers, find out what they are more interested in, or learn about changes in the market. Questions are also great for more personal posts. In Figure 16-5, you see a Facebook post created by one of the book's authors.

Figure 16-5

Being Nice

When you're tempted to respond in kind when you see someone being nasty on social media, remember that what you say when you post online becomes an eternal part of the Internet record. Recent history is littered with examples of public (and private) individuals causing a scandal when they get caught up in the moment, forgetting that the whole world is potentially listening.

warning

If you descend to the level of someone who is provoking you with taunts, insults, or plain old blockheaded stupidity, you risk turning off people who would have otherwise been happy to connect and share with you. Worse, you could get caught up in an escalating *flame war,* where other people jump into the conversation to issue threats, denunciations, and even attempt to blemish your reputation in the real world by contacting your boss (or customers) to tell them what you've been up to.

On the other hand, just a few kind words at the right time, in the right places, can boost your popularity and make people think of you as a kind, benevolent, level-headed force for good in the world.

Some social media experts say that a good guideline is that you should have at least seven positive interactions each time you engage with a social media platform. It's as easy as clicking Like on a Facebook posting, retweeting a particularly clever tweet, or repinning a delicious-looking Pinterest recipe. Not only does "spreading the love" make people feel that you care about them, but social media services respond by promoting the things that you say onto the feeds of the people that you have interacted with.

remember

We suggest that you not overdo these interactions, or you run the risk of coming off as smarmy and manipulative.

Your social actions should come from an honest place. If you're just Liking or commenting on other people's posts in the hopes that they will pay attention to you, it's equivalent to the kid on the playground trying to bribe the other kids with the cookies from his lunch so that they will be his friend. That doesn't usually lead to valuable long-term relationships.

tip

If you're being "spammed" by overly friendly users bombarding you with too much attention, you can unfriend or block them. If they cross the line into outright abuse or stalker behavior, most social media platforms (such as Facebook, as shown in Figure 16-6) provide tools that will allow you to report their behavior and get them warned, banned, or suspended.

facebook

⌂ Help Center ▸ Report Something   English (US)

How to Report Things

Don't Have an Account?

Report a Violation

Report a Bug

Bullying

Tools for Addressing Abuse

Tools for Parents & Educators

Intellectual Property Issues   ›

Image Privacy Rights

Give Us Feedback

Tools for Addressing Abuse

Don't have a Facebook account?

Learn more about how you can report potential abuse on Facebook.

5 Things You Can Do

1. Send a message to the person responsible for posting

2. Unfriend the person to remove them from your friend list

3. Block the person from contacting you

4. Report the person if their behavior is abusive

5. Use privacy settings

Figure 16-6

Being Consistent

The two ways to be consistent on your social media profiles are

▶ Be consistent with what you say.

▶ Be consistent with when you say it.

Of course, don't assume that after you establish your personality, you are never allowed to deviate from what you talk about. It's okay — in fact, it can be a welcome relief — to broaden your focus from time to time. Say you're known on Tumblr for posting photos of the latest heavy-duty rock-climbing gear, but then you suddenly switch to posting your favorite creampuff recipes. That would be such a drastic change in tone and content that most of your followers might suspect that your account has been hijacked.

The second key to consistency is to post, update, and interact at regular intervals. For many people, who log on to social media sites and get lost there for hours, this isn't much of a challenge. However, mindless surfing is not (surprise!) productive. We recommend being a little more mindful of your activities, particularly if you're hoping to use social media to build credibility and authority, or for business purposes.

remember

When you shift gears, give a little explanation to your audience as to why.

Establish a clear and consistent schedule for your social media sessions. Say, set aside Mondays for posting ways to schedule your work week, or tools that you can use to prioritize. Wednesdays can be about planning for the weekend, and Fridays are good for a round-up of the week's funniest viral videos. Or you can segment what you do according to the time of day — post quirky items first thing in the morning to give people a smile over their morning coffee, and then switch to more business-related subjects in the afternoon.

tip

Being consistent can help you build an audience and benefit people who take the time to follow you.

Making Relevant Recommendations

After you build an audience, one of the keys to retaining their attention is to ensure that what you're talking about is relevant. Some people find this to be easy and instinctual, but all of us are prone to drifting off into our own interests, forgetting that not everybody is fascinated by the same things that we are. What a moody 14-year-old with multiple facial piercings finds funny will probably not be the same as what makes an 86-year-old granny snicker over her knitting.

With that in mind, here are some guidelines to follow that will keep you on track:

▶ **Listen.** The cardinal rule for interacting on social media is much the same as the old saying, "You have two ears and one mouth, so you should listen twice as much as you talk."

remember

Keeping abreast of the latest memes, abbreviations, embarrassing errors, and unsolved mysteries does more than make you look like the coolest kid on the playground. It provides you with insight into how to take the conversation one step further, rather than telling people things that they already know.

▶ **Diversify.** This is a little counterintuitive. Having what social media experts describe as "wide antennae" means that you pay attention to a lot of different sources of information. Being able to bring something new and interesting to the conversation (that still relates to what is being discussed) means that you are adding value to your community.

tip

We suggest you set aside time each week to browse sites that represent opposing points of view. Everyone needs to have their homework checked, even if the person who is arguing against you is quite clearly wrong in every conceivable way (as they so obviously are).

▶ **Think before you post.** There is definitely some value in being the first in your community to bring a fact or an occurrence to an everyone's attention, but there's a difference when it comes to expressing your personal opinion. The Internet is full of people flying off the handle, having knee-jerk reactions, going nuclear, or whatever phrase you want to use to express shouting before they think. There are enough people like that already. Be different.

▶ **Blend.** One of the most valuable things you can do is to take information from a wide variety of points of view and then find a common thread in all of them that ties it all together in a new way. Giving people a new way to look at the relationships between familiar objects, institutions, or people is a really good way to surprise and delight your followers.

You'll know that you're being relevant when your followers seek out your opinion, they share what you post to their followers, and they tell you, "I've been wanting to meet you! I've been reading what you say about. . . ."

Index

D

E

• Z •

About the Authors

Janine Warner is the founder and creative director of DigitalFamily.com, a full-service interactive design and training agency that offers web and mobile design, content strategy, SEO, social media, and Internet marketing services.

Janine's skills as a "techy translator" helped her land the deal for her first book in 1996. Since then, she's written or coauthored more than 25 books, including *Web Sites Do-It-Yourself For Dummies, Mobile Web Design For Dummies,* and every edition of *Dreamweaver For Dummies.* She has also created more than 100 hours of training videos about web design for top-rated online learning sites, including creativeLIVE, lynda.com, and KelbyOne.

Since 2001, Janine has run her own business as an author, a consultant, and a speaker. Over the years, she's worked with one of Russia's largest publishing companies in Moscow; traveled to New Delhi to speak at Internet World India; consulted with newspapers in every major city in Colombia; and worked with media companies and other businesses in more than a dozen other countries. (She speaks fluent Spanish.) Janine has also taught courses at the University of Miami and the University of Southern California and been a guest lecturer at more than 20 universities in the United States and abroad.

When she's not traveling, she is based in southern California where she lives with her husband, David LaFontaine, manages DigitalFamily.com, and occasionally takes a break to run on the beach.

Dave LaFontaine is a writer, researcher, and multimedia content producer whose work has earned him invitations to lecture and train journalists, NGOs, and pro-democracy groups all over the world. Dave's curiosity and willingness to use himself as a human lab rat help him keep up with technology trends, test the latest digital tools, and produce the Sips from the Firehose blog.

Dave teaches online multimedia and digital publishing at the Annenberg School of Journalism at USC, where his students have used the design templates and techniques pioneered by this book to trick out their own profiles.

David got his start on the Internet in 1991, when he cracked the case of his (then) cutting-edge Zeos 386-25 computer to install a 2400-baud modem, and joined Prodigy and CompuServe. He was fascinated by the way users formed communities online to share news, collaborate to create new businesses, develop their own shorthand argot language, and devise new and exciting ways of insulting each other for violating the unwritten rules.

David grew up reading science fiction, and is often amazed by the way technologies that only hard-core nerds dreamed about have come to be taken for granted by billions.

Dedication

To the untold billions of people connecting via social media: May you find ways to create something as touching, funny, beautiful, and delightful as the examples we feature in the book.

Authors' Acknowledgements

Janine: More than anything, I want to thank all the people who have read my books or watched my videos over the years. You are my greatest inspiration, and I sincerely enjoy it when you send me links to your websites and connect with me on social media. You'll always find my e-mail address and links to my social profiles on my websites at http://jcwarner.com and www.digitalfamily.com.

Special thanks to David LaFontaine, my partner in all things digital and analog, whom I've shared so much with over the years, including writing this book together. You are my best friend — ever.

Thanks to the entire editorial team on this book: Rebecca Senninger and Teresa Artman for their attention to detail and careful editing; Jon McFarland for reviewing all the technical details; and Amy Fandrei for shepherding this book through the development and publishing process.

Over the years, I've thanked many people in my books — family, friends, teachers, and mentors — but I have been graced by so many wonderful people now that no publisher will give me enough pages to thank them all. So let me conclude by thanking everyone who has ever helped me with a web site, book, video, or any other aspect of the writing and research that go into these pages. Okay, now I think I can go to sleep tonight without fearing I've forgotten anyone.

Thank you, thank you, thank you.

David: I'd like to thank all the great teachers and mentors that turned me on to reading and writing throughout my career. From my grade-school teachers reading my essays aloud to the class, so that everybody could enjoy what I wrote, to my college professors questioning my use of the word "yeoman," you've all encouraged me to develop this gift I apparently have for stringing one word after another.

I'd like to thank all the thousands of artists, designers, and quirky individualists all over the world who put hours into designing social media profiles "just because." In the course of researching and looking for examples in this book, I laughed and learned from every one of you. There would not be enough room in a thousand books to do justice to all the creativity that exists on the Internet. If you, dear reader, find something that just delights you, send it to me via www.davidlafontaine.com.

Special thanks to Janine Warner, for being my sounding board and reeling me back a bit when I go off on one of my rhetorical flights of fancy. You have an amazing talent for taking my overwritten, overwrought sections of purple prose and reducing it to something actually readable. A giggle from you is more inspiring than a dozen positive Amazon reviews (although if any of you readers feel like competing, go to it).

I'd like to give a special shout-out to America's librarians. As a boy, just walking through the doors of the local public library filled me with a sense of incredible excitement and awe. And, of course, to my mom and sisters, who used to sit with me on the couch as I worked my way through the stacks of library books, sharing with me the joy of the written word (and keeping me from using my crayons to "improve" the stories I loved so much).

Thanks, everybody.

Publisher's Acknowledgments

Acquisitions Editor: Amy Fandrei

Project Editor: Rebecca Senninger

Sr. Copy Editor: Teresa Artman

Technical Editor: Jon McFarland

Editorial Assistant: Anne Sullivan

Sr. Editorial Assistant: Cherie Case

Special Help: Virginia Sanders

Project Coordinator: Erin Zeltner

Cover Image: ©iStockphoto.com / cienpies

ple & Mac

d For Dummies,
Edition
8-1-118-72306-7

one For Dummies,
Edition
8-1-118-69083-3

cs All-in-One
r Dummies, 4th Edition
8-1-118-82210-4

X Mavericks
r Dummies
8-1-118-69188-5

ogging & Social Media

cebook For Dummies,
Edition
8-1-118-63312-0

cial Media Engagement
r Dummies
8-1-118-53019-1

ordPress For Dummies,
Edition
8-1-118-79161-5

usiness

ock Investing
r Dummies, 4th Edition
8-1-118-37678-2

vesting For Dummies,
Edition
8-0-470-90545-6

Personal Finance
For Dummies, 7th Edition
978-1-118-11785-9

QuickBooks 2014
For Dummies
978-1-118-72005-9

Small Business Marketing
Kit For Dummies,
3rd Edition
978-1-118-31183-7

Careers

Job Interviews
For Dummies, 4th Edition
978-1-118-11290-8

Job Searching with Social
Media For Dummies,
2nd Edition
978-1-118-67856-5

Personal Branding
For Dummies
978-1-118-11792-7

Resumes For Dummies,
6th Edition
978-0-470-87361-8

Starting an Etsy Business
For Dummies, 2nd Edition
978-1-118-59024-9

Diet & Nutrition

Belly Fat Diet For Dummies
978-1-118-34585-6

Mediterranean Diet
For Dummies
978-1-118-71525-3

Nutrition For Dummies,
5th Edition
978-0-470-93231-5

Digital Photography

Digital SLR Photography
All-in-One For Dummies,
2nd Edition
978-1-118-59082-9

Digital SLR Video &
Filmmaking For Dummies
978-1-118-36598-4

Photoshop Elements 12
For Dummies
978-1-118-72714-0

Gardening

Herb Gardening
For Dummies, 2nd Edition
978-0-470-61778-6

Gardening with Free-Range
Chickens For Dummies
978-1-118-54754-0

Health

Boosting Your Immunity
For Dummies
978-1-118-40200-9

Diabetes For Dummies,
4th Edition
978-1-118-29447-5

Living Paleo For Dummies
978-1-118-29405-5

Big Data

Big Data For Dummies
978-1-118-50422-2

Data Visualization
For Dummies
978-1-118-50289-1

Hadoop For Dummies
978-1-118-60755-8

Language &
Foreign Language

500 Spanish Verbs
For Dummies
978-1-118-02382-2

English Grammar
For Dummies, 2nd Edition
978-0-470-54664-2

French All-in-One
For Dummies
978-1-118-22815-9

German Essentials
For Dummies
978-1-118-18422-6

Italian For Dummies,
2nd Edition
978-1-118-00465-4

📖 Available in print and e-book formats.

Available wherever books are sold. **For more information or to order direct visit www.dummies.com**

Math & Science

Algebra I For Dummies,
2nd Edition
978-0-470-55964-2

Anatomy and Physiology
For Dummies, 2nd Edition
978-0-470-92326-9

Astronomy For Dummies,
3rd Edition
978-1-118-37697-3

Biology For Dummies,
2nd Edition
978-0-470-59875-7

Chemistry For Dummies,
2nd Edition
978-1-118-00730-3

1001 Algebra II Practice
Problems For Dummies
978-1-118-44662-1

Microsoft Office

Excel 2013 For Dummies
978-1-118-51012-4

Office 2013 All-in-One
For Dummies
978-1-118-51636-2

PowerPoint 2013
For Dummies
978-1-118-50253-2

Word 2013 For Dummies
978-1-118-49123-2

Music

Blues Harmonica
For Dummies
978-1-118-25269-7

Guitar For Dummies,
3rd Edition
978-1-118-11554-1

iPod & iTunes
For Dummies, 10th Edition
978-1-118-50864-0

Programming

Beginning Programming
with C For Dummies
978-1-118-73763-7

Excel VBA Programming
For Dummies, 3rd Edition
978-1-118-49037-2

Java For Dummies,
6th Edition
978-1-118-40780-6

Religion & Inspiration

The Bible For Dummies
978-0-7645-5296-0

Buddhism For Dummies,
2nd Edition
978-1-118-02379-2

Catholicism For Dummies,
2nd Edition
978-1-118-07778-8

Self-Help & Relationships

Beating Sugar Addiction
For Dummies
978-1-118-54645-1

Meditation For Dummies,
3rd Edition
978-1-118-29144-3

Seniors

Laptops For Seniors
For Dummies, 3rd Edition
978-1-118-71105-7

Computers For Seniors
For Dummies, 3rd Edition
978-1-118-11553-4

iPad For Seniors
For Dummies, 6th Edition
978-1-118-72826-0

Social Security
For Dummies
978-1-118-20573-0

Smartphones & Tablets

Android Phones
For Dummies, 2nd Edition
978-1-118-72030-1

Nexus Tablets
For Dummies
978-1-118-77243-0

Samsung Galaxy S 4
For Dummies
978-1-118-64222-1

Samsung Galaxy Tabs
For Dummies
978-1-118-77294-2

Test Prep

ACT For Dummies,
5th Edition
978-1-118-01259-8

ASVAB For Dummies,
3rd Edition
978-0-470-63760-9

GRE For Dummies,
7th Edition
978-0-470-88921-3

Officer Candidate Tests
For Dummies
978-0-470-59876-4

Physician's Assistant Exam
For Dummies
978-1-118-11556-5

Series 7 Exam For Dummies
978-0-470-09932-2

Windows 8

Windows 8.1 All-in-One
For Dummies
978-1-118-82087-2

Windows 8.1 For Dummies
978-1-118-82121-3

Windows 8.1 For Dummies
Book + DVD Bundle
978-1-118-82107-7

 Available in print and e-book formats.

Available wherever books are sold. **For more information or to order direct visit www.dummies.com**

Take Dummies with you everywhere you go!

Whether you are excited about e-books, want more from the web, must have your mobile apps, or are swept up in social media, Dummies makes everything easier.

For Dummies is the global leader in the reference category and one of the most trusted and highly regarded brands in the world. No longer just focused on books, customers now have access to the For Dummies content they need in the format they want. Let us help you develop a solution that will fit your brand and help you connect with your customers.

Advertising & Sponsorships

Connect with an engaged audience on a powerful multimedia site, and position your message alongside expert how-to content.

Targeted ads • Video • Email marketing • Microsites • Sweepstakes sponsorship

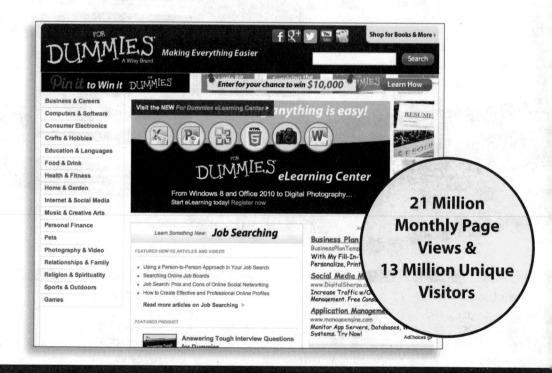